OTHER BOOKS IN THIS SERIES

Your Daily Walk:
365 Daily Devotions to Read
Through the Bible in a Year

Youthwalk:
Sex, Parents, Popularity,
and Other Topics for Teen Survival

FAMILY WALK™

Bruce H. Wilkinson
Executive Editor

Paula A. Kirk
Editor

Calvin W. Edwards
General Editor

Walk Thru the Bible Ministries
Atlanta, Georgia

Zondervan Publishing House
Grand Rapids, Michigan

Family Walk
Copyright © 1991 by Walk Thru the Bible Ministries
All rights reserved

Published by Zondervan Publishing House

Requests for information should be addressed to:
Walk Thru the Bible Ministries or   Zondervan Publishing House
P.O. Box 80587   Grand Rapids, Michigan 49530
Atlanta, GA 30366

Library of Congress Cataloging-in-Publication Data

Family Walk: love, anger, courage, and 49 other weekly readings for your
family devotions/ Walk Thru the Bible Ministries
    p. cm.
    ISBN 0-310-54241-3
    1. Family—Prayer-books and devotions—English. 2. Devotional calendars.
3. Bible—Devotional use. I. Walk Thru the Bible
(Educational Ministry).
BV255.F334   1991
249—dc20   91—11979
                                                    CIP

Cover and interior design by Michelle Beeman
Cover photo by The Image Bank
Cartoons by Martha Campbell

Printed in the United States of America

95 96 97 98 99 00 01 02 /❖ DH / 14 13 12 11 10 9 8 7

DEDICATION

When God brought Walk Thru the Bible into existence, little did I know the quality of laborers He was simultaneously preparing to enter that field with me. This volume is dedicated to two of those most faithful friends and co-laborers, Bert and Shirley Stumberg.

It is almost impossible for me to think of Walk Thru the Bible without thinking of them, so faithful and forward-looking has been their fellowship over the years. As a dedicated Christian couple, they have invested a generous portion of all that they are and have—their time, talent, and treasure—to seeing that Walk Thru the Bible could fulfill its mission. In fact, I firmly believe that on the day God called my wife, Darlene, and me, He also called Bert and Shirley.

The entire Walk Thru the Bible family, and especially Darlene and I, have been so blessed from this wonderful couple's partnership over the years. May God continue to bless their own "family walk"!

Bruce H. Wilkinson
Executive Editor

ACKNOWLEDGMENTS

Family Walk: Love, Anger, Courage, and 49 Other Weekly Readings for Your Family Devotions is a fresh, new compilation of topical studies from the *Family Walk* devotional guide published by Walk Thru the Bible Ministries. We are grateful to everyone who worked so faithfully on this magazine during the past 10 years. We especially appreciate the vision and leadership given WTB in publishing, first by Harvey Warner, then by Don Holloway, and more recently by Calvin Edwards.

Special thanks for great ideas and hard work go to our *Family Walk* design and production team: Michelle Beeman, Martha Comeaux, Robyn Holmes, Stuart McLellan, and Myra Wilkinson. Their commitment to excellence and attention to detail has made this book a pleasure to produce. Their desire to invest their time and talent in work that makes a lasting difference in the lives of God's people makes them a joy to work with.

INTRODUCTION

Family Walk is carefully designed to help parents train their children to apply biblical truths to everyday situations. With this book, parents have a tool to open communication about the vital issues families face today and to find the answers in God's Word.

Family Walk will help you and your children establish the Scriptures as your foundation for living in this chaotic and insecure world. As you discover practical applications for family problems in *Family Walk*, your child will see the Bible in a new light. No longer will the Bible simply be a book of exciting stories about things that happened long ago. Instead, your children will see the Bible as a vital resource for a happy and successful life. As you and your children grow spiritually and become confident in God's love, you will become more secure as a family.

We at Walk Thru the Bible Ministries are thrilled to join with Zondervan Publishing House to make this Bible reading guide available to you. The common purpose of our ministries is to help Christians become grounded in the Scriptures.

Bruce H. Wilkinson
President and Executive Editor

HOW TO GET THE MOST OUT OF *FAMILY WALK*

Family Walk is arranged by topics for you and your children to explore together each week. You can start with the first topic or just jump in at any point in the book. Simply put a check in the accompanying box to keep your place.

Day One of each topic brings your family a definition of the topic and a key Bible verse. The primary Scripture portion for Day One is the key verse, and we encourage you and your children to read it aloud several times and perhaps even memorize it. Use the cartoon as a discussion starter or just have a good laugh together.

Days Two–Five are divided into these three sections:

> **An opening story** helps your family focus on the question for the day.

> **Take a Look** guides you to a passage in God's Word that gives insight into the biblical answer to the day's question. Let your children find the passage in their Bibles and read the selection aloud. Or let them read the verse that is printed in italic type. Encourage your children to mark that verse in their own Bibles and reread it at some point during the day.

> **Take a Step** reveals useful ways you can practice what you learn. Through discussion about the Scripture you read, references back to the opening story, and concrete action your family can take, Take a Step is designed to generate conversation about the issues young people face today.

We encourage you to be sensitive to your children's needs and questions. Stop at any point to discuss what you're reading and how it relates to your situation. Spiritual growth is a process that takes place over time. **Family Walk**, if used consistently, is a tool that will give your family, and its individual members, opportunities to prepare for the challenges that will come your way.

WALK THRU THE BIBLE MINISTRIES

Walk Thru the Bible Ministries (WTB) unofficially began in the early 1970s in Portland, Oregon, with the teaching of Old and New Testament surveys of the Bible. Dr. Bruce H. Wilkinson was looking for a way to innovatively teach the Word of God so that it would change people's lives.

Dr. Wilkinson officially founded WTB in 1976 as a nonprofit ministry. In 1978 WTB moved to its current home in Atlanta.

From these small beginnings WTB has grown into one of the leading Christian organizations in America with an international ministry extending to 21 countries in 30 languages. International branch offices are located in Australia, Brazil, Great Britain, Singapore, and New Zealand.

By focusing on the central themes of Scripture and their practical application to life, WTB has been able to develop and maintain wide acceptance in denominations and fellowships around the world. In addition, it has carefully initiated strategic ministry alliances with more than one hundred Christian organizations and missions of wide diversity and background.

WTB has four major outreach ministries: seminars, publishing, leadership training, and video training.

Since it began its seminar ministry two decades ago, WTB has instructed more than one million people worldwide through seminars taught by more than two hundred highly qualified, well-trained teachers. People of all ages and religious persuasions have developed a deeper understanding of the Bible through these unique Old and New Testament surveys, and many have come to know Christ in a new and more personal way. WTB's seminars actively involve the audience in the learning process through memorable hand signs, and note-taking is prohibited!

WTB's publishing ministry began in 1978 with the launching of *The Daily Walk* magazine. Since then WTB Publishing has continued to develop additional publications that enable individuals, families, and churches to maintain a regular, meaningful habit of daily devotional time in the Word of God. The publications include *Closer Walk,*

Family Walk, LifeWalk, and *Youthwalk.* WTB is one of the largest publishers of devotional magazines in the Christian community.

The third strategic ministry of WTB is the training of Christian leaders and communicators. Launched in the late 1980s, The Applied Principles of Learning (APL) training conference for teachers, pastors, and parents has rapidly become the most widely used interdenominational teacher training program in North America. Dozens of certified WTB instructors regularly conduct this life-changing course in schools, churches, businesses, and colleges. In addition, WTB's Leadership Dynamics curriculum is an integral part of the regular and ongoing discipleship training in hundreds of churches.

The newest and fastest growing ministry of WTB is the Video Training curriculum outreach. In just a few short years, the WTB creative team has developed a number of leading video courses that have enjoyed widespread distribution. "The Seven Laws of the Teacher" featuring Dr. Howard G. Hendricks equips church school teachers to effectively prepare and teach Bible lessons that capture attention and motivate lifechange. "Master Your Money" weaves a contemporary drama through the six-part presentation by Christian financial planner Ron Blue as he trains people to maximize their effectiveness as stewards. Thousands of churches use these and other fine WTB video series with their congregations each year.

Walk Thru the Bible Ministries has had a consistent history of strategic ministry since its beginning more than fifteen years ago. The call of the Lord has been clear and consistent on the organization as it strives to help fulfill the Lord's Great Commission. The highest ethics and standards of integrity are carefully practiced as Walk Thru the Bible lives out its commitment to excellence not only in ministry but also in its internal operational policies and procedures. No matter what the ministry, no matter where the ministry, WTB focuses on the Word of God and encourages people of all nations to grow in their knowledge of Him and in their unreserved obedience and service to Him.

For more information about Walk Thru the Bible's publications, videos, or seminars in your area, write to Walk Thru the Bible Ministries, P.O. Box 80587, Atlanta, Ga 30366 or call (404) 458-9300.

CONTENTS

NEW STARTS

"*T his is like the movies,*" *Jerry thought to himself as the cell block gates clanged shut behind him. But it wasn't a movie. It was real—as real as the day Jerry first entered prison. The judge had sentenced him to ten years, but now, after only five, he was being paroled—given a new start.*

"*And I'll do it,*" *he promised himself. "I won't mess up this time. I'll start over and do it right . . . "*

But six months later, the cell block gates clanged shut a second time behind Jerry. Once again, he was starting over.

◆ THINKING ABOUT NEW STARTS

At the beginning of each year we think about new starts, **fresh opportunities to do something or be something different**—new beginnings, second chances.

The blank pages of the new calendar urge us to improve. We make resolutions to be more patient, to study harder, to diet, to exercise, to practice our music, to read the Bible every day. For many of us, the resolutions we make on January 1 are as hard to keep as it was for Jerry to go straight.

But new starts are possible—if we make them with God's help! The Apostle Paul wrote these encouraging words to the church:

● KEY VERSE ON NEW STARTS

If anyone is in Christ, he is a new creation; the old has gone, the new has come! (2 Corinthians 5:17).

▲ LOOKING AHEAD

This week we'll talk about new starts from God's perspective. You can get off to a good start by answering these questions: "What is one thing we did as a family last year that we would like to do again? What is one thing we would like to do differently in the coming year?"

After everybody's had a chance to answer, mark your family calendar with the dates you'll need to remember. But before you make final plans, read Proverbs 3:1-2.

"My whole family made New Year's resolutions. Dad's eating more bran, Mom's eating more fruit, and I'm eating more cake."

If at first you don't succeed, you're still okay!

*I*t's impossible, Mom. Just look at this mess. It's hopeless. And Miss Hodges is going to grade this project on Friday. I'll probably make a D in Home Ec, and it'll go on my permanent record. All because I can't put in one lousy zipper."

"Cindy," her mother replied as she carefully examined the skirt her daughter was sewing, "what you did was put the zipper in backward. All you have to do is take it out and start over. It's not hopeless. You've done a great job so far, and when you correct this mistake your skirt will be beautiful. You'll probably make an A—and you'll have something new to wear!"

◆ TAKE A LOOK / Genesis 3:14-24

From sewing a skirt to practicing the piano to building a relationship, God gives us many opportunities to start over—to learn from our mistakes and move forward.

New starts are necessary because we are imperfect people who live in an imperfect world. The Bible teaches that when God first created the world, everything was perfect—sinless. But when Adam and Eve disobeyed God, death and decay entered the world. From that time on, all things (including you) have experienced the effects of sin.

The entrance of sin into the world is sometimes called the "fall of man." Read the account of how it happened and what its tragic results were in Genesis 3:14-24.

▲ TAKE A STEP

Though the penalty of Adam and Eve's sin was death, God promised that one day someone would come to crush the head of the serpent who had tempted them to disobey God (Genesis 3:15). He gave them a new start—a hope for the future. And that hope was fulfilled in Jesus Christ:

Because of his great love for us, God, . . . made us alive with Christ even when we were dead in transgressions—it is by grace you have been saved (Ephesians 2:4-5).

Even though everyone and everything still experience the effects of sin, God offers a fresh beginning through Jesus Christ. That's comforting news whether your name is Adam, Eve, or Cindy!

Today, as you close your family time, reread the Key Verse for this week. Aren't you glad God doesn't give up on you—even when you are sometimes tempted to give up on yourself? Tell Him thank you right now!

Q

Why is it often necessary to start over?

A

New starts are sometimes necessary because sin came into the world.

M om, Dad, I've got to talk to you. I've done something terrible, and you're going to hate me for it." As 15-year-old Becky spoke, her lip quivered and she began to sob. Mr. and Mrs. Lewis knew this was serious.

"Becky," her dad said gently as Mrs. Lewis gave Becky a tender hug, "you're very special to us. We won't stop loving you, regardless of what you've done. Whatever it is, we'll work it out together. Now, come sit by me and tell me what's wrong."

"Oh, Dad, I can't . . ." Becky's voice broke again.

"Becky, you've got to. We can't help you until we know what the problem is. Once you've told us, we can all begin to look for the best way to set things right."

"Okay, but you won't like what you hear . . ."

◆ TAKE A LOOK / Psalm 51:1-4, 13-17

Mr. and Mrs. Lewis loved their daughter and encouraged her to confess what she had done. They knew that to make a new start, you have to have a starting point—a time when you face up to what you've done and are willing to make it right.

He who conceals his sins does not prosper, but whoever confesses and renounces them finds mercy (Proverbs 28:13).

King David provides a good model to follow. At one point in his life he committed two terrible sins—adultery and murder. He thought no one knew what he had done. But God knew and sent a prophet to tell the king so.

David realized he could not escape the *consequences* of his wrong actions. But he also knew that if he *confessed* those actions and was sincerely sorry, God would forgive him. Read David's confession in Psalm 51:1-4, 13-17.

▲ TAKE A STEP

New starts are necessary because we are sinful people living in a sinful world. We make mistakes—sometimes deliberately, sometimes accidentally. Often we are like King David and behave sinfully in our relationships with other people.

When we sin, a new start is possible only when we admit that sin and are willing to make it right. Think back to Becky and her parents. How did Mr. Lewis encourage Becky to admit her wrong action? What did Becky know about her parents that gave her confidence that she would be forgiven?

Where do I start when my world falls apart?

Q

How can I start over?

A

New starts can happen when I admit I was wrong and am willing to make things right.

A broken law and a broken heart

Becky's voice trembled as she began. "Oh, Dad, I'm so ashamed. You remember when I was baby-sitting to earn Christmas money? Well, one night Mrs. Morris left her tiny diamond earrings on the table. I tried them on . . . and then I just put them in my pocket. I don't know why I did it—I know it was wrong." Becky paused. She started to chew on her lip.

"Becky," her mom interrupted, "is there more?"

"Well . . . I put them in a jeweler's box and gave them to Liz for Christmas. Liz couldn't believe I had given her such an expensive gift, and she wore them all the time. It was awful. I wanted to take the earrings back, but by then I couldn't.

"Then last night Liz baby-sat for the Morrises. Right away Mrs. Morris spotted the earrings. She called Liz a thief. When Liz told her I had given them to her, Mrs. Morris was furious. She told Liz neither of us could every baby-sit for her again. Now Liz hates me, Mrs. Morris hates me, and nobody will ever trust me again. I'm so sorry. Please forgive me."

Q

How can I help someone else start over?

A

New starts often begin with Christlike forgiveness.

PARENT:
Teach your child the importance of confession by being quick to admit when you are wrong. It's hard, but well worth it!

◆ **TAKE A LOOK / Luke 22:59-62; John 21:15-19**

Peter, a disciple of Jesus, also needed a new start. He had promised to stick by Jesus no matter what. But on the very day of Jesus' death, Peter denied Him—*three times!* Read Luke 22:59-62 to see how Peter felt about his failure. Then turn to John 21:15-19 to see how Jesus responded to Peter after His resurrection. As you read, look for clues that show you how to help someone else who is going through a "Peter Problem."

▲ **TAKE A STEP**

Peter had denied Jesus three times. By giving Peter three opportunities to express his love for Jesus, our Lord showed Peter that He forgave him and accepted him completely. This is the kind of forgiveness that helps others start over, the kind described in Ephesians 4:32:

Be kind and compassionate to one another, forgiving each other, just as in Christ God forgave you (Ephesians 4:32).

In Becky's confession, she showed true sorrow for what she had done. She had broken God's law; she had grieved her parents, and had gotten Liz in trouble. Becky realized that people now thought she was untrustworthy. From this starting point, what should she do next? If you were her mom or dad, what would you tell her to do?

Mom and Dad have sure been super," Becky thought. "They knew what I did was wrong and that I really felt bad about it. They could have treated me like the family outcast—but they didn't. Or they could have just ignored the problem and let me get away with it, but they didn't do that either."

The stolen earrings were returned to Mrs. Morris. Becky apologized to her friend Liz and assured everyone that Liz had not been involved in taking them. Everything should have been back to normal. But Becky's eyes told another story.

"Oh, Mom," Becky cried softly, "Richard asked me to go to the Valentine Banquet . . . but when some of the girls in the youth department heard about it, they told him they couldn't believe a Christian guy would go out with a thief. I've done everything I can to make things right. What if people won't forget?"

◆ **TAKE A LOOK**
2 Corinthians 2:5-8; Philippians 3:10-14
"Forgetting what is behind." Sometimes it's easier for you to do than it is for those your actions have affected.

After the Apostle Paul became a believer in Jesus, other Christians had a hard time forgetting the suffering he had caused. Even the leaders of the church "were afraid of him, not believing that he really was a disciple" (Acts 9:26). For three long years, only the Lord knew that Paul was sorry for his past and was no longer a threat to the church.

Turn now to 2 Corinthians 2:5-8 and read Paul's own words describing how believers should treat someone who has sinned, confessed, and repented—someone who needs a new start. Then read Philippians 3:10-14 to learn how Paul found strength to start over, even though others wouldn't forget his painful past.

▲ **TAKE A STEP**
Like Paul, Becky repented of her sin. She confessed it to God, to her parents, and to everyone else involved. She knew God forgave her because . . .
If we confess our sins, [God] is faithful and just and will forgive us our sins (1 John 1:9).
Becky did what she could to make things right. But she couldn't control the hurtful things unforgiving people thought and said about her. On the basis of the verses that you have just read, what advice would you give her now?

If God can forgive me, why can't others?

What happens if others won't forget the past?

A

I can still experience God's forgiveness, make a new start, and leave the past behind.

WORSHIP

*P*icture this scene. It is 12:30 p.m. on an average Sunday in an average church in Anytown, U.S.A. Hymns have been sung, the offering has been collected, prayers have been prayed, Scripture has been read, and the pastor has preached. Now the ushers collect the discarded bulletins in the empty sanctuary. But instead of throwing them away, the ushers tally what has been scribbled on them:

15 pictures of cars, planes, spaceships, and laser guns
7 grocery lists (lettuce, tomatoes, detergent, ice cream)
8 things-to-do lists (laundry, car repair, call Mabel)
5 collections of doodles and designs
6 tic-tac-toe games
The worship service is over . . . but did worship ever begin?

◆ THINKING ABOUT WORSHIP

What does worship mean to you? Is it long boring services . . . majestic hymns . . . quiet voices? Regardless of your past experiences, worship can—and should—be one of the most exciting parts of your life. The psalmist calls us to worship with these words:

● KEY VERSE ON WORSHIP

Come, let us bow down in worship, let us kneel before the Lord our Maker (Psalm 95:6).

▲ LOOKING AHEAD

Worship is **being aware of who God is, and telling Him so.** It is declaring the "worth" of God—the many things He is and does that make Him such a wonderful God to get to know.

The Doxology is a worship song sung in many churches. The

word *doxology* comes from a Greek word meaning "to give a praiseful opinion of someone"—exactly what we do when we worship God! Begin your week by singing its worshipful words:

Praise God from whom
all blessings flow.
Praise Him all creatures
here below.
Praise Him above ye
heavenly hosts.
Praise Father, Son, and
Holy Ghost. Amen.

S itting in church with his older sister, six-year-old Jerry just couldn't seem to sit still. He slouched in the pew, squirmed and wiggled, talked out loud, and pulled the ponytail of the girl in front of him.

Heads began to turn. This was getting embarrassing! At last a lady with a kind face moved up from the row behind and sat down beside Jerry. Firmly she placed her arm around him and encouraged him to sit up straight. Nothing seemed to work.

At last she took his hand in hers, bent low, and whispered in his ear, "This is God's house, Jerry. You must sit still and be quiet."

Jerry's eyes widened. Slowly he looked around the sanctuary. Then he turned to her and declared in a voice loud enough to be heard 10 rows away, "Well, He must not be home 'cause I sure don't see Him anywhere!"

◆ **TAKE A LOOK / Revelation 4:2-11**

Like Jerry, you cannot see God in the buildings built to honor Him. But God is *very* real. In fact, He is seated on the throne of the universe. He is King of Kings and Lord of Lords!

When the Apostle John (one of the original 12 disciples) was a very old man, God gave him a vision of a magnificent throne where God Himself was seated. Something very special was happening around that throne. Living creatures were busy worshiping God.

Day and night they never stop saying: "Holy, holy, holy is the Lord God Almighty, who was, and is, and is to come" (Revelation 4:8).

Catch a glimpse of our holy God by reading John's exciting description of Him in Revelation 4:2-11.

▲ **TAKE A STEP**

Worship is very important to God. The full-time job of the four living beings and the 24 elders John saw in his vision was worship—*giving God the praise He deserves.*

Close your family time today by having each family member read verse 11 aloud. What reason does this verse give for worshiping God?

One of the reasons the angels and elders in heaven are praising God right now is because He created *you.* What an exciting thought! That should be reason enough for you to sing His praises throughout the day. He is your worthy Creator.

If this is God's house, why isn't He home?

Q

Whom should I worship?

A

I should worship the God who created all things, including me.

The best family and the best job in the world

Why shouldn't I quit school?" asked Peter angrily. "There's no reason to keep trying. There probably won't be any jobs when I graduate anyway."

Bitterly, the young man confronted his pastor. "Look at my dad. He worked all those years—just for the family, he said—and now our family is falling apart. It doesn't make sense."

"Pete, I know your family has had a difficult time," Reverend Miller interrupted. "But your life still has meaning and purpose." He paused for a thoughtful moment, then continued.

"How would you like to become part of a family that will never break up and find a job that's tailor-made for you—a rewarding, meaningful job? Would you like that?"

"Who wouldn't," Peter replied. "But what's the catch?"

Q

Why should I worship?

A

Worship gives purpose and meaning to my life.

◆ TAKE A LOOK / Revelation 5:11-14

Like Peter, we wake up every morning to a world gone wrong. Christians and non-Christians alike suffer injustice, violence, broken homes, poverty, illness, and misunderstanding. Is it really possible to be happy when things you wish were *all right* turn out *all wrong?*

Yesterday you learned that worship in heaven never stops. God deserves worship because He is the Creator. Revelation 5:11-14 pictures another scene of worship, this time involving "the Lamb." As you read, try to discover who the Lamb is, and why He too is worthy of worship.

▲ TAKE A STEP

The Lamb of God is none other than Jesus Christ, the One who "takes away the sin of the world" (John 1:29). And why is He worthy of our worship? John describes it this way:

"With your blood you purchased men for God from every tribe and language and people and nation" (Revelation 5:9).

Earthly families will sometimes disappoint us; and unexpected tragedy may come our way. But God has given meaning and security to life by making it possible for us to become a part of His heavenly family. Once we are a part of that family, He has a job for each of us: the job of worshiping Him "in spirit and in truth" (John 4:24).

Peter thought there must be a catch for something that good to become his. And there is! Find out what it is in 1 John 5:11-12.

He's coming! Dad's coming up the driveway!" The door slammed behind the seven-year-old twins as they ran to meet their father arriving home from work.

From now till bedtime, their time belonged to him—and his time to them. After dinner and their daily Bible reading, Dad listened to their music (John Thompson, Book One), heard about their day, or had a rough-and-tumble time before bath. Then they piled into bed while Dad read from a favorite book.

The minutes zoomed by, and before they knew it, it was 8:00 and time for Dad's familiar words, "Okay, team, lights out!"

◆ **TAKE A LOOK / Revelation 5:13**
You might say the twins "worshiped" their father. During the special hours between "Dad's coming!" and "Lights out!" their lives revolved around his because they loved him.

In a similar but infinitely greater way, God wants His children to worship Him—to make Him the center of their lives. Yesterday you read a description of heavenly worship and thought about the question, "Why should I worship?" Today, read again Revelation 5:13 and think about the question, "How should I worship?"

"To him who sits on the throne and to the Lamb be praise and honor and glory and power, for ever and ever!" (Revelation 5:13).

▲ **TAKE A STEP**
Worship is easier when you understand four terms: *praise, honor, glory,* and *power.* (Can you find and circle those words in the verse above?)

We *praise* God by recognizing Him as the Creator and thanking Him for the things He has made—sunsets and rainbows, fragile flowers and mighty trees.

We *honor* God by giving Him the credit He deserves. When you get an *A* on a test, who gets bragged on—you, or God who gave you a sharp mind?

We give God *glory* by magnifying His name. We tell others about His mighty works so they can praise Him too!

We recognize God's *power* when we acknowledge that He alone is able to meet our needs each day.

Put one of those words into practice as a family today!

How do I love you? Let me count the ways . . .

Q

How should I worship?

A

I should worship by giving my powerful God the praise, honor, and glory He deserves.

"I'll love you forever and a day"

The elderly couple stood with their sons, daughters, grandchildren, great-grandchildren, and many friends to repeat the marriage vows they had made 50 years before.

No one really noticed the "bride's" wrinkled face or the "groom's" stooped shoulders, so radiant were their faces on this Golden Wedding Anniversary.

Later, at the reception, everyone was gently teasing them to learn the secret of their long life together. With a twinkle in her eye, the 74-year-old great-grandmother announced, "Well, we made a promise to each other 50 years ago, and so far we've kept it. He promised to pay me a special compliment and say 'I love you' every day . . . and I promised to believe him."

◆ TAKE A LOOK / John 17:20-23

Through the good times, the bad times, and all the in-between times, love grows stronger between two people who are committed to each other. Often those two people begin to act alike as they become *one* with each other.

Worship is like that. It is God's way of helping you become one with Him in character and conduct. But it takes time—and time is what busy families seem to lack. When *can* you worship?

Have you ever gone to bed singing a song . . . and found in the morning that same song was still on your mind? That was no accident!

Try the same thing with worship. Before you go to sleep tonight, take a minute to give God **praise**, **honor**, and **glory** for being who He is: the great God of **power**. As you develop the habit of worshiping God at bedtime, rise-and-shine time, and other times in between, you'll find yourself becoming "one" with God. You'll like the things He likes, want the things He wants, do the things He desires. You'll discover your life becoming the answer to the prayer Jesus prayed in John 17:20-23! Read that prayer again together.

Q

When should I worship?

A

Worship God as often as you think of Him— morning, noon, and night.

▲ TAKE A STEP

Close this week by doing what the psalmist suggests:

Come, let us bow down in worship, let us kneel before the LORD our Maker; for He is our God (Psalm 95:6-7).

As the family kneels or folds their hands in reverence, have the oldest member read verses 3-7 of Psalm 95. Personalize it by substituting the words *you* and *yours* for *him* and *his*.

HOLINESS

"R yan, you've got to get those crayons off the table now," Angela announced with all the authority of an older sister. "Mom'll be home soon, and I've got to set the table."

"Aw, Angie, I'm almost done. Let me finish coloring."

"Okay, okay. Five more minutes. What is that thing, anyway?"

"A present for Mom," Ryan replied. "I'll wrap this drawing around a jar and put flowers in it. I think it will help Mom feel happy."

And Ryan's mother did feel happy when she found the decorated peanut butter jar in the center of the table—complete with its curious arrangement of brown pine needles. "They were the only flowers I could find," Ryan explained.

◆ THINKING ABOUT HOLINESS

Ryan's bouquet of pine straw wasn't very colorful or fragrant. But to his mother, it was beautiful! Beautiful because she knew the gift came from Ryan's heart—an expression of his love for her.

God too knows the hearts of His children. Though we don't always *act* as we should, He is looking for an *attitude* of obedience to His commands that comes from hearts that love Him.

● KEY VERSE ON HOLINESS

As obedient children, do not conform to . . . evil desires. . . . But just as he who called you is holy, so be holy in all you do (1 Peter 1:14-15).

▲ LOOKING AHEAD

The meaning of the word *holy* is **"set apart."** Just as you have items in your home (china, silverware, special clothes for Sunday) set apart for a special purpose, God does too. Read Genesis 2:3 to discover the first thing God called holy.

What do you think God meant in Exodus 20:8 when He commanded His people to "remember the Sabbath day by keeping it holy"? How do you keep that day of rest set apart from other days of the week?

"For breakfast I had a bowl of cereal with oat fiber, wheat fiber and rice fiber, but no moral fiber."

Nobody's perfect— not even parents!

Q

What is holiness?

A

Holiness is having a hatred for sin and a character like God's.

Already Mrs. Adams had cautioned Mike and Melinda at least three times to "settle down . . . remember what I said . . . don't play so rough." But their silly behavior got louder and louder.

Now as they waited for their mother to serve dinner, everything seemed to be funny. Melinda turned over a chair (laughter). Mike accidentally spilled his milk (more laughter).

"This is not funny at all!" Mrs. Adams suddenly shouted. "I've had enough." (More giggles.)

But Mrs. Adams wasn't kidding. She turned, picked up the dinner plates, raised them over her head, and dropped them with a crash in the middle of the kitchen floor! (Complete silence.)

"Now that I have your attention," she announced calmly to her two startled children, "Go to your rooms . . . now!"

As a bewildered Melinda tiptoed past, she whispered, "Mom, I don't understand. It's just not like you . . . "

◆ **TAKE A LOOK / Psalm 99**

Melinda was right. Her mother's behavior was definitely out of character. But the truth is, everyone loses control from time to time and does something he or she later regrets.

Everyone, that is, *except* God. All of God's acts are always in harmony with His character, and His character (as we learned yesterday) is holy. That means He is good in all His thoughts, actions, and attitudes. He has never done—nor will He ever do—anything that is less than perfectly right, good, just, fair, merciful, kind, and loving. The holiness of God sets Him apart from anything and everything that is wrong or evil.

The holiness of God is so important that heavenly beings constantly praise Him for it, crying:

"Holy, holy, holy is the LORD Almighty; the whole earth is full of his glory" (Isaiah 6:3).

▲ **TAKE A STEP**

Holiness is sinlessness. Anything that is sinful cannot be holy.

God hates sin—and He wants you, as His child, to detest it too. After reading Psalm 99, see if you can think of three things you *do not* do—and three things you *do*—because you want to be a person who is holy (set apart).

A fter two days, the rain finally stopped. Keith and Kevin could hardly wait to go outside. "Just be sure to stay dry," their mother warned as she bundled them into warm jackets. "And come when I call."

Thirty minutes later, Mrs. Sanders looked out the window. There, soaked from head to toe and splashing in the nearest mud puddle, were her two young sons. As she removed their soggy clothes, she heard the first sneeze. "I wouldn't be surprised if you both catch colds," she scolded. "Why didn't you obey me?"

Five-year-old Kevin thought a minute, then gave his truthful reply: "Well, Mom, it was more fun not to."

◆ TAKE A LOOK / 1 Samuel 8:4-9, 17-19

Keith and Kevin's decision to disobey their mother and play in the mud puddles is like the decision many people make about holy living: "It's more fun not to."

In Old Testament times God led the Israelites to a land all their own—the Promised Land. He would be their King and show them how to be a holy nation, set apart for God and different from the other nations around them.

But gradually the Israelites took up the sinful ways of their neighbors. Soon they demanded an earthly king.

Read about "The Country Where God Was King" in 1 Samuel 8:4-9, 17-19. Compare what God says in 1 Thessalonians 4:7-8 about those who refuse to be holy.

▲ TAKE A STEP

In demanding an earthly king, the people of Israel ignored the consequences of their choice. In the same way Kevin and Keith didn't think about the sore throats that might result from getting wet on a cold day. They thought their mother was trying to spoil their fun. Actually she wanted them to have the best kind of fun.

For your own good, God wants you to live a holy life:

Let us purify ourselves from everything that contaminates body and spirit, perfecting holiness out of reverence for God (2 Corinthians 7:1).

Holiness through obedience to God is not simply a nice idea. It is the *only* path to true happiness! How might Keith and Kevin have pleased God—and avoided three days in bed—by putting that verse to work?

Everybody's doing it, so why can't I?

Q

Why does God want me to be holy?

A

Holiness is part of God's plan for my happiness.

PARENT:
Explain to your child the "why" behind some of the restrictions you have placed on certain activities. Let your child share how he or she feels about the restrictions.

Holiness is hard work— and heart work

The emergency call had come late Friday night, and the Andersons were leaving instructions with their two teenagers:

"Rob, you can reach us at Grandpa's house," Mr. Anderson said. "We won't be back until late tomorrow, so you'll need to start the Saturday yardwork. The garage could also use a good cleaning. Do as much as you can, and we'll finish it next week."

"Rachel," Mrs. Anderson continued, "there's a casserole in the refrigerator for lunch, and here's money for dinner out. About the housework—just make sure the laundry is folded, and tidy up the house a bit. Okay?"

Upon returning home late Saturday night, the Andersons found the lawn half-mowed and the garage still cluttered and unswept. But they entered a house that was tidied up, cleaned, and polished.

Q

Why is holiness more than a list of do's and don'ts?

A

Holiness is obedience with a willing heart.

◆ **TAKE A LOOK / Matthew 15:1-9**

Rob and Rachel followed their parents' instructions. But each had a different attitude toward the tasks. Rob did very little, using the excuse, "We'll finish it next week." He did just enough to avoid punishment. Rachel, on the other hand, did more than she was asked to do.

In Jesus' day a group of religious leaders, called the Pharisees, thought they were being holy because they were keeping God's law better than anyone else did. Eventually, however, keeping the rules became more important to them than having attitudes that pleased God. Read Matthew 15:1-9 to learn what Jesus said about the Pharisees' attitudes and actions.

▲ **TAKE A STEP**

Jesus used strong language to teach the Pharisees a lesson about holiness—and their own hearts.

God's Word is God's will. It is one of the most important ways He guides us. We should always obey God's laws. But holiness is more than keeping a list of do's and don'ts. God is looking for hearts that are "thirsty" to do His will!

As the deer pants for streams of water, so my soul [heart] pants for you, O God. My soul [heart] thirsts for God, for the living God (Psalm 42:1-2).

Rob could learn an important lesson from his sister Rachel in wholehearted holy living—a lesson the Pharisees were seemingly too busy to learn. What do you think that lesson is?

Marshall felt special. He was the only person by that name in his entire kindergarten class—in fact, in his whole school! But he was quickly discovering that a shorter name like Ted or Joe would sure be a lot easier to write.

The letter l was easy—just a straight line. But that upper case M and the s—those were two tough letters.

Head bent in concentration, his pencil tightly clenched in his hand, Marshall tried once more to write his name. Suddenly, he felt Mrs. Lucas's gentle hand on his. "Those M's are pretty hard, aren't they, Marshall? Let me get you started."

She bent down, took his small hand in her larger one, and guided the pencil slowly, carefully over the paper. Marshall grinned at the result: a perfect upper case M.

◆ TAKE A LOOK / John 14:15-27

We learned yesterday that holiness is not simply a list of do's and don'ts. It is obedience to God's will coming from a heart that wants to obey Him and be like Him more than anything else. But just as Marshall lacked the muscle control to form the letters of the alphabet, so too the child of God needs help to live a holy life.

Even the 12 men (called disciples) who spent three years traveling with Jesus were not able to do His will without a power greater than their own. And so, before Jesus died, He promised to send the Holy Spirit to live within them and be their Helper. Read the exciting promise Jesus made in John 14:15-27.

▲ TAKE A STEP

The power you need to live a holy life doesn't come from a pill. Rather, it comes from a Person— the Holy Spirit—who is present in the life of every child of God.

The Holy Spirit takes the truth of God's Word and teaches you what holy living is all about: being aware of sin, confessing your sins to God, avoiding Satan's traps, filling your heart and mind with God's thoughts. Then, once you know what to do, the Holy Spirit gives you the power to do it!

For it is God who works in you to will and to act according to his good purpose (Philippians 2:13).

Close your family devotional time today by reading the words of Ephesians 3:16-19 aloud as your family prayer for holiness.

Heavenly help for holy living

Q

Where does the power to live a holy life come from?

A

God's Spirit gives me the power to live a holy life.

LEISURE

W hat is this life if, full of care,
We have no time to stand and stare.
No time to stand beneath the boughs
And stare as long as sheep or cows.
No time to see, when woods we pass,
Where squirrels hide their nuts in grass.
No time to see, in broad daylight,
Streams full of stars, like stars at night. . . .
A poor life this if, full of care,
We have no time to stand and stare.

From "Leisure," by William Henry Davies in A CHILD'S TREASURY OF VERSE, compiled by Eleanor Doan. Copyright 1977, Zondervan Publishing House. Used by permission.

◆ THINKING ABOUT LEISURE
"It's a waste of time to stand and stare," you might protest. But is it really?

We can divide each day God has given us into 24 hours . . . 1,440 minutes . . . 86,400 seconds. But no matter how you divide it, *all* your time belongs to the Lord. And that means, whether working or relaxing, you need this attitude in your heart:

● KEY VERSE ON LEISURE
This is the day the LORD has made; let us rejoice and be glad in it (Psalm 118:24).

▲ LOOKING AHEAD
Most people think about leisure as a vacation—two weeks spent going "somewhere" exciting and doing "something" fun. But leisure isn't something you have to wait for. Leisure is any **planned pause in your regular routine.**

"Mother will never be able to rest on her laurels. If they're green, she'll cook 'em!"

Were you aware Jesus told His disciples to enjoy leisure time? Read Mark 6:30-32 to see what their mini-vacation included.

Swap stories from your family's unforgettable vacations: "I remember when . . ."

If I had only a short time to live, I would immediately contact all the people I had ever loved, and I'd make sure they knew I really loved them. Then I would play all the music that meant most to me and I would sing all my favorite songs. And oh! I would dance. I would dance all night.

"I would look at my blue skies and feel my warm sunshine. I would tell the moon and the stars how lovely and beautiful they are. I would say 'goodbye' to all the little things I own, my clothes, my books and my 'stuff.' Then I would thank God for the great gift of life, and die in His arms."*

Make sure to play a little every day

◆ **TAKE A LOOK / Leviticus 23:39-43**

What would *you* do if you knew you had only a short time to live? The college student who wrote the above essay realized that happiness can only be found today—now—by enjoying the people around us, the things God has made, and the companionship of God Himself.

The Bible describes many joyful occasions for the nation of Israel—leisure times of feasting and celebrating happy times marked by good food and pleasant memories. Israel's seven annual feasts are described in Leviticus 23. Read about the "Feast of Booths" (also called the Feast of Tabernacles) in verses 39-43. Can you discover why it was called by that unusual title?

▲ **TAKE A STEP**

You do not have to go somewhere or buy something to be happy. You can discover happiness in moments of leisure by celebrating the fact that *this* day is special. The psalmist describes the secret of happiness this way:

Blessed are those who . . . walk in the light of your presence, O LORD. They rejoice in your name all day long" (Psalm 89:15-16).

Just as God planned special times of feasting and remembrance for His people, you can plan pauses in your routine to enjoy each once-in-a-lifetime, never-to-be-repeated day God gives you! Turn back to Genesis 1 and refresh your memory regarding what God created on each day of the week (Day One: light and darkness; Day Two: water and sky; etc.). Each day this week, pick one category of God's creation and thank Him for it. Today, think about all the kinds of *light* you enjoy each day and what life would be like without it.

Q

Why is it important to take time for leisure?

A

Leisure time reminds me that each day is a special gift from God.

*From *The Secret of Staying in Love*, by John Powell, S.J. Copyright 1974, Argus Communications, a division of DLM, Inc., Allen, Texas 75002. Used by permission.

Take time to be a child again

Q

Is leisure simply doing nothing?

A

Leisure time at its best involves play, not just rest.

PARENT: Many communities offer short, inexpensive courses in crafts, water safety, and other helpful skills. Taking a class may uncover hidden talents in you and your child.

O n weekends the earthmoving equipment was silent and the site was deserted—except for the children. As mountain climbers, they swarmed over the hills of dirt piled to the side of the new road. As warriors they defended the castle at the top. As bobsledders, they slid down the slopes on cardboard sleds. As race car drivers, they made trails and jumps for their bikes.

For another group of children miles away, the moss that spread between the roots of a large oak tree became a small world of make-believe. Tiny twigs, acorn caps, and leaves were transformed by imagination into roads and houses, castles and kingdoms, princesses and pirates.

◆ **TAKE A LOOK / Ecclesiastes 11:9–12:7**

Children play hard and rest well. As God's beloved children, shouldn't we enjoy life that way?

Jesus said, "I have come that they may have life, and have it to the full" (John 10:10). This doesn't mean we should never work. It does mean that more than any other group of people, Christians should live life to the full!

There's no verse in the Bible that says, "Go out and play." But there is a Scripture that says:

Remember your Creator in the days of your youth (Ecclesiastes 12:1).

The author of Ecclesiastes describes how the passing of time can rob us of some of the happy activities we enjoyed earlier in life. At the conclusion of the book (Ecclesiastes 11:9–12:7), you'll discover a word picture of old age. Growing older can be a rich, rewarding time; but running, jumping, and playing become more difficult with each passing year. (If you don't believe it, just ask Mom or Dad.) As you read those verses, see if you can match each phrase with the part of the body it describes: weak eyes, toothless mouth, old bones, weak knees, or deaf ears.

▲ **TAKE A STEP**

When was the last time you played catch? Caught a fish? Told jokes until you couldn't stop laughing? Went barefoot in the grass? Splashed in a puddle? Walked in the rain? Took a nap in a hammock? Enjoyed a nature hike?

Plan a family fun time for later in the week. Fly a kite, take a walk, toss a ball, wade in a creek, splash in a puddle, build a sandcastle. Let your imagination stretch and soar as you plan. But whatever you do, do it just for fun!

*T*he physics and chemistry courses in high school never got people excited. We used a book that was actually called "Dull," and I really absorbed more physics by learning it from my friends. I read lots of college outline physics books. But then someone would say, "Hey, I learned some quantum physics last night, and it's not so hard," and the rest of us would get so jealous we'd go out and get some physics textbooks to learn it ourselves.

The math courses were very good, but there was no calculus. I learned it in the lunchroom from friends. . . . What you become in life depends partly on whom you go to school with.

I might as well go to summer school

◆ TAKE A LOOK / Matthew 25:14-30

How often do you spend time learning something new—just for the fun of it? The words above were spoken by Dr. Sheldon Glashow, a Nobel Prize winner who discovered as a student that what he learned in his leisure time was as important as what he learned in class. If he had limited himself only to what he heard in classrooms, he might never have understood the marvels of physics or developed his scientific talents.

Some people think that leisure time means empty time, but *leisure* can mean *learning*. Jesus told the parable of a rich man who gave each of three servants a different amount of money (called talents). He then went on a journey; but when he returned, he asked the servants what they had done with his money. As you read this parable in Matthew 25:14-30, try to imagine what *you* would have done with *your* talents.

Q

How can learning be leisure?

A

Leisure time used for learning can multiply the talents God has given me.

▲ TAKE A STEP

Just as the servants were responsible for their money, you are responsible for how you use the time, talents, and abilities God has given you.

For everyone who has will be given more, and he will have an abundance. Whoever does not have, even what he has will be taken from him (Matthew 25:29).

You might never win a Nobel Prize, but you can use your leisure time to stretch your mental, spiritual, and physical muscles by learning or doing something new: fix something you have that doesn't work, try a new recipe, memorize a Bible verse. Say, how *will* you use your leisure time this week to make your "talent" multiply?

With a vacation like this, who needs work?

Q

How long should leisure time last?

A

Leisure time needs to last long enough for people to be refreshed.

PARENT:
Vacations offer opportunities for unforgettable times of family worship—if you plan for them.

*T*he Wilsons were on their way at last—Dad, Mom, Evie (9), Jonas (4), Jordan (8 months), and Grandma (age unknown). With a trunk full of beach equipment they set out on a six-hour drive to their rented beach cabin and a much-needed two-week vacation.

One hour into the trip, Jonas got carsick. Two hours along, the baby developed heat rash. At the three-hour mark, Evie and Jonas declared war in the back seat. At five hours, Dad took a wrong turn. At seven hours, Mom was ready to go back home.

During the next 10 days, the Wilsons endured blistering heat, crowded beaches, five cases of sunburn, and countless frazzled nerves. When they finally returned home, Dad couldn't wait to get back to work. Mom vowed never to leave town again. And Grandma joined a senior citizens' vacation club!

◆ **TAKE A LOOK / Deuteronomy 5:12-15**

For many families the summer vacation is the highlight of the year. It's saved for, planned for, and anticipated all year!

The idea of taking a well-deserved rest from your work is not new. After six days of creation God rested on the seventh day and set it apart (Genesis 2:3). Years later, God's people—the Israelites—found themselves enslaved in the land of Egypt, working 365 days a year with no time to worship or rest. After Moses led them out of bondage in the dramatic events of the Exodus, God reaffirmed the importance of a day of rest. Discover the name of that day by reading Deuteronomy 5:12-15.

▲ **TAKE A STEP**

For the Wilsons, a two-week vacation became more *work* than *rest*. But whether your family takes a long trip each year or only rests one day a week, that time should be a change of pace from your regular routine—a chance to be refreshed in mind, body, and spirit.

For anyone who enters God's rest also rests from his own work, just as God did from his (Hebrews 4:10).

Make the most of your vacations—whether they are long or short, a month or a weekend. Begin your creative planning by having each family member describe his or her dream vacation. Then make your family vacation plans for this year (or next). And when you go, relax and don't feel guilty!

SUCCESS

*W*hen Mr. Williams, the chemistry teacher, announced the homework assignment, Wade took one look at the problems, closed his book, crossed his arms, and stared out the window. "This is impossible," he thought. "I'll never learn to do these awful equations."

Wade had always been a good student—and chemistry hadn't seemed all that tough at first. But in four weeks, Wade had failed three tests! Every day as the class moved further ahead, Wade fell further behind. But worse than that were the feelings Wade began to have about himself. He began to wonder if he could do anything right.

◆ THINKING ABOUT SUCCESS

Like most students, Wade wanted to succeed in school. In the world today there are many ways to measure success. Money, ability, beauty, intelligence, and grades are just a few of the "measuring sticks" for success. **Success is meeting up to the standard you are being measured by.** In Wade's case, that standard was a C for a passing grade in chemistry.

Sometimes we may feel as if we've failed because we use the wrong "yardstick" to measure progress. For example, if Wade thought he needed to get 100 percent on every test in order to succeed, he would think he failed even if he got a 90! So it's important to know whose standard is the right one.

● KEY VERSE ON SUCCESS

You will have success if you are careful to observe the decrees and laws [of] the LORD (1 Chronicles 22:13).

▲ LOOKING AHEAD

Begin your study of success this week by reading Joshua 1:9 to find God's key to success. Then for fun, find a yardstick or ruler, and measure how long each family member's right foot is. If the standard of success was, "The person with the shortest foot wins," who would win at your house?

"Don't guess I have to worry about success going to my head."

This yard-stick is an inch too short

Because Karl was always so quick to tell about his day, tonight's silence was very unusual.

"Karl," his mother began, "is something wrong?"

"Naw, Mom, I can handle it," he mumbled without looking up.

Now his parents were concerned. "Is there something we can do to help?" his father asked.

"Dad, it's okay. No big deal. Really."

"Karl!" His father's voice was stern now.

"Well, I . . . uh . . . I got kicked out of school for three days," he blurted out quickly.

Mrs. Ellis gasped. Mr. Ellis scowled. But before either could respond, Karl shook his head and grinned.

"I'm just kidding. Actually, I did get in trouble, but I didn't get suspended. I just have to stay after school tomorrow because I was cutting up in class."

◆ **TAKE A LOOK / 1 John 2:15-17**

Karl jokingly made his *bad news* sound like *good news* by comparing it with really *bad news*. Success is like that. It really doesn't mean much until you have something to measure it by.

Some people think having a great deal of *money* is the "yardstick" of success. But if that were true, then Jesus was a failure. He had to pay His taxes with a coin found in a fish's mouth!

Another "measuring stick" some people use is *clothes*. But stop and think; when Jesus died, He owned only one garment. Was Jesus successful? It all depends on how you measure His life.

You can read about God's standard for success in 1 John 2:15-17.

▲ **TAKE A STEP**

From God's point of view Jesus was successful because like the psalmist, He could say from the heart:

I desire to do your will, O my God; your law is within my heart (Psalm 40:8).

Making money, wearing expensive clothes, being seen with the right people—none of these is an accurate way to measure success. For that you need God's words in the Bible, the only true "measuring stick" for successful living.

Discuss some of the ways people you know measure success. Is it by making money, looking good, doing well in studies or sports?

After you've looked at your "yardsticks," have each person read Psalm 40:8 out loud. There's no better prayer you can pray if success is your goal!

Q

How can I know how to measure success?

A

I must measure success by the standard of God's Word.

Disappointment covered the team like a soggy blanket. They had come so close, only to lose in the final few seconds. Now on the long ride home, the team members were trying to cheer each other up by reliving some of the exciting plays during the game.

"Could you believe that basket John made just before the buzzer at halftime? He must have been unconscious!"

"Tony, you were really hot. Another game like that and you'll be a starter next year for sure."

And on and on. But no amount of talk could change the final score, and at last someone spoke the words all were thinking.

"If the refs had just called that last foul, we would have won. Those guys must be blind. It's their fault we lost . . ."

◆ **TAKE A LOOK / Luke 18:10-14**

Do you remember the last time your teacher handed back test papers? Did you hear comments like these: "I made an *A*!" . . . "He gave me an *F*."

If we fail, it's someone else's fault; if we succeed, we take all the credit.

But God doesn't look at your grades or the number of trophies on your shelves. God measures how well you follow His Rulebook, the Bible. Jesus told a parable that illustrates what God thinks of man's success stories. Read it in Luke 18:10-14.

▲ **TAKE A STEP**

Jesus said the tax collector went home "justified." The Pharisee did not. *Justified* means "not guilty" before God. What made the difference in the way God saw them?

The Pharisee thought a successful man was one who did many good deeds—prayer, fasting, giving money—in order to make friends with God. The tax collector knew he could never do enough good deeds to please God. The Pharisee was *proud* of himself; the tax collector was *ashamed* of himself and counting on God to forgive him. Together, they show what this verse means:

"Everyone who exalts himself will be humbled, and he who humbles himself will be exalted" (Luke 18:14).

The team was disappointed at losing the big game. But blaming the referees wasn't the answer. What can they learn that will help them be successful in future games, *regardless of the final score?*

Losers don't always finish last

Q

How does God define success?

A

Success with God means doing things His way.

PARENT: *Analyze the "measuring sticks" you use with your child. Are they fair, just, and merciful? Do you avoid comparing one child's behavior with another?*

Everydoby can learn to reab, can't they?

Q

What if I don't have what I need to succeed?

A

I will succeed if I let God's strength be seen in my weakness.

None of his classmates knew Mike had a problem. They liked his bright, pleasant attitude and his sense of humor. But when it came to school work, everyone thought he was a failure—someone who didn't try very hard and probably didn't care.

But Mike did care. He did try. In fact, he had been trying hard ever since first grade when he began learning to read and write. Day after day, hour after hour, Mike had tried to learn to read. But he was always behind, and his grades were always disappointing. He just couldn't seem to catch on.

Though many of his classmates thought of him as a failure, Mike, his parents, and the few teachers who understood his situation knew that in many ways he was a success. For Mike suffered from severe dyslexia (dis-LEX-ee-ah)—a condition which causes letters of the alphabet to appear backward, making it very difficult to learn to read.

◆ **TAKE A LOOK / 2 Corinthians 12:7-10**

When Mike opened a book, he did not see what other students saw. Instead, his brain scrambled the printed words. So when Mike was measured by the standards used for average readers, he seemed to be a failure instead of a success.

Like Mike, we all experience failure because of our human limitations. But God doesn't expect *everyone* to be able to do *everything*. He has given us different abilities, and He uses our weaknesses to show us how much we need Him.

The Apostle Paul also had a weakness in his life—and it was there for a very important reason. See if you can discover both the *what* and the *why* of Paul's weakness by reading 2 Corinthians 12:7-10.

▲ **TAKE A STEP**

Paul reminds us of the secret of success:

I delight in weaknesses. . . . For when I am weak, then I am strong (2 Corinthians 12:10).

Failure in the eyes of those around you isn't nearly as important as success in the eyes of God. And that kind of success comes as you allow God's strength to shine through your weakness.

Even Mike with his reading problem could show others God's power at work in his life. Can you identify an area of your life where you can do the same?

*I*t wasn't because Karla didn't know better. She knew what the Bible says. Her youth pastor had even taught a course on "Dating and Sex," and her mom had given her good instruction. But none of that mattered now. She had done the wrong thing, and now there was a baby on the way.

And so 15-year-old Karla sat weeping in her pastor's office. "Nobody knows—not Mom and not my boyfriend—not yet, anyway. Help me, please, Pastor. Just tell me what to do. I didn't want it to turn out this way . . . "

◆ TAKE A LOOK / Judges 16:18-30

Do you remember our definition of success? It is *meeting up to the standard we are being measured by.* But what happens when we sin and fall far short of doing what pleases God?

The life of Samson will help answer that important question. Samson was the leader of the nation of Israel, but he fell in love with the beautiful Philistine woman Delilah—*one of the enemies of God's people.* After he revealed the secret of his strength to her, Delilah cut off his hair. Samson's enemies easily captured him. They blinded him and put him in prison. Samson looked like a hopeless failure.

But the story has a surprise ending. Read Judges 16:18-30 to discover how God turned Samson's failure into success.

▲ TAKE A STEP

In many ways, Samson was a failure. Even though he was the strongest man in the world, Samson couldn't control his weaknesses. But after his terrible failure, Samson discovered that the Lord was willing to forgive him and use him again.

No sin is too big for God to forgive; no failure too great for God to overcome. The secret of success is to agree with God:

If we confess our sins, he is faithful and just and will forgive us our sins and purify us from all unrighteousness (1 John 1:9).

Karla needed that forgiveness and cleansing as never before in her life. By talking with her pastor, she was taking the first step toward confessing her sin. It wouldn't be easy, but with God's help she was going to make it through the tough months ahead. If you were her friend, how would you encourage Karla now?

Failure may be the back door to success

Q

What should I do if I fail?

A

If I fail, I need to confess my sin and accept God's forgiveness.

PARENT: *Discuss with your child the difference between grudges, getting even, and enjoying God's cleansing and forgiveness.*

ANGELS

E very Saturday morning, millions of American children sit in front of TV sets watching the amazing adventures of the Superfriends, powerful defenders of justice and right.

With their wonderful powers, Superman, Wonder Woman, Aquaman, and others rescue people in trouble, defeat nasty villains, and protect nations from evil dictators—all in the "nick of time."

But everyone knows the Superfriends are just pretend. Nobody could ever fly like that, move through the oceans with such ease, or have such power at their fingertips . . . could they?

◆ THINKING ABOUT ANGELS

To be sure, no human being has that kind of power. But there is a group of heavenly "Superfriends"—spirit beings created by God and called "angels."

The name *angel* comes from a word meaning "to deliver a message," and that's exactly what angels are—**God's messengers.** The Bible speaks of angels over 300 times and tells us much about them: They have great power but are not all-powerful; they are usually invisible but sometimes can be seen; they are organized like an army; they worship before God's throne; and they protect God's people.

● KEY VERSE ON ANGELS

Are not all angels ministering spirits sent to serve those who will inherit salvation? (Hebrews 1:14).

"Unless your name's Daniel, I'd get down."

▲ LOOKING AHEAD

The Superfriends get their power from a TV writer's imagination. Just imagine how exciting it's going to be this week learning about *real* super beings who get their power from God!

You'll see one way angels help believers as you read Psalm 91:11. Can you think of an Old Testament person who was guarded and helped by angels? For the answer, look in Daniel 6:22.

*T*his would be a special present for Daddy. The appointment with the photographer was for 1 p.m., but the "getting ready" had started the night before when Mother had washed and dried Mandy's long blond hair. Now dressed in lacy white tights, black slippers, and a pink frilly dress, three-year-old Mandy looked like a sweet, cotton-candy cloud.

"Hold still now, I'm almost done," her mother urged as she tied a pink ribbon around Mandy's carefully combed curls. Then stepping back to admire her work, Mother exclaimed with delight, "You look just like an angel!"

Oh, if I had the wings of an angel . . .

◆ TAKE A LOOK
Genesis 3:21-24; Revelation 22:16

Little girls may sometimes look sweet enough to eat, but they never *really* look like an angel.

According to the Bible, angels are messengers of God. They are powerful beings created by God to serve Him in heaven, on earth, and throughout the universe. Although angels may sometimes look like human beings, they are not human. Some (called *cherubim*) are guardians of God's honor; some (called *seraphim*) have six wings and stand in God's presence.

Angels are not always gentle either. Sometimes their job is to bring God's judgment upon wicked people. The two angels who came to warn Lot that God was going to destroy the wicked cities of Sodom and Gomorrah are examples of angels who didn't bring good news (Genesis 18:16–19:29).

Nearly every book of the Bible mentions angels. Today, look at the *first* place where they are mentioned (Genesis 3:21-24), the *last* place (Revelation 22:16), and one place in-between (Psalm 103:20-21). Keep pencil and paper handy this week, and see how many things you can learn about these remarkable beings who do God's will.

Praise the LORD, you his angels, you mighty ones who do his bidding, who obey his word (Psalm 103:20).

▲ TAKE A STEP

Did you discover the one important way that Mandy *could* resemble an angel? Of course! She could learn to do God's will. For Mandy that means obeying God's Word. You too can obey in the same way. You don't have to be as "cute as an angel" to be as obedient as one!

Q

How are angels different from people?

A

Angels are different from people because they are spirit beings.

It's a fight with an invisible enemy

Oh, Mom, isn't there something you can do? I feel like I'm on fire, it hurts so bad."

"Sweetheart, I wish I could do something, but you'll just have to wait this one out. The doctor said it will be two or three more days before you feel well enough to go back to school."

"Mom, I feel so dumb. All I wanted to do was keep my summer tan. Now I'll look horrible for months."

"Well, I'm thankful you didn't damage your eyes. Sun lamps can be very dangerous. What I don't understand is why you let Leslie talk you into this."

"I don't know, Mom. It looked safe, and it didn't even feel hot. How was I to know I was going to turn into a French fry?"

Q

Are there really "good" angels and "bad" angels?

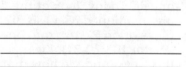

TAKE A LOOK / 1 Peter 5:8

Judy suffered a nasty burn because she didn't know about invisible rays of light. In a similar way, understanding angels—the invisible spirit beings who inhabit our planet—can keep us from getting spiritually burned.

The Bible teaches us there are *good* angels who do God's will, and *bad* angels called "demons" who rebelled against God and became His enemies. Demons and their leader Satan are busily trying to stop God's plan and destroy God's children.

For your Bible study today, do some Scripture sleuthing. Have one or two family members look up the following verses while another records the facts you learn in the space provided.

A

Angels who rebelled against God are evil beings called "demons."

Reference	Clues about the Enemy
1 Peter 5:8	_____
John 8:44	_____
2 Corinthians 4:4	_____
2 Corinthians 11:14	_____
Ephesians 2:2	_____

PARENT:
Discuss with your child some ways in which the names of Satan (father of lies, god of this world, angel of light) depict his activities.

TAKE A STEP

Though Satan and his demons are determined enemies of God (and we need to be aware of their tricks), it is also important to realize that God's power is greater than theirs.

The One who is in you is greater than the one who is in the world (1 John 4:4).

That means in the fight between God and Satan, God will ultimately win. Since we're on God's side, we will win too. Read the final score in Revelation 20:10.

*T*hat night after her two children were in bed, the shaken young mother shared the day's terrifying events.

"When I took the car to the garage," she began, "the mechanic told me to drive his car until ours was ready. His back seat was piled with stuff and there were no seatbelts, so I told the kids to sit real still in the front seat. Jeannie was in the middle and Joel was by the door." She paused to take a breath.

"Just as I was turning left onto the four-lane, I saw the passenger door swinging open. Before I could stop him, Joel grabbed for the door, fell out of the car, and disappeared. I thought he had rolled under the car. There was a car coming up on the right side, and my first thought was, 'It's going to hit him—or I'm going to run over him.' But before I could stop, there was Joel sitting on the seat with the door closed! When I asked him what happened, he said he rolled over and over, and then it felt like somebody just picked him up and put him back on the seat."

◆ **TAKE A LOOK / Psalm 34:7; 91:9-14**

Seeing an angel is a rare event. The Bible records only 32 times when angels appeared to people. When they did, it was usually under special circumstances (such as Daniel in the lions' den, or Gabriel telling Mary she would become the mother of God's Son).

Even though angels are usually *invisible*, they are not inactive. Some of them are busy protecting us from danger. Jesus mentioned these guardian angels when He cautioned His disciples not to look down on little children. Why? Because . . .

"Their angels in heaven always see the face of my Father in heaven" (Matthew 18:10).

Read what else the Bible has to say about these heavenly helpers in Psalm 34:7 and Psalm 91:9-14.

▲ **TAKE A STEP**

Probably every family can tell a story of protection like the one you read today. Accidents don't just happen. And it is no accident that angels are busy protecting us from the circumstances and dangers that are not a part of God's plan.

Retell one or two accounts when a member of your family was protected from harm. Then close your time together today by thanking God for His daily protection and for the unseen bodyguards He uses to keep your family safe.

All night, all day, angels watchin' over me

Q

What do guardian angels do?

A

Angels guard and protect God's people.

Fighting a battle we've already won

Q

How can knowing about angels help me?

A

Angels are on the "winning team"— and so am I if I'm saved.

PARENT: On the topic of the angelic conflict, we recommend Satan is No Myth by J. Oswald Sanders, The Adversary by Mark Bubeck, and the fiction books This Present Darkness and Piercing the Darkness by Frank Peretti.

Don't you dare tell me. I don't want to hear."

"Aw, come on, Cindy, everyone wants to know what they're getting for their birthday. I saw Mom wrapping it yesterday. It's a . . . "

"DON'T!" Cindy exclaimed. "I like surprises, and you're going to spoil it if you tell me."

But Cindy's little brother just grinned. He liked nothing better than to tease his big sister. "Just wait. When you're not looking, I'm going to sneak up and whisper it in your ear."

"Mother," Cindy yelled, "make Craig promise not to . . . "

"R-A-D-I-O!"

◆ TAKE A LOOK / Romans 8:35-39

Cindy wanted her birthday present to remain a mystery until she opened it. She didn't want Craig spoiling the surprise by telling her in advance. But in real life, it's sometimes nice to know ahead of time how things are going to turn out once they're "unwrapped": that important test, Grandpa's serious illness, the championship game.

The Apostle Paul knew that life doesn't always work out the way we might hope. Sometimes when things go all wrong, we may even wonder if God still loves us.

Satan and his army are at war with God, and because we are God's children, that means Satan is at war with us, too. Is he strong enough . . . or smart enough . . . or big enough . . . or mean enough to separate us from God's love? That's a very important question! Romans 8:35-39 gives the encouraging answer.

▲ TAKE A STEP

Fighting a war is never easy. Fighting a war against an invisible enemy is even tougher. But fighting a war against an invisible and powerful enemy sounds hopeless from the start!

That's why it's important to remember that the spiritual war with Satan has already been won. Jesus Christ made sure of that. His death and resurrection show that He conquered sin, Satan, and death once and for all. That's why the Apostle Paul can say with confidence:

I am convinced that . . . neither angels nor demons . . . will be able to separate us from the love of God that is in Christ Jesus our Lord (Romans 8:38-39).

Are you convinced? Then tell God so right now!

LOVE

The two young men, friends since seventh grade, had been camping together for a week. Now, packed and ready to hike out, they were enjoying one last swim in the icy river.

Suddenly, David noticed that Brent was in trouble. Without a thought for his own safety, he dived in to help his friend. As he reached Brent and hooked his arm around him, David felt the fierce pull of the strong current. It had almost overpowered his friend; now it threatened to sweep them both down stream.

"Hold on, we'll make it," David panted as he started towing Brent to shore. Then suddenly it hit—the cramp that every swimmer dreads.

◆ THINKING ABOUT LOVE

Love is more than warm fuzzy feelings. Sometimes it's courage, as with David and Brent. At other times it is kindness, unselfishness, or patience. But in all its many forms, love is **meeting another's needs without expecting something in return.**

You don't have to say "I love you" to communicate it, either. David showed his love for Brent by risking his life. He was a living example of what Jesus meant when He said these words to His disciples:

● KEY VERSE ON LOVE

"Greater love has no one than this, that he lay down his life for his friends" (John 15:13).

▲ LOOKING AHEAD

On a large piece of poster board copy the words of 1 Corinthians 13:4-7. Read those words together now and each day this week. Each time you read, discuss a different characteristic of love.

You might even like to choose a portion of the chapter (one or two verses) and compose a tune to match the words. Think of this chapter as God's love letter to you—a message worth taking to heart!

"I hope she recognizes this as a labor of love. She's not gonna recognize it as breakfast."

Love is the glue that holds life together

*T*he baby was a "preemie." He had been born two months early and needed a great deal of special care. He was placed in an incubator and cared for round the clock in a "neonatal" (newborn) nursery. Special machines checked his breathing, heartbeat, and temperature.

But even though machines saved the baby's life, he needed something no machine could provide: a loving human touch. *So, several times a day, his mother came to the nursery, put on germ-free clothing, and held her tiny baby. She rocked him, sang lullabies, fed him, and whispered tender words. The days and weeks went by, and the tiny infant grew and thrived. When he weighed five pounds, his proud parents took him home.*

◆ TAKE A LOOK / 1 Corinthians 12:31–13:3

"Have You Hugged Your Child Today?" is a familiar bumper sticker that carries an important message: Children need to be loved in order to grow.

Doctors and nurses know that sick babies can't grow unless they are held and cuddled. People who work in nursing homes often bring in puppies and kittens for the elderly people to pet. They have learned that happiness comes from giving and receiving love.

Modern science has discovered what God told us in the Bible long ago: Love makes a difference. The Apostle Paul says it this way:

If I give all I possess to the poor . . . but have not love, I gain nothing (1 Corinthians 13:3).

Read about this powerful force for good—and what life would be like without it—in the last verse of 1 Corinthians 12 and the first three verses of chapter 13.

▲ TAKE A STEP

Paul wrote about things that are important: speech, knowledge, faith, even life itself. But without the all-important ingredient of love, these things are worth nothing. They amount to zero.

In the life of the premature baby boy, all the machines, medicines, and manpower in the world couldn't do what his mother's gentle touch and tender words could do.

By the way, when was the last time you told another family member, "I love you"? Turn to the person on your right and tell him or her . . . right now! It's "special treatment" everyone needs!

Q

Why does love make a difference?

A

Love makes a difference because without it everything else adds up to nothing.

A daughter-in-law gives up her part-time job to care for her elderly mother-in-law.

A couple spends a Saturday painting a widow's house.

An older brother celebrates his younger brother's promotion, even though he knows he will never achieve an equal position.

A teenage boy rises when his grandmother enters the room and holds the chair for his aunt at dinner.

The parents of a runaway daughter keep a light in her room, believing that one day she will come home.

What do these and countless other actions have in common? They all say "love" in a way no one can miss.

◆ TAKE A LOOK / 1 Corinthians 13:4-7

Love is a lot like *light*. Though light appears to be white, in fact it is many different colors. If you pass a beam of light through a prism, you will see it break apart into the colors of a rainbow. But chances are, you don't often think about the different parts of light. You simply enjoy their effects.

The effects of love in your life are like that. You experience love daily without thinking too much about it—that is, until it's no longer there! Then you miss it.

Love has many "parts." It can be seen in many different ways. Some of those ways are listed for you in 1 Corinthians 13:4-7. From the poster you made on Day One read together the parts of Paul's "spectrum of love."

▲ TAKE A STEP

When your parents try to protect you or when they treat you with patience, they are saying "I love you." When you trust your parents or do something kind for them, you are telling them "I love you."

Contrary to what some people say, love is *not* a feeling or an emotion. It is an act of your will in which you say, "I will treat that person as Christ would. I will try to meet his needs without expecting something in return."

A few minutes ago you read examples of five people who put love to work. Can you match each *action* of love with the corresponding *attitude* of love that Paul mentions in verses 4-7?

"[Love] always protects, always trusts, always hopes, always perseveres" (1 Corinthians 13:7).

By any other name, love is still the same

Q

How can I recognize love at work?

A

Love is at work when I see its effects.

PARENT: Let the "spectrum of love" reflect on your family by asking your child to identify examples of love in your home: "Mom washes my gym clothes, Dad drives for my paper route, sister helps with the vacuuming . . . "

You can't take it with you . . . unless it's love

Q

Why is love so important?

A

Love lasts forever.

Fourteen-year-old Rosemary finally persuaded her grandmother to show her the things in the cedar chest—that treasure box full of Grandmother's keepsakes. What an adventure it was!

"Grandma, did you actually wear this?" Rosemary giggled, holding up a faded wedding dress. "It's so skinny! And this hat. How could you have worn that?"

Each discovery sent Rosemary into gales of laughter. The "good old days" sure were different! But there were sad moments, too, especially when Rosemary found the christening dress of her grandmother's first baby—the little girl who had died suddenly from measles.

Now they were sitting side by side on the bed, carefully turning the brittle pages of a photo album. Suddenly, Rosemary squealed, "Grandmother, is that you? In a model T? We read about those old cars in history last week. Tell me what it was like to ride in one."

◆ TAKE A LOOK / 1 Corinthians 13:8-13

Have you ever ridden in a droshky, stanhope, cabriolet, or model T? Have you ever worn a wimple? Like Grandmother's treasures, the fads and inventions of yesterday have become the antiques of today.

In 1 Corinthians 13:8-13, the Apostle Paul speaks of three things that were very important to the people living in his day—things they valued and thought would last forever. But they were wrong. Each of the three would fail to pass the test of time. See if you can find all three as you read those verses, along with the one thing that will last forever!

▲ TAKE A STEP

Why is love so important? Why is it the best thing anyone could ever hope to have, do, or be? Because . . .

Love never fails . . . (1 Corinthians 13:8).

Love is what *lasts*. It is what makes life worth living. Love endures forever because "God is love" (1 John 4:8), and God endures forever. The one thing you will find in heaven and on earth, the one thing that will outlive even Grandmother's cedar chest full of memories, is *love*.

Do you have a treasure chest at your house? Photo albums . . . hope chest . . . picture gallery? Spend a few minutes thinking about a loved one those treasures remind you of. After all, you'll be loving that person throughout eternity!

I hate her. She's horrible and I hate her."
With that angry outburst, Alicia fell sobbing across her bed. "Oh, honey," her mother soothed, "I know Mrs. McCormack seems mean and unfair at times. But hating her won't make the situation better. You're just hurting yourself and making both of you miserable."

"Mom, she's the meanest teacher I've ever had. She never even tries to be nice to anyone in the class. No matter how hard I try, it's impossible to do anything that pleases her. She criticizes everybody. And she won't let anyone be nice to her either. I've tried, Mom, I really have. But I don't think anyone *could* love Mrs. McCormack."

◆ TAKE A LOOK / Luke 6:27-36

The world is full of people who are hard to love. Parents who abuse their children, old people who complain constantly, children who are disrespectful and disobedient. Loving someone who is mean, self-centered, bitter, or proud is not an easy assignment—even if that someone is yourself!

Some people are easier to love than others, but God does not want us to pick and choose those we will love. Instead, He commands us to love every-one—even people we might want to label unlovely:
"Love your enemies, do good to those who hate you" (Luke 6:27).

Luke 6:27-36 contains some of the most challenging words in the whole Bible. Have each family member read one verse out loud until you have finished all nine verses.

▲ TAKE A STEP

On Day One we defined love as "meeting the needs of another without expecting something in return." But to *define* love is really the easy part. It is much more difficult to *do* the loving thing—especially if the person you are trying to love is as unlovely as Mrs. McCormack.

Think about a person whom *you* find difficult to love. Perhaps it's your teacher . . . or a classmate . . . or even another family member. Do you *feel* like loving that person? Probably not! But did Jesus command you to *feel love* for your enemy? No! He said *do good* to your enemy. That means that regardless of how you feel toward another person, you can *choose* to show love. That was the choice Alicia faced with her teacher.

Whom is God asking you to love today?

Don't wait for a feeling before you start loving

How can I learn to love?

A

I can learn to love by choosing to love people who seem hard to love.

LISTENING

P ushing to get dinner ready before six, Mrs. Hewitt hardly noticed when fifteen-year-old Michael stuck his head around the corner and called, "Hey, Mom, Chuck and I are in the garage. We're working on the car." She didn't pay much attention either when Mike came in a short time later and asked if she had any little plastic bags, "you know, the kind you put sandwiches in."

But late that evening, as she drove into the garage after a PTA meeting, her eyes opened wide in horror. The hood of the family's other car was open. Beside it was Mr. Hewitt's tool box. And all around, carefully placed in little plastic bags, lay the parts the boys had removed. If only she had listened . . .

◆ THINKING ABOUT LISTENING

For Mrs. Hewitt, Michael's words had "gone in one ear and out the other." She heard what he *said*, but missed what he *meant*.

Listening, our topic this week, is the ability to **reach behind the words to find the message that is being shared.** It is an important skill for two reasons:

1. Listening helps us understand what others are saying.
2. Listening helps us communicate more clearly and completely.

The writer of Proverbs gives this instruction:

● KEY VERSE ON LISTENING

Let the wise listen and add to their learning (Proverbs 1:5).

"Mrs. Reed says to tell you I'm having trouble with my ears. Everything goes in one ear and out the other."

▲ LOOKING AHEAD

A good listener must do more than simply hear the words someone is speaking. A true listener tries to understand and share the speaker's feelings.

Start the week by testing your listening skills. How many sounds can you identify from right where you are sitting? Can you hear a car passing? a dog barking? a clock ticking? Can you detect 20 different sounds?

Now test your spiritual listening skills by reading James 1:23-24 together.

D ean was was working happily with his dad, tying the newspapers into bundles for recycling.

Suddenly, his father cocked his head. "Dean," he asked, "What's that song you're singing?"

"Oh, it's just something I heard on the radio. I kinda like it."

"But son, have you really listened to what you're singing? It took me a while to catch on, but the words of that song are telling you to do something wrong."

"Aw, Dad, I don't really pay attention to the words. I just like the music. I don't really mean what I'm singing."

◆ TAKE A LOOK / 1 John 4:1-6

While Dean was listening to the music he liked, the words were being planted in his mind. Without even knowing it, Dean was in danger of being "brainwashed" because he was not listening wisely.

In a world filled with many different messages, it is important to know what each one really means. To do this we must learn to listen carefully —and to measure the things we hear by God's standard of right and wrong. That way we will be learning to . . .

Take captive every thought to make it obedient to Christ (2 Corinthians 10:5).

Sometimes lies come cleverly disguised to look like the truth. But 1 John 4:1-6 will help you tell *which* is *which!*

▲ TAKE A STEP

To listen wisely sounds like one of the easiest skills in the world. In fact it's one of the hardest. To listen wisely you must shut out other sounds and voices, and focus on what is *really* being said. Listening takes practice, but it's well worth any effort it takes.

Try an exercise in listening this evening. As a family, select a television program you have watched before, but this time really *listen* to what is being said.

When the program is over, ask and answer these questions: "What kind of lifestyle did the program show? Were law and order respected? Were the 'heroes' good and pure in their actions, or evil and immoral? Was the show marked by violence or peace?"

As a family, discuss how you can put 2 Corinthians 10:5 to work in your home.

Put your ears on alert

Q

What does it mean to listen wisely?

A

Listening wisely means measuring what I hear by God's truth.

Please may I have your undivided attention?

Kent had planned a long time for this weekend. He had saved for a new rifle, taken the required hunter-safety course, and double-checked to be sure he hadn't forgotten anything. Then overnight, his carefully laid plans fell apart. His best friend Mark got sick and couldn't go.

At breakfast the next morning, Kent told his parents what had happened. But as he talked, his mother started clearing the breakfast dishes. Kent's dad gave an occasional absent-minded "uh-huh" as he read his morning newspaper. Angrily, Kent left his breakfast half-eaten and stormed out of the kitchen. "It's no use talking to you," he mumbled. "You don't even care enough to listen . . . "

◆ TAKE A LOOK / Luke 10:38-42

In the minds of many teenagers, the number one communication problem is *parents who won't listen*. In the minds of many parents, the number one communication problem is *teenagers who won't talk*.

Communication problems are not limited to the home, either! You find them at work, school, and even in the church. Everyone wants to be heard, but good listeners are rare. The Book of Ecclesiastes reminds us that . . .

There is a time for everything . . . a time to be silent and a time to speak (Ecclesiastes 3:1, 7).

Two sisters, Mary and Martha, provide a helpful example of why listening is so important. One was a doer, the other a listener. See if you can discover which sister was the better listener as you read together Luke 10:38-42.

▲ TAKE A STEP

Martha was not *wrong* in doing the housework. After all, what would *your* house look like if the dishes were never washed and the floors were never vacuumed? But her problem was that she got "distracted by all the preparations that had to be made." Her attention was drawn away from what Jesus was saying. By contrast, Mary gave her undivided attention to Jesus. She did the most important thing *first* by listening to Jesus.

Think back to Kent and his parents. How do you think they all could have been better listeners? What might Kent's mom and dad have learned if they had only taken the time to listen?

What three things would you like to see happen at your house to improve communication?

Q

Why is a listener everyone's friend?

A

A good listener sets aside other things and pays attention.

*T*he young couple was in a world all their own. For two hours they sat opposite each other in the restaurant. His hot chocolate grew cold; the ice in her glass melted. They ate very little. Waitresses moved around them clearing other tables. Other customers came and went. They didn't even notice.

He did most of the talking. She said very little, but listened intently. It was obvious to everybody that he was the center of her world, and vice versa. Though few words were actually spoken, many things were being said—and heard! Their love for each other was growing because they were taking the time to listen.

◆ TAKE A LOOK / 1 Kings 12:3-8, 13-14, 16

The couple in the restaurant was young and in love. But really, it could have been anyone: a father and daughter, grandmother and grandson, two friends sipping a soda after school. Listening isn't just a skill for lovers!

In the Old Testament, you'll read the account of a king who lost his kingdom because he had never learned to listen. He was insensitive to the feelings of his people. He heard the words they said, but missed the feelings behind those words.

The king's name was Rehoboam. Though you've perhaps never heard of him, it's likely you've heard of his famous father (Solomon) and grandfather (David). When Rehoboam was crowned king, the people sent representatives to him, pleading with him to lower their taxes. Read about Rehoboam's response and the people's revolt in 1 Kings 12:3-8, 13-14, 16.

▲ TAKE A STEP

Because Rehoboam refused to listen to wise counsel, his kingdom went through a civil war. And that doesn't happen just in nations; it can happen in families as well.

The Bible has this timely warning for dads:
Fathers, do not exasperate your children; instead, bring them up in the training and instruction of the Lord (Ephesians 6:4).

One of the most exasperating things you can do to anyone is not to listen. At the end of your Bible time today, ask God to help your family to make listening a daily part of your busy schedule. Look each person in the eye, give her (or him) your undivided attention, and really listen—with both your head and your heart!

Listen with your heart, not just your ears

How can I be a good listener?

A

I am a good listener when I give the other person my undivided attention.

Friend, can you lend me your ears?

Q

What are the rewards of being a listener?

A

By being a good listener I may help others solve their problems.

PARENT:
When was the last time you set aside a half-hour just to listen to whatever your child might want to say?

During the difficult days of the Civil War, President Abraham Lincoln called an old friend to Washington, D.C. to ask his advice on a crucial issue.

When his friend arrived, President Lincoln began to discuss his ideas for freeing the slaves and issuing the Emancipation Proclamation. He spoke of reasons why he should do this, what the results would be if he did, and what would happen if he did not. He told his friend what other leaders in Washington and around the country thought of his idea, and what the nation's newspapers were printing about him.

After leaving the President late that night, the friend realized that Mr. Lincoln had never actually asked for his advice. The President, in trying to make an important decision, had simply needed someone to listen to him.

◆ TAKE A LOOK / Mark 5:24-34

Many people who need help to solve a problem hesitate to confide in a friend. They are afraid others will reject them, laugh at them, or not take them seriously if they speak about what is really bothering them.

Mark 5:24-34 records an event from the life of Jesus which shows how fear can keep people from opening up to share their needs. As you read, look for the way in which Jesus showed Himself to be a good listener.

▲ TAKE A STEP

The woman who had been sick for years was at first afraid to share her need with Jesus. But when she did, He showed that *her* burden had now become *His* burden.

For every person who needs your *advice*, there are probably dozens who simply need your *acceptance*—a listening ear, a tender heart, a little bit of your time, or a warm hug.

Accept one another, then, just as Christ accepted you (Romans 15:7).

Allowing others to talk through their problems is a great way to help them solve those problems—often without saying a word!

For the next few minutes, why not open a "Family Listening Clinic" at your house. Give each person in your family two minutes to say whatever is on his or her mind. No questions, comments, or interruptions allowed! Close your clinic—and your week—by thanking God for the power of a listening ear.

PROVERBS

*H*ere's a riddle for you: What do Samson (the Bible character) and
Bilbo Baggins (the make-believe hobbit) have in common?
Answer: They both love riddles.

Riddles are a fun way to have a few laughs. But on occasion, they
can be serious business. Did you know there is a life-and-death riddle in
the Bible for you to answer? Read it now and see if you know the answer:

"I love those who love me, and those who seek me find me.
With me are riches and honor. . .
My fruit is better than . . . gold . . .
Whoever finds me finds life and receives favor from the LORD.
But whoever fails to find me harms himself;
All who hate me love death." Who am I?

◆ THINKING ABOUT PROVERBS

The riddle you just read is found in Proverbs 8:17-19, 35-36. To
find the answer, turn to Proverbs 8:11, and there you'll discover a
treasure more precious than rubies! The Book of Proverbs also
describes that priceless treasure this way:

● KEY VERSE ON PROVERBS

*Wisdom is supreme; therefore get wisdom. Though it cost
all you have, get understanding (Proverbs 4:7).*

▲ LOOKING AHEAD

Wisdom is one of the most
valuable things on earth. But
how do you get it? Can it be
bought? Is it something you
can learn?

The Book of Proverbs
answers these questions and
more. The first nine chapters
tell us how important wisdom
is. The rest of the book gives us
about 900 practical ways to
put God's wisdom to work.

For today, look in Proverbs
17:6 to find the answer to this
riddle:

"Children's children are a
crown to the aged, and
__(who?)__ are the pride of
their children."

*"They won't let you pray in
school, but they sure expect you
to have the wisdom of Solomon."*

Only a fool would ignore God's wisdom

Decide as a family whether each of the following statements is wise or foolish. Place an F or W in the blank beside each.

____ **Teenage girl:** "C'mon, let's go. Your mom will never find out. We'll just tell her we went to a late movie."

____ **Third-grader:** "Even though the test isn't until next week, I'll learn my multiplication tonight. Then I can play."

____ **Businessman:** "I can charge Joe a high price for this work. He has lots of money."

____ **Teenage boy:** "My dad didn't graduate from high school, but he's still my dad—and that means I need to obey him."

____ **Mother:** "I really don't want to go to that baby shower. I'll just say I'm sick."

◆ **TAKE A LOOK / Proverbs 1:1-9**

Sometimes you'll hear it said that wisdom comes from experience—and that's partially true. The hard knocks that come from making mistakes are an effective way to learn lessons. But God's Word says that the principles of wisdom can—and should—be learned before they are needed.

As you read Proverbs 1:1-9, see if you can spot the four kinds of people who will profit from reading God's "book of wisdom." (Hint: Look at verses 4-5.)

Who needs wisdom?

A

The Book of Proverbs shows us that everyone needs wisdom.

▲ **TAKE A STEP**

We live in a day when it seems as if everyone is taking a how-to class. Only a short drive from where you live, you'll probably find classes offered on a wide range of subjects: how to speed read, swim, paint, work a computer, ride a motorcycle, build a house, start your own business. While no one ever grows too old to learn something new, the best time to learn is when we are still young—before we learn many of life's lessons the hard way. Where should we begin? Proverbs tells us to begin at the beginning!

The fear of the LORD is the beginning of wisdom (Proverbs 9:10).

Go back to the five statements at the top of the page. Reword each statement that you said was foolish to show how that person might truly fear and obey the Lord.

You may think we're old-fashioned, Diana, but that's the rule in this family. If you go to the game without us, you must come home with the person you went with. We don't want you riding with just anyone."

"But, Dad, I wouldn't ride with someone I didn't know. Give me a break. Nothing will happen."

"I'm sure you might know the person, Diana, but you might not know enough to be safe. Once you get into someone else's car, you don't have any control. If that person decides to drive too fast, drink a beer, or go somewhere you don't want to go, you can't do a thing about it. Your mom and I want to know who you're with. So the matter is settled. Okay?"

But the expression on Diana's face said, "Well, maybe . . . "

◆ **TAKE A LOOK / Proverbs 1:10-19**

Diana's parents knew more about the facts than Diana did. Statistics show that most auto accidents involve drivers who have been drinking; people drink more and drive more recklessly on weekends than during the week; and teenage drivers have more accidents than any age group. Diana's parents were being wise by keeping their daughter away from a potentially dangerous situation.

Wisdom lies in knowing both *what* to do and *what not* to do, *whom* to follow and *whom not* to follow. The Book of Proverbs tells how to handle many dangerous situations—but it also tells about many situations to avoid altogether! Watch for "danger signs" as you read Proverbs 1:10-19.

▲ **TAKE A STEP**

Peer pressure—doing something because everyone else is doing it—helps to explain why some people get in with the wrong crowd, do wrong things, and wind up in trouble. While everyone wants to be part of a group and to feel accepted, the warning of wisdom is very clear:

If sinners entice you, do not give in to them (Proverbs 1:10).

Spend a few minutes talking about times when you experience peer pressure and face temptation to do the wrong thing. After you talk about some specific situations, discuss how you can work together as parent and child to face unpleasant peer pressure. How can you strengthen good associations? How can good communication help?

Caution! Danger just around the bend

Q

What does wisdom do for me?

A

The wisdom of the Book of Proverbs warns me of dangers to avoid.

PARENT:
When was the last time peer pressure influenced you? Give both a positive and a negative example from your own experience as you discuss peer pressure with your child.

How to avoid becoming a headline

*H*ey, Diana, you and Phyllis want to go get a pizza after the game? A bunch of us are going. I'll take you home afterward."

"That'd be fun, Steve, but my dad is really strict about who I ride with. He'll be really mad unless I come home with Phyllis's mom. That's who we came with."

"C'mon, Diana," Phyllis broke in, "I'll call mom and tell her we're riding with Steve. Then she won't have to come out in the cold to get us. Your dad will never know."

"Phyllis, if I go, my dad will find out for sure. I'll call him to come get us. That's better than disobeying."

"Aw, who cares? I don't much like that crowd anyway. We can phone in a pizza order when we get to my house. Let's go call my mom and tell her we're ready."

◆ **TAKE A LOOK / Proverbs 2:1-5, 11-15**

The next day, both Diana and Phyllis sighed a prayer of thanks when they read Steve's name under this headline: "Local Teen Arrested for Drinking and Driving." The wisdom of Diana's parents in protecting her from a dangerous situation—and her own wisdom in obeying them—made the difference.

The writer of Proverbs speaks of this "protective work of wisdom" in chapter 2 of his book. But there is a big *if*. As you read 2:1-5, look for the attitude you must have before God's wisdom can help keep you from harm. Then read verses 11-15 and see how that wisdom works.

▲ **TAKE A STEP**

"Caution—Slippery When Wet." Everyone has seen signs like that on the highway. Those signs are there, not to spoil your fun, but to alert you to dangerous spots along the road and keep you from having a nasty accident.

The Book of Proverbs is filled with danger signs, warning travelers on the road of life where the slippery places are. Laziness, anger, adultery, rebellion—Proverbs warns about these and many other danger spots.

Close your family time by reading a verse no family member should face the day without!

He who scorns instruction will pay for it,
but he who respects a command is rewarded
(Proverbs 13:13).

You might even take time for each person to write his own copy of that important warning!

Q

What does wisdom warn about?

A

The wisdom of Proverbs warns of danger spots in the road of life.

*T*ry combining your listening skills with the wisdom you've learned from Proverbs this week. Have Mom or Dad read the following statements one by one. After each statement, see if you can discover a corresponding Proverb from the list in the "Take a Look" section.

1. "We've been married 20 years, and that person is still the joy of my life."
2. "Joe, sneak me a copy of the test and I'll give you $5.00."
3. "Son, I don't like to punish you, but I can't allow you to be disobedient."
4. "Listen, Ellen, I promised not to tell, but . . . "
5. "Just tell Mrs. Jackson you lost your homework. She won't know you didn't do it."
6. "Studying's a drag; let's go play basketball."

◆ **TAKE A LOOK**
Here's what God says about those six actions:
a. "He who spares the rod hates his son, but he who loves him is careful to discipline him" (13:24).
b. "He who finds a wife finds what is good" (18:22).
c. "A wicked man accepts a bribe in secret" (17:23).
d. "Diligent hands will rule, but laziness ends in slave labor" (12:24).
e. "A gossip betrays a confidence, but a trustworthy man keeps a secret" (11:13).
f. "The LORD detests lying lips, but he delights in men who are truthful" (12:22).

▲ **TAKE A STEP**
The Book of Proverbs contains some words of wisdom on most of the topics in this book. Three of those topics are listed below beside three chapters from Proverbs. See who can be the first one to find a verse related to each of the topics in those chapters. Or assign a chapter and topic to three different family members.

Peace—Proverbs 29
Growth—Proverbs 13
Mankind—Proverbs 8

Did anyone notice that the chapters of two topics (Peace and Mankind) contained *two* different verses on those topics? If so, let that family member have an extra serving of dessert for dinner.

(Correct answers are: 1b, 2c, 3a, 4e, 5f, 6d.)

You'll never run out of the riches of wisdom

What are the rewards of wisdom?

The Book of Proverbs shows me that the rewards of wisdom are safety and blessing.

PEACE

I *n the space of less than a year, headlines like these made front-page reading in the nation's newspapers:*
  "Airliner Destroyed by Terrorist. No Survivors"
  "Divorce Rate Hits All-Time High"
  "Car Bomb Kills Innocent Bystanders"
  "Teenage Girl Abducted from Shopping Mall"
  "New Findings Show Murder on the Increase"
  Is it any wonder that someone has defined peace as "that one brief moment of silence when everyone is standing around reloading"?

◆ THINKING ABOUT PEACE
Peace is very rare. Of the last 3,500 years of human history, less than 300 have been free from war. And yet world leaders meet to talk about peace; demonstrators demand it; and everyone hopes it will happen.

God clearly commands us to pursue peace as individuals, and He promises a special blessing for those who are peacemakers (Matthew 5:9). Because God never gives a command that He doesn't expect us to obey, it's important to remember this verse:

● KEY VERSE ON PEACE
If it is possible, as far as it depends on you, live at peace with everyone (Romans 12:18).

▲ TAKE A STEP
This week we'll see that peace is more than the absence of war. Peace is **the inner calm that comes when your relationships are right**—your relationship with God, yourself, and others.

"Bruce Sims achieved peace through strength today."

Find today's newspaper and cut out some articles dealing with war and peace. Why do you think nations cannot maintain peace?

Now read Luke 2:14 and imagine that your family was with the shepherds that night. Since your country was not fighting a war at that time, what do you suppose the angel meant? Would you have recognized the angel's words as the world's most important "peace announcement"?

*M*other, where did Bradley learn to act like that?" Beth watched her two-year-old brother with amazement. Seconds ago he had been quietly looking at the picture books his grandmother kept especially for him. But suddenly he had decided to "read" Grandpa's Bible that was lying open on the coffee table.

As Bradley reached out for it, his mother saw him and moved it away. Squealing in anger, Bradley climbed on the couch and reached out again. "No, Bradley," his mother said firmly, putting him back on the floor.

But Bradley's mind was made up. Once again he tried to climb on the couch. Once again his mother "upset" his plans. And finally, little Bradley had had enough. Throwing himself on the floor, he unleashed a fit of anger, kicking his legs and crying loudly.

◆ TAKE A LOOK / Colossians 1:19-22

Where do babies learn to act like that? The answer may surprise you: They never have to learn to be disobedient, selfish, or angry.

Like every human being since Adam, Bradley was born with a sin nature—a "knack" for sinning. Though his mother and father would have to train him to be honest, kind, and thankful, they would never have to train him to lie, disobey, or be selfish.

He, like every member of the human race, was born "at war" with God, separated from Him by sin. God sent His Son, Jesus Christ, to make a way of peace for men and women, boys and girls. When Jesus died on the cross,

He was pierced for our transgressions, he was crushed for our iniquities; the punishment that brought us peace was upon him, and by his wounds we are healed (Isaiah 53:5).

Read more about this Peacemaker in Colossians 1:19-22.

▲ TAKE A STEP

Peace with God is the place where all other kinds of peace begin. You cannot really be at peace with yourself . . . with your parents . . . with your brothers and sisters . . . with your teachers . . . until you have first made peace with God through the Prince of Peace, Jesus Christ.

Hold hands as a family and say together the verse for today, Isaiah 53:5.

Don't bother to teach me, I already know how

Q

How can I be at peace with God?

A

Peace with God comes through the Peacemaker, Jesus Christ.

Don't hit me because you're mad at yourself!

Standing at the kitchen window, Greg's mother saw her son come across the backyard like a storm gathering force. She watched him slam the gate, kick two garbage cans, and angrily shove his dog aside. Clearly the peaceful afternoon was in danger of being spoiled.

Seconds later the garage door banged, then the kitchen door. Almost before she could turn around, Greg threw his book bag on the floor and glared at her.

"Why'd ya bake oatmeal cookies again?" he growled. "Can't we have some decent snacks for a change? Only sissies and babies like Todd want oatmeal," and he made an ugly face at his little brother.

◆ TAKE A LOOK / Philippians 4:6-7

Later that evening after Greg apologized for his behavior, the truth came out. He was mad at himself for failing a math test. Not knowing how to handle his feelings of frustration properly, he took them out on *others*.

From time to time, stormy feelings build up inside us all. Sometimes, like Greg, we feel like striking out at others—acting rudely or cruelly toward people we genuinely love. But this kind of angry response only makes the problem worse, and we sin against the other person. Instead, the Bible gives this command:

"In your anger do not sin": Do not let the sun go down while you are still angry, and do not give the devil a foothold (Ephesians 4:26-27).

The best way to avoid taking your anger out on others is to take it to the Lord in prayer. Philippians 4:6-7 will show you another key for being at peace with yourself and others.

▲ TAKE A STEP

There's an invisible thief on the loose, but you'll have no difficulty seeing the trouble he leaves behind in homes, schools, and offices. His name? *Worry.* His companions? *Anger* and *frustration.*

When worry comes into your life, he is looking to steal one of the most precious possessions you own—your *joy.*

Has that thief been at work in your life? If so, now would be a good time to lock him up. Philippians 4:6 tells us how: by "prayer and petition, with thanksgiving."

If Greg had shared his *problem* with God, instead of venting his *anger* on his family, how might the above story have had a peaceful ending?

Q

Why is it important to be at peace with myself?

A

Peace with myself helps me be at peace with others.

PARENT:
Moodiness and stormy feelings in your child sometimes have physical causes. Proper diet and adequate rest are a must for preschoolers and teenagers alike.

---

*T*hrough a deep sleep Mr. Baxter heard a whisper. "Dad, Dad, wake up. We need you. We've got to take Jim to the hospital. He's bleeding bad."

With those words Mr. Baxter came alive and ran down the hall. There he found 14-year-old Jim with a washcloth covering his face. Beside him on the floor lay four boxing gloves. As Jim lowered the cloth, Mr. Baxter saw the evidence of a broken nose.

"Jerry," he asked as he turned to the older boy, "what were you two doing? It's 1 A.M."

With tears in his eyes, Jerry explained. "Jim's always bugging me and he says I'm always bugging him. So we just decided to have it out. We didn't mean for anybody to get hurt."

◆ TAKE A LOOK / Genesis 32:6, 16, 20; 33:3-10

Keeping the peace is not easy. Restoring peace after a conflict is even harder. But God loves peacemakers. That's why He instructs us to . . .

Make every effort to live in peace with all men and to be holy (Hebrews 12:14).

The first book of the Bible records the conflict between two brothers. Jacob cheated Esau, his older twin. In return Esau hated Jacob. Instead of brotherly love, suspicion and fear filled that family.

Finally Esau determined to kill his brother, and Jacob ran for his life. Many years later they met again, and Jacob was still afraid of his brother Esau who was coming to see him . . . with 400 armed men! So Jacob made "every effort to live in peace." Read about Jacob's peacemaking efforts in Genesis 32:6, 16, 20; 33:3-10.

▲ TAKE A STEP

Jacob's "every effort" included being the first to try to restore peace. In addition, he showed an attitude of humility; he was willing to earn the right to be heard; he paid a price in order to make peace; and he trusted God with the outcome.

Here's a humorous poem that might help your family the next time you face a conflict!

Push, pull, pinch, and hit;
Don't get your way and throw a fit.
Mom is sad, Dad gets the paddle
You're sent to your room 'til your temper settles.

Oh no, wait just a minute.
Life is better when love is in it.
Giggle, cuddle, hug, and grin—
That's the way I want to win.

I'd rather win with love than war.

How can I be at peace with other people?

Peace with others begins when I am willing to take the first step.

Endless war . . . or endless peace?

Stan could hardly wait. Tonight the whole family—and his best friend Randy—were coming to celebrate his sixth birthday. As each person arrived bearing a colorfully wrapped present, Stan eyed it carefully. He had already told his grandparents, aunts, uncles, cousins, mom and dad—and yes, even Randy—exactly what he wanted. He sure hoped there wouldn't be any surprises!

After the cake was served, Stan was allowed to open gifts. And what do you suppose he got? GI Joe the Marine, GI Joe the Ranger, GI Joe the Sea Trooper, GI Joe the Copter Trooper, and GI Joe the Medic. And when he opened the last box to find a tank and a helicopter, his excitement was complete.

"C'mon, Randy," he exclaimed, "let's go play. We've got enough men to have a really good war."

◆ TAKE A LOOK / Matthew 24:3-14

In his childhood innocence, Stan talked about a "really good war." But is there such a thing? All around the world today, people are concerned about the threat of war. In fact, world leaders constantly search for ways to end wars and keep peace among the world's nations.

Perhaps you have wondered, "Will there ever really be a peaceful world?" According to the Bible, the answer is *Yes!* Jesus knew there would be many wars in the world before He returned. And so He comforted His disciples with some hope-filled words you won't want to miss! Find and read them right now in Matthew 24:3-14.

▲ TAKE A STEP

Working for peace is a worthy goal in any generation. After all, it was Jesus Himself who said "Blessed are the peacemakers" (Matthew 5:9).

But the world will never know lasting peace until Jesus Christ, the Prince of Peace, returns to rule as King of kings and Lord of lords. Then—and only then—will it be true that . . .

Of the increase of his government and peace there will be no end (Isaiah 9:7).

Stan and Randy might enjoy playing war, but conflict between people or world powers is no game. Is there an unresolved conflict going on in your family? Call a family council, make sure everyone knows the facts, and discuss the situation until you reach a "peaceful" solution. Pray together that God will help your family live at peace with one another.

Q

Will the world ever have lasting peace?

A

Peace in the world will come when the Prince of Peace returns.

SERVING

*T*wenty 3rd-graders sat wide-eyed as their teachers read to the end of the story: " . . . And so, because of the magic looking glass, Miss Minka could choose who and what she wanted to be, simply by making a wish." Then the teacher closed the book and looked at the children. "What would you like to be if you could choose?"

"I'd like to be a movie star!"

"I want to be an astronaut."

"I think it would be fun to be in the circus."

"I'm going to drive race cars."

"I'm going to be a nurse."

Now pretend for a moment it's your turn. What would you like to be if you could choose any occupation in the world?

◆ THINKING ABOUT SERVING

Ask 100 people what they would like to be, and you will get about 100 different answers! But hardly ever will anyone say, "I want to be a servant."

That's easy to understand. Who wants to serve others if he can be served by others? Who wants to be a slave when he can be a celebrity?

But this week we'll talk about what could make you want to choose a life of serving others.

● KEY VERSE ON SERVING

Jesus Christ, the greatest "celebrity" who ever lived, said this: "I am among you as one who serves" (Luke 22:27).

▲ TAKE A STEP

Follow Jesus' example by finding creative ways **to selflessly move to meet the needs of others.** Do the dishes *without* being asked, give Dad a back rub, help Sis with a project, or fix Mom a wake-up cup of coffee. The possibilities are endless. Read Colossians 3:22-24 to discover whom you are actually serving when you serve other people.

"I'll have to admit I'm going to miss the parental goods and services."

Everyone loves service with a smile

O h, dear," Mrs. Ramsey muttered as she stirred the last few drops of milk into the potatoes. "I forgot to get another quart of milk." She dried her hands, got some money from her purse, and called to her son Ethan. Slowly he slouched into the kitchen.

"Isn't dinner ready yet? I'm starved."

Mrs. Ramsey explained, "I need you to ride your bike over to the store and get some milk. It will only take a few minutes."

"Aw c'mon, Mom. Let Dad go in the car. It's too cold to ride my bike."

"No, Ethan, your father's resting. He's been working very hard this week. And besides, it was warm enough to play football just 30 minutes ago! Now go on."

"Aw, Mom, why do you need milk for the potatoes? Just use water. I hate being treated like a slave."

Q

What does it mean to be a servant?

◆ TAKE A LOOK / Mark 10:35-45

Ethan had the wrong idea about who the real servants were in his family. He loved to eat the meals his mother made, using food she bought with his father's hard-earned money. But Ethan hadn't learned to appreciate the things his parents did to make his life happy. He simply expected them as his rights.

Two of Jesus' disciples also had a wrong idea about their rights in God's family. They thought, "If we just ask first, Jesus will have to give us the best places." Read what Jesus said about their request in Mark 10:35-45.

A

Serving is seeing a need and selflessly meeting it.

▲ TAKE A STEP

When was the last time you saw an ordinary person praised on the front page of your newspaper? Instead, we usually applaud those who do the greatest things: make the most money, catch the longest pass, climb the highest mountain. Yet, Jesus in His answer to James and John showed that true greatness comes through serving others.

"Whoever wants to become great among you must be your servant" (Mark 10:43).

Who is the "greatest" servant you know—a person who sees the needs of others and selflessly moves to meet them? It may be a parent or grandparent . . . pastor or close, personal friend. This week would be a wonderful time to recognize that person's greatness with a card, a small gift, or a phone call—something that says, "I'm thankful for the way you serve me!" And a good place to begin is with those who serve you at home.

68/SERVING DAY TWO ❑

Day after day the missionary nurse travels over Thailand's dangerous mountain trails, treating the victims of leprosy and tuberculosis. Month after month the evangelist visits the garbage dumps of Cairo, Egypt, to share the gospel with the thousands of garbage pickers who come there each night to look for meager provisions for their families.

And in a quiet American neighborhood, a family very much like yours helps an elderly lady who has cancer by cleaning her house, preparing her meals, and giving her the attention she needs during the final weeks of her life.

◆ **TAKE A LOOK / Matthew 25:31-46**
A classified ad for the job of a servant might read like this: "WANTED: Unsung hero for challenging position. Long hours, low pay, few promotions. Only people totally committed should apply."

That's not the kind of job most people are looking for today. Most want a job with "good money . . . excellent benefits . . . paid sick leave . . . vacation . . . retirement . . . frequent promotions."

Jesus gave His disciples a job description in Matthew 25:31-46. As you read those verses, try to decide which of the two "ads" you just read more closely matches that of a disciple.

▲ **TAKE A STEP**
Every Christian has a God-given job to do: the job of sharing the good news about Jesus with those who haven't heard (Matthew 28:19-20). But people who are hungry aren't too interested in what you have to say. At least not before they have a hot meal.

In the passage you just read, Jesus doesn't mention teaching or preaching. He talks instead about helping needy people. He says that those who meet the needs of others are serving Him.

"Whatever you did for one of the least of these brothers of mine, you did for me."
(Matthew 25:40).

Perhaps you live in a neighborhood where people are not hungry, thirsty, cold, or in prison. But there are other needs just as important: the need of a friend, a listener, a helper. And there's no better way to earn the right to be heard than by first showing yourself to be a servant. Plan now what your family will do to help open the door for sharing the gospel in your community.

Q

How can I serve God and others?

A

I serve God and others by treating others as I would treat Jesus Christ.

It's a dirty job, but we love to do it!

Parents of the glee club members were organizing committees to help in the district festival at their school. Ticket committee . . . program committee . . . refreshment committee . . . publicity committee . . . parking committee . . . clean-up committee. Each glee club member would be assigned to serve on his or her parent's committee.

As the Copeland family drove home after the meeting, Keith sat silently staring out the car window. Finally he blurted out, "Dad, why did you have to volunteer for the clean-up committee? That's the worst job of all. We'll have to work harder and longer than anyone. I hate it. Someone else will have to help because I'm *just not going to.*"

◆ TAKE A LOOK / Matthew 23:1-12

Keith let his pride get in the way of serving his parents, fellow students, and God. He was so busy thinking about himself that he didn't have time to think about others. He wanted to *be served,* but not to look for ways to *serve others.*

When Jesus was on earth, He criticized the Pharisees, a group of religious leaders who thought they were serving God when in fact they were serving themselves. Read what Jesus said about them in Matthew 23:1-12. Can you discover why they were "blind," even though with their physical eyes they could see just fine?

▲ TAKE A STEP

To obey the command of Deuteronomy 6:8, the Pharisees proudly wore small boxes containing written portions of Scripture on their arms and foreheads. But by doing "everything for men to see," they were actually *disobeying* Deuteronomy 6:6, which states that God's commands are "to be upon your hearts."

Pride has a way of keeping God's command-ments out of our hearts. The **P** in pride says "I am concerned about my POSITION." The **R** says "I want my RIGHTS." The **I** is in the center and says, "I am most IMPORTANT." The **D** says, "My DESIRES are more important than yours." And the **E** says "I EXPECT everyone to agree with me." But Jesus said,

"Whoever exalts himself will be humbled, and whoever humbles himself will be exalted" (Matthew 23:12).

Pride was keeping Keith from being a servant in his glee club and in his family. What would you say to show that *humility* is the path to *happiness*?

Q

What gets in the way of serving?

A

Pride and selfishness get in the way of serving.

*A*fter the wealthy businessman's funeral, family and friends gathered for the reading of the will. Two sons and a daughter had traveled many miles, thinking their wealthy father's money would at last be theirs. Finally the lawyer began to read:

"I, Frederick C. Grant, being of sound mind, do hereby make this last will and testament. One-half of the proceeds of my estate is to be divided among my three children. The remaining half is to be given to John Morris, my faithful servant and friend, as a reward for his years of faithful service . . . "

◆ **TAKE A LOOK / 1 Corinthians 3:12-14**

Heirs wait for the reading of the will. Workers wait for payday. Students wait for grades and graduation. Athletes compete for trophies. But is there a reward for being a faithful servant of God?

Not long before His death Jesus comforted His disciples with these words:

"Whoever serves me must follow me; and where I am, my servant also will be. My Father will honor the one who serves me" (John 12:26).

The Bible often speaks of rewards for faithful service. Can you match the following statements with the verse or verses from which each was taken?

1. God's rewards are "out of this world." They often come after death, not before.

2. God's rewards are not based on the impressiveness of your work, but on the attitude of your heart.

3. God never forgets an act of service. He *will* reward it in due time.

The passages to match with the statements are:
(a) 1 Corinthians 3:12-14; (b) Matthew 16:27; (c) Colossians 3:23-25.

▲ **TAKE A STEP**

Are you working for earthly praise or eternal rewards? It's not hard to tell! Just ask yourself, "*Why* did I do what I did? Was it to make a name for myself or to magnify the name of Jesus? Was it to *serve* or *be served?*"

Mr. Grant's will was a disappointing surprise for his greedy children. But there will be no disappointment for any servant of Christ when God honors those who have faithfully served Him.

The time to begin working for future rewards is now. Discuss how you can use your talents and abilities to serve God and others.

A king's wage for a servant's work

Q

What are the rewards of being a servant?

A

Serving Christ faithfully results in eternal rewards.

Answers:

1–b; 2–a; 3–c.

GROWTH

*S*ometimes the mother-to-be could hardly believe what was happening. She would feel her tummy and wonder, "Am I really going to have a baby?"

The new little life began with two cells no bigger than the period at the end of this sentence. As the cells united and then divided again and again, the baby was slowly developing into a little person, complete with heart and lungs, arms and legs.

Then one day it happened! The mother felt an odd flutter in her tummy—like a butterfly flapping its wings. Though the birth was still months away, the mother knew her baby was growing.

◆ THINKING ABOUT GROWTH

Perhaps you've watched a newborn kitten change from a tiny ball of fuzz into a beautiful full-grown cat. Or you planted a kernel of corn in the ground and watched day by day as a green shoot poked up through the dirt and grew into a fine, tall cornstalk. Maybe your parents have marked *your* growth each year on a wall or doorway.

Growth is the process of **change which can be measured and seen in a living thing.** Everything that is living is also growing. But unlike plants and animals that only grow physically, God wants us to grow in many different ways. When He was young, even Jesus had to learn to walk and talk, read and write.

"Don't worry, dear. You'll grow."

● KEY VERSE ON GROWTH

Jesus grew in wisdom and stature, and in favor with God and men (Luke 2:52).

▲ TAKE A STEP

This week we will explore four different ways in which God wants us to grow. And as we do, we'll measure ourselves to see how much growth there has been recently.

Did your parents keep a record of your birth weight and height (perhaps in a baby book)? If so, find it now, and compare your height and weight today. Then read 2 Thessalonians 1:3 to discover two other areas of growth you can experience. How can you tell if your love for each other is growing?

*T*he date was July 20, 1969. More than a quarter million miles from earth, an American astronaut took the first-ever spacewalk on the moon. Do you remember his now famous words? "That's one small step for man, one giant leap for mankind."

Fifteen-year-old Merrilee had been much too young at the time to remember anything about it—only 11 months old, to be exact! But according to her baby book, that was the very day she took her first step too. There weren't as many people watching . . . and her walk lasted only a few seconds. But her parents thought it was such an important stage in her development that they wrote it down.

◆ TAKE A LOOK / Psalm 139:13-16

You may not remember your first wobbly step, but for you and your parents it was a big event!

When you decided to launch out on that all-important first step, over 100 million sense cells in each of your eyes gave you a picture of your goal. Your inner ear supplied information about gravity and balance. Nerves in your neck and joints guided the movement of your arms and legs.

Put it all together, and it spells "one giant step"—for *you!*

Long ago, the psalmist David recognized God's wonderful design in the human body and penned this prayer:

I praise you because I am fearfully and wonderfully made (Psalm 139:14).

Join the psalmist in praising God for the miracle of the human body by reading Psalm 139:13-16.

▲ TAKE A STEP

Your physical body has been growing and changing ever since the day you were born. That's why your life has been marked by so many firsts: your first tooth . . . first haircut . . . first step . . . first time to shave . . . first date. The body God has given you is an amazing creation, and it is the only body you'll have this side of heaven! That means you need to give it proper food, exercise, rest, and protection from things that can harm it.

But the greatest miracle about your body is this amazing fact: It is not *your* body! It actually belongs to someone else. Do you know who? Of course you do . . . but 1 Corinthians 6:19-20 will remind you, just in case you've forgotten!

What do you mean, your shoes are too small?

Q

What can I learn from my physical body?

A

My physical growth reminds me to praise my wonderful Creator.

But if I read too much, I might go blind

You have a choice," the teacher said as she handed out the reading assignment. "This semester you may read three short books from this list, or one long one—Moby Dick by Herman Melville. I hope you choose to read Moby Dick. But I'll warn you in advance —it's not an easy book. But whatever your choice, you must read to pass the course. Class dismissed."

In the hallway everyone had an opinion about the reading assignment they had just been given.

"What a dumb class. I really hate to read."

"What good is all that fiction stuff anyway? It's just pretend. I'd rather watch TV anytime."

But one lone voice came to the teacher's defense: "Hey guys, have you ever thought that reading something besides TV Guide might be good for you? There's a lot of great stuff in print. I'm going to read Moby Dick."

Q
How can I grow mentally?

A
Growing mentally means learning to think as God would have me think.

PARENT: Vocabulary is important. Games like Scrabble and Password are good vocabulary builders. And nothing beats reading good books.

◆ **TAKE A LOOK / Philippians 4:8-9**

Thinking is the God-given ability to reason, to plan, to invent, to remember, to believe. It is what makes the difference between humans and the rest of God's creation.

Just as your physical body needs exercise in order to grow and develop properly, so your mind needs exercise if it is to reach the potential God has placed within it. The Apostle Paul, one of the keenest thinkers of his day, understood this principle. Read his directions for mental gymnastics in Philippians 4:8-9.

▲ **TAKE A STEP**

There is a saying from the world of computers: "Garbage in, garbage out." What you put into a computer is what you get out. And the same can be said of your mind: What you feed it in the form of thoughts and messages is what you will get out of it. Pure thoughts, pure mind; dirty thoughts, dirty mind. That's why it's so important to . . .

Prepare your minds for action (1 Peter 1:13).

Reading good books together (yes, Mom and Dad, even *Moby Dick*) is one good way to do that. And of course, the *best* way is to read together the *best* Book—God's matchless Word, the Bible.

Pick a short Bible book you have never read as a family (such as Ruth or Jonah) and make it your family reading project this week! Take a few minutes to tell the family about a book or story you recently enjoyed reading.

I t was one of those tragic endings to an event every-one thought was going to end "happily ever after."

The nine-month pregnancy had gone so well. The mother-to-be's labor pains began early in the morning, and by noon it was clearly time to make the drive to the hospital. Eagerly the young couple looked forward to the arrival of their new baby.

But then, suddenly and unexplainably, something went terribly wrong. The baby was stillborn—dead at birth. Now instead of tears of joy, there were tears of sadness. The baby would never grow up, because it had never experienced a "live birth."

Before you can grow, you have to be born

◆ TAKE A LOOK / John 3:1-8

That's not a happy story, and thankfully it doesn't happen often. But it does make an important point: Before you can have growth, you must have *life*.

Do you remember the four ways in which Jesus grew? " . . . in wisdom [that's mentally] and stature [that's physically], and in favor with God and man" (Luke 2:52). Growing "in favor with God" means learning to do the things that please God. But in order to *please* God, you must be *related* to Him by birth. Just as you began to grow physically after your physical birth, you can grow spiritually only after you have had a spiritual birth.

Does that sound a bit confusing? It confused at least one person Jesus shared it with! His name was Nicodemus, and he couldn't understand how anyone could be born twice. Meet him right now and learn about the "new birth" by reading John 3:1-8.

▲ TAKE A STEP

Everyone knows what it means to be *born:* That's how you entered the family of your earthly father and mother. And the physical birth process is a helpful "picture" of what it means to be "born again." By being born again you enter the family of your heavenly Father.

To all who received [Jesus], to those who believed in his name, he gave the right to become children of God—children born not of natural descent, . . . but born of God (John 1:12-13).

Have you been born physically? Of course! Just ask your parents. Equally important, have you been born spiritually? If so, then you have *two* birthdays to celebrate, not just *one*.

Q

What does it mean to grow in favor with God?

A

Growing in favor with God begins with being born into His family.

It's hard to swallow a dose of bad manners

Don had looked forward to the youth department's spring banquet. The food would be fantastic, but even better would be the chance to go with Ellen. Later that evening, though, Don's face told a sad story: The party had been a disaster! Don's father decided to investigate.

"Dad, it was awful. When we got there, Ellen just sat in the car. I couldn't figure out what was wrong. Finally, she got out . . . and then I knew she'd been waiting for me to open the door. When we got inside, I realized that she was the only girl not wearing a corsage. But the worst part was the meal . . . "

"Wasn't the food good?" Don's father asked.

"Oh, it was super. But they gave each person two plates and three forks. What in the world is a guy supposed to do with three forks? I just know Ellen had a lousy time. "

◆ **TAKE A LOOK / Daniel 2:10-19**

Life does have its embarrassing moments—some accidental and some that we bring upon ourselves!

The Bible says that Jesus grew "in favor with God and man." Not only did He do things which pleased God, He was also gracious in His dealings with people. Sensitive to the feelings of others, Jesus looked for ways to *serve,* rather than be served.

Daniel, a young man who lived long before Jesus, also grew in favor with man. In fact, his wise, polite behavior once saved his life. One night the king had a very disturbing dream. When his "wise men" couldn't tell him what it meant, the king grew furious. His wise men were not only in danger of losing their *jobs,* they were in danger of losing their *lives!* Then Daniel heard about the problem. As you read Daniel 2:10-19, watch how he responded with tact and politeness.

▲ **TAKE A STEP**

Whether at a banquet or a backyard barbeque, *[Love] is not rude (1 Corinthians 13:5).*

Someone who is growing in favor with man learns the manners and customs of society and doesn't needlessly hurt others' feelings by being rude or insensitive.

Don sure had some homework to do. What did he need to learn in order to be growing in favor with people in general and with Ellen in particular? Can you name any areas in which your manners need polishing?

Q

What does it mean to grow in favor with man?

A

Growing in favor with man includes learning and practicing good manners.

PARENT:
Does your child practice good manners? An ounce of instruction can avoid a ton of embarrassment!

MANKIND

*Y*ears ago in India, a man's widow would be thrown into the flames of his funeral pyre to be burned alive with her husband's body. In ancient China, unwanted baby girls were left outside the city walls to die. Some tribes in Africa believed that twins were abnormal and left one (or sometimes both) of the twins under a thorn bush to die. Even in "civilized" 20th-century America, some children who were born with extreme defects were left in hospitals to die without food and water because the parents did not want to accept the responsibility of caring for a severely handicapped child.

◆ THINKING ABOUT MANKIND

Facts like these are sad and shocking. But they raise a key question: How important is human life?

Some scientists think that people are not really different than animals or complex machines. And if human beings are only "machines," then they can be "discarded" if they are born handicapped, or become too old or sick to be useful.

How important is human life? Not only is that a question people are asking today, it's one the psalmist David asked God many centuries ago.

● KEY VERSE ON MANKIND

"When I consider your heavens, . . . the moon and the stars, which you have set in place, what is man that you are mindful of him, . . . that you care for him?"
(Psalm 8:3-4) .

▲ LOOKING AHEAD

The answer to David's question is this: Human life has special value because God created it.

Start your week by reading the rest of Psalm 8. Just think—you are the "crowning part" of God's creation, right down to your freckles and pigtails! And by the way, where are you in relation to the angels? What about the rest of creation?

"No. I do not accept the Big Bang Theory."

Molecules, monkeys, and me

As the McClendons sat down to dinner, Mindy announced with a chuckle, "You should have been in my science class today! Mr. Green was lecturing about the 'Big Bang' theory of how the universe began. I raised my hand and asked, 'Mr. Green, what you're telling us doesn't seem right to me. The stuff that exploded in the Big Bang had to come from somewhere, didn't it?'

"He just glared at me a couple of seconds and then said, 'Science has no way of knowing what happened before the Big Bang.' When everyone in the class laughed, I guess he realized how 'unscientific' his answer sounded! I think he was mad."

◆ **TAKE A LOOK**
Genesis 1:1, 21, 25-26; 2:7, 21-22

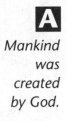

Where did human beings come from?

As concerned parents, the McClendons had taught their children to recognize—and reject—theories that try to explain the way things are but leave God out of the picture. Another is the question, "Where did human beings come from?"

God's record of creation and the beginning of life on earth is found in Genesis—the book of "beginnings." Read God's account of the beginning in Genesis 1:1, 21, 25-26; 2:7, 21-22.

A

Mankind was created by God.

▲ **TAKE A STEP**

The Biblical account of how humanity came into existence is totally different from the theories presented in many classrooms and textbooks. The Bible states clearly:

And the LORD God formed man from the dust of the ground and breathed into his nostrils the breath of life, and man became a living being (Genesis 2:7).

By contrast, the theory of evolution—which is often taught as if it were fact—assumes that all living things came from a single cell, and by a series of slow changes over millions of years, developed into complicated creatures.

Evolution is an attempt to explain how life began without God being involved. But as Mindy pointed out, you can't have a Big Bang unless you have something to go "boom"—and that means *Someone* had to create *something!*

God is the Someone, and the something is the heavens and earth, exactly as He reveals in His Word. Mindy knew that. Do you?

*T*wo-year-old Terry had learned to play the "Name Game" with his parents and grandparents. As he ran around the room, Terry would point to an object and wait for someone to say its name: "chair." Then Terry would grin and repeat what he had heard: "chair." Some of his words were hilarious! When Terry pointed to one piece of furniture and his grandmother said "piano," the best Terry could manage was "nanno." But no one seemed to mind. On and on the game went, while Terry learned to speak and think.

Throughout the game, the family poodle Fritz dozed on his bed. He didn't have the slightest interest in what was going on! In fact, to him, it seemed silly.

◆ **TAKE A LOOK / Genesis 1:27-31; 2:7**
Two-year-old children and two-year-old dogs have a lot in common. They both eat, sleep, play, and get into mischief. But in many important ways, people and poodles are very different, because only people are made "in God's image."

In the beginning when God made everything, He said:

"Let us make man in our image, in our likeness, and let them rule over the fish of the sea and the birds of the air, over the livestock, over all the earth, and over all the creatures that move along the ground" (Genesis 1:26).

That's why people own poodles, and not the other way around. Because you were made in God's image, you have the ability to speak and think, to give and receive love, to tell the difference between right and wrong. You have a will that enables you to make right choices. And most important, you have a spirit that actually enables you to communicate with God.

Read about the way you were made in the image of your Creator by reading Genesis 1:27-31; 2:7.

▲ **TAKE A STEP**
Without even knowing it, baby Terry was enjoying some of the benefits of being made in God's image when he was playing the "Name Game." Today, you too can be *happy* that you are *human!* Do something that only human beings can do: Write a poem, enjoy a sunset, tell someone you love him or her, take a poodle for a walk!

Close your family time by doing something else only people can do: Thank God for making *you!*

Made like Him so I can choose Him

Q

What does it mean to be created in God's image?

A

Because I am made in God's image, I can communicate with Him and can choose right from wrong.

Could it feel so right, and still be wrong?

Wes stood in the junkyard with his dad. There before him was the car he had worked for so long. He thought back to the day he had bought it. He remembered the smell of the interior, the glistening paint, the hum of the engine. Now that beauty was ruined. Though Wes was fortunate to have gotten out of the accident alive, he was heartbroken every time he looked at the car. The basic shape was still there—it was his car, no doubt about it—but it was so bent and scratched, Wes knew it would never be the same again.

◆ **TAKE A LOOK / Genesis 2:15-17; 3:6, 17-19**

People are not mechanical objects. But like Wes's car, we are no longer what our Manufacturer intended us to be when He made us. What went wrong with God's original design?

God's design included giving people a choice. They were free to choose to *obey* God's command; they were equally free to choose to *disobey*. The possibility of making the *wrong* choice showed that mankind really did have freedom to make the *right* choice. People are not robots.

God gave Adam one command to obey. Discover what it was by reading Genesis 2:15-17. Then turn ahead to 3:6,17-19 to see what Adam did with his freedom.

▲ **TAKE A STEP**

Adam's disobedience was sin. The result of that sin was *death*. And when Adam sinned, he died in two ways. First, he died *spiritually*. His perfect communication with God was broken. Then Adam began the long, slow process of dying *physically*.

Because of sin, Adam was no longer the same person God had created. His disobedience caused a change in his basic nature that would be passed on to all his descendants.

Just as sin entered the world through one man, and death through sin, [so] in this way death came to all men, because all sinned (Romans 5:12).

The consequences of Adam's sin were awful. Like Wes's car after the accident, it was barely possible to recognize the Maker's work. Wes's car could be repaired at the body shop, but where do you find help for a life that has been wrecked by sin? Romans 5:15-19 will give you the name of the master Repairman who specializes in cases like Adam's . . . and yours! When you find His name, close your family time by telling Him, "Thank You for dying that I might have new life!"

Q

What went wrong with the human race?

A

Mankind's disobedience brought sin and death; Jesus' death brought new life.

*T*hree-year-old Katie's favorite treat was going with her mom and dad for an ice cream cone. She had learned to distinguish three different flavors—vanilla, strawberry, and chocolate. Daddy's favorite was strawberry, Mommy liked vanilla, but Katie's favorite by far was chocolate!

Tonight as the family sat around the small table in the ice cream shop, Katie suddenly noticed a dark-skinned man sitting at the next table. Her big blue eyes got even bigger as she waved her spoon and exclaimed, "Look, Daddy, a chocolate man!"

◆ **TAKE A LOOK** / Genesis 11:1-9; Acts 17:26-27
Although Katie's innocent shout embarrassed her parents, she was actually learning an important truth: The God who created the world made many different "flavors" of people!

We often group people by the ways they are different from us—the color of their skin, the shape of their eyes, the language they speak. Sometimes one group or individual may treat others badly because of those differences. But the differences are not nearly as important as the fact that *all* men came from *one* man.

"From one man [God] made every nation of men, that they should inhabit the whole earth" (Acts 17:26).

In a sense, we are all "blood brothers." But early in the history of mankind, something happened that made it hard for us to talk to one another and put barriers between different groups of people. Turn in the Old Testament to Genesis 11:1-9 and read about an important event from the "dawn of human history." Then find Acts 17:26-27 to see why God did what He did.

▲ **TAKE A STEP**
Just imagine how much more people could accomplish if everyone spoke the same language! But, like the dwellers in Babel, we would want to take the credit for everything we did. And that is the very reason why God established language barriers.

The world's many languages make communication difficult, but God still wants people from every nation, tribe, and language to know Him. Close this week by praying for a missionary who is working in another language group. The missionaries and the people they work with are your brothers and sisters in the family called "Human"!

We're all blood brothers under the skin

Q

Why are there so many different kinds of people?

A

Because mankind is divided by language, culture, and race, people have many differences.

EASTER

F or the Howard family, spring was the favorite season of the year. Tender leaves budding, daffodils poking up through the ground, birds singing, Easter vacation on the horizon.

But there was one thing about spring that no one in the Howard family enjoyed. Two weeks before Easter, that dreaded ordeal called spring-cleaning would begin. Mrs. Howard would suddenly become a drill sergeant, ordering the troops (Mr. Howard and the three children) to attack the enemy (the accumulated dirt and grime of the winter). Curtains were cleaned, windows washed, carpets shampooed, walls scrubbed, floors waxed. Furniture was moved and closets were emptied. From top to bottom the Howard house had to sparkle!

◆ THINKING ABOUT EASTER TRADITIONS

What do you think of when you think of spring? If you're like most people, you probably don't think about spring-cleaning! And yet, in many homes spring-cleaning is as traditional at Easter time as baskets and bonnets, bunnies and eggs.

Like the traditions we celebrate during the Christmas season, Easter traditions are empty if they do not point to Jesus Christ, the One whose resurrection caused the angel to exclaim:

● KEY VERSE ON EASTER TRADITIONS

"He is not here; he has risen, just as he said" (Matthew 28:6).

"What could I say? They are her most Eastery shoes."

▲ TAKE A STEP

This week we'll think about some of the traditions of Easter, **customs handed down from one generation to the next,** to help us remember the events of that very special day.

Take turns sharing what you most enjoy at Easter! Is there a special meal Mom prepares? A sunrise service the family attends? A favorite hymn you enjoy? Then, to understand the real meaning of Easter, read John 20:1-8 and summarize what we celebrate in two words: _____ _____ .

*F*rankie Howard hated spring-cleaning. Being the oldest of three children and the only boy, he felt housework was a perfect way to waste time. So this year Frankie decided to add a little excitement to cleanup day.

Mom had handed out assignments, and any time now Frankie's six-year-old sister would be dusting the furniture in the den. Quietly, Frankie slipped into his room and dug out one of his treasures—an enormous black rubber spider. Unnoticed by his sister, he placed it on top of the television, then headed back to his room to see what would happen. He was soon rewarded with a terrifying scream.

"Spring-cleaning might be fun after all!" thought Frankie—until he heard his father's stern voice: "Franklin James Howard . . ."

◆ TAKE A LOOK / Exodus 12:1-15

How did spring-cleaning ever become a tradition?

Each year the Jewish people celebrate Passover to remember how God freed them from slavery. Passover points backward to the lamb whose blood was put on the door of each house so that God's people would be safe when the Lord "passed over" to kill the firstborn of the Egyptians. Passover also symbolized the time when the Lamb of God would die to take away the sin of the world (John 1:29).

Read God's specific instructions in Exodus 12:1-15 about how His people were to prepare, eat, and celebrate this special feast.

▲ TAKE A STEP

For seven days after Passover, every Jewish house was to be totally free of leaven (yeast). In the Bible, leaven is often a symbol of sin. Taking all leaven from the house was to be a picture of removing all sin from the heart.

What better way to be sure that every speck of leaven was out of the house than by a thorough spring-cleaning! And the process also portrayed another cleansing—this one of human hearts:

The blood of Jesus, [God's] Son, purifies us from all sin (1 John 1:7).

This year as you do your spring-cleaning, look for anything in your house that does not honor God: books, magazines, records, games, or toys. As you sweep out the dirt, sweep out anything else that might defile your home.

A perfect way to ruin a perfect Saturday

Q

What can I learn from spring-cleaning?

A

The Easter tradition of spring-cleaning reminds me that my life needs to be cleansed of sin.

You can't get into heaven wearing sneakers

Mrs. Willis had stretched her budget to the limit getting four children ready for Easter. The girls were picture perfect in their white lacy hats and ruffled dresses. And the boys were wearing new shirts and sweaters. It was a fine-looking family!

Now dressed in their new outfits and ready for church, the children stood restlessly while Mr. Willis prepared to take the annual Easter picture. Suddenly Mrs. Willis noticed the shoes Benjie was wearing. Not his good black ones, but his old sneakers—the ones with holes in the toes.

"Benjamin, why are you wearing your play shoes?" his mother asked in her most no-nonsense tone. "Go to your room right now and put on your black shoes."

"I can't, Mom. I left them at Gramp's last week."

Q

Why should I wear new clothes at Easter?

◆ **TAKE A LOOK / Romans 6:1-5**

Benjie wasn't very concerned about looking his "Sunday best." Perhaps no one had explained the tradition of wearing new clothes at Easter.

Soon after Jesus' resurrection, His followers began the custom of baptizing new believers on the day before Easter. Those who were baptized, wore new clothes to remind them of their new life in Christ. Read Romans 6:1-5 to discover why baptism is such a beautiful picture of that new life.

A

The Easter tradition of wearing new clothes reminds me of new life in Christ.

▲ **TAKE A STEP**

Later, when the early Christians began to be persecuted, they were forced to meet secretly. Those who wanted to join them were carefully prepared for the hardships they would face. Part of that preparation was a 40-day fast during which they ate no meat or eggs, until at last they were baptized on the night before Easter. Before long, this entire 40-day period came to be called Lent, from the Anglo-Saxon word *lencten*, which means "lengthening days."

The fasting period ended at Easter when the feast of the Resurrection and the wearing of new clothes reminded the Christians of their new life in Christ.

He has clothed me with garments of salvation and arrayed me in a robe of righteousness (Isaiah 61:10).

Benjie might have been able to sneak into church with his sneakers on, but there is no way to sneak into heaven. That's a privileged place reserved for those who are wearing the "righteousness of Christ." Is that a part of *your* wardrobe?

*F*our-year-old Connie was worried. The Easter egg hunt was tomorrow, and Mommy couldn't find her Easter basket anywhere.

"Well, Connie, we'll just have to make one." And with that, Mrs. Johnson set about with crayons, scissors, and a brown paper sack. In minutes, the "basket" was ready.

Connie enjoyed the egg hunt. She didn't know why a big rabbit was there . . . or why she was looking for brightly colored eggs. But she certainly was having a good time! Do you know where the idea of an Easter bunny and Easter eggs came from?

◆ **TAKE A LOOK / 1 Corinthians 15:20-24**

Decorated baskets lined with straw make a perfect nest for the candy eggs that the "Easter bunny" brings—or so the tradition goes. But try as you might, you won't find anything about eggs or bunnies in the Bible. So where did the ideas come from?

When the early Christians began to give up certain foods during the season of Lent (remember yesterday's reading), one food they stopped eating for a time was eggs. When the feast time finally arrived, eggs were dyed red to remind people of the joy of Christ's resurrection. The hard shell of the egg reminded some people of the tomb which "broke open" when Jesus rose from the dead.

And the Easter bunny? His origin is even harder to trace! Bunnies are known to spend the winter in dark, tomb-like holes and then emerge full of joy and gladness in the spring. In any case, these two traditions were brought together as one.

They are fun traditions, to be sure. But they have nothing to do with the true meaning of Easter. Remind yourself of that truth by reading 1 Corinthians 15:20-24 right now!

▲ **TAKE A STEP**

Easter is first and foremost a celebration—not just of the new life we see in nature each spring, but of the resurrection of Jesus from the dead. It's a time to praise God as the Apostle Paul did:

Thanks be to God! He gives us the victory through our Lord Jesus Christ! (1 Corinthians 15:57).

Whether or not bunnies, baskets, and colored eggs are part of your Easter celebration, don't forget the *real* reason for the season: our resurrected Savior whose empty tomb shouts to the world, "He is alive!"

Cracking the mystery of the Easter egg

Q

Is there a real Easter bunny?

A

The Easter traditions of eggs and bunnies are pretend; but the reason for the season is Jesus' resurrection.

Don't look now, but somebody moved Easter

Doyle was finishing his homework at the kitchen table. Suddenly he looked up and asked, "Hey, Mom, what's the date today?"

"I forget, Doyle. Let me check." She glanced at the calendar on the wall. "It's April 6."

"Oh yeah. Thanks." Doyle jotted the date at the top of his paper. Then he got a quizzical look on his face.

"Mom, how do we really know what year it is or even what day? Where did our calendar come from in the first place?"

"Now that's a good question . . . and I'm not sure I have a good answer. Let's get the encyclopedia and look it up."

◆ TAKE A LOOK / Genesis 1:14-19

Have you ever wondered why Christmas is always on December 25, but Easter changes each year?

The rotation of the earth around the sun gives us the unit of time called the year (365 days) The calendar that corresponds to the sun's movement is called the solar (365-day) calendar. But the movement of the moon is also important. About every 30 days it circles the earth, giving us the unit of time called the "mo[o]nth." Calendars based on the moon are called lunar (360-day) calendars.

Various civilizations have developed different calendars—some very simple, others quite complicated. But each kind of calendar was actually based on a system which God originally designed. Read Genesis 1:14-19 to discover God's purpose behind the sun, moon, and stars.

▲ TAKE A STEP

In the 1580s, a church leader named Gregory combined the solar and lunar systems to establish a new calendar based on the year Jesus was believed to have been born. The Gregorian calendar is still used today. Under that system, Christmas was given a set date: December 25. Easter, on the other hand, always comes on the first Sunday after the Jewish Passover. Because Passover is based on a lunar calendar, its date varies from year to year. Thus, the date of Easter reminds Christians once a year that . . .

Christ was sacrificed once to take away the sins of many people (Hebrews 9:28).

That event is marked for time and eternity, and nothing can change it! Not even the sun, moon, and stars.

Q

Why is Easter always on a different date?

A

Easter is related in time and meaning to Passover, which is based on a lunar calendar.

NEW LIFE

*W**ere you there when they crucified my Lord?*
Were you there when they crucified my Lord?
Oh, sometimes it causes me to tremble, tremble, tremble—
Were you there when they crucified my Lord?

You may have sung that old spiritual, but have you ever stopped to realize that if Jesus is your Lord then you were *there!*

You were there in God's eyes when the sins of the world—including your own—were laid on Jesus. You were there—dead because of sin—when He was laid in the tomb. You were there—alive in Him—when Jesus rose up from the grave.

◆ THINKING ABOUT NEW LIFE

New life, **the spiritual life that Jesus gives to those who believe in Him,** is possible because of the miracle of Easter. That week of agony in the life of Christ makes possible a new life of victory for you today! Here's how the Apostle Paul describes it:

● KEY VERSE ON NEW LIFE

We were therefore buried with him . . . in order that, just as Christ was raised from the dead through the glory of the Father, we too may live a new life (Romans 6:4).

▲ TAKE A STEP

This week we'll travel back in time, and through the eyes of people who were there, we'll view "the week that changed the world."

Another word that means the same thing as New Life is *metamorphosis*. Find a dictionary or encyclopedia, look up that word, and read what it says. This will help you understand why the butterfly is often used as a symbol for new life.

As you think about the new life Christians have, read what the Apostle Paul says in Romans 7:4. Then close your family time today by singing the song at the top of this page.

"I played the cocoon last year."

But I only did what my heart told me to do

Pilate was troubled. He prided himself on keeping the peace in the Jewish colony he ruled for the Roman government. But to condemn an innocent man to death—that was going too far and Pilate wasn't at all happy about it.

Early that morning the Jewish leaders had brought Jesus to him, demanding the death penalty. Pilate had listened to Jesus' accusers, questioned Jesus himself, and then returned the verdict: "I find no basis for a charge against him" (John 18:38; 19:4).

But the Jewish leaders were determined. They wanted this man dead. What was Pilate to do? His wife had been warned in a dream that the man was innocent. There was absolutely no reason to order the death penalty.

Q

Why is new life necessary?

A

New life is necessary because of my sinful heart.

◆ **TAKE A LOOK / John 19:4-16**

As far as we know, Pilate never left his comfortable palace to go out to Golgotha, the place of crucifixion. But he was there. He was there because he had given in to the demands of the Jewish leaders, even though Jesus was innocent. He was there because he had listened to the cries of the crowd instead of the whisper of his own conscience. He was there because he was afraid to stand alone.

In a word, Pilate was there because of *sin.* As you read John 19:4-16, see how many reasons you can find why Pilate gave in to the angry cries, "Crucify Him!"

▲ **TAKE A STEP**

Perhaps you've heard someone say, "If *I'd* been there, I wouldn't have done what Pilate did." But is that really true? Pilate did what he did because of the condition of his heart. And according to the prophet Jeremiah—an expert on human hearts—that condition is universal.

The heart is deceitful above all things and beyond cure. Who can understand it? (Jeremiah 17:9).

Because of his sinful heart, Pilate listened to the cry of the crowd. Though he probably thought of himself as a man who was good, kind, and fair; when the pressure was on, the true condition of his heart became clear.

Share with each other a time when *you* sinned in a way you never thought you would . . . by telling a lie . . . stealing . . . hitting someone in anger. As each person shares, finish this sentence: "Because of my sin of _____ , I was there when they crucified my Lord."

A s a Roman soldier, the centurion had seen his share of executions. He had no reason to believe this one would be any different. Another death, another day's work.

But as the hours dragged on, the centurion realized this was not an ordinary crucifixion. The crowd was large and angry. By contrast, the "criminal" looked peaceful and loving. And then there was that peculiar sign over the accused's head: "THIS IS JESUS, THE KING OF THE JEWS." Jews shouting cruel insults at their own king? It didn't make sense.

"Can't they even let a condemned man die in peace?" the centurion thought to himself. "If this crowd gets out of control, I'll be the one who gets the blame." And so, as the day wore on, the centurion moved closer to the foot of the cross. And it was there he saw firsthand the remarkable death of a remarkable Man.

◆ **TAKE A LOOK**
Matthew 27:45-47, 50-54; Luke 23:44-48
If you had experienced the Crucifixion through the eyes and ears of the centurion, what would you have seen and heard?
- A face filled with kindness instead of cruelty
- Words of forgiveness instead of vengeance
- An innocent man dying for the guilty
- Holy God forsaking His sin-bearing Son

Read Matthew 27:45-47, 50, 54 and Luke 23:44-48 for two accounts of the centurion's reaction to the death of Christ. .

▲ **TAKE A STEP**
"Were you there when they crucified my Lord?" The centurion was there. He saw the darkness come over the land for three long hours . . . heard the last words of Jesus . . . felt the earth move under his feet. He saw and came to a startling conclusion about the man from Galilee:

"Surely this man was the Son of God!"
(Mark 15:39).

Like Pilate, the Jewish rulers, and the angry crowd, many people today refuse to see God at work. They look at the evidence of Jesus' life and death, but come to the wrong conclusion—or no conclusion at all.

Pretend for a moment that you are the centurion. Tell the family what evidence from Jesus' life and death has convinced you that He really is who He claimed to be—God's Son and your Savior.

A death unlike any other

Q

Why is Jesus' death essential for new life?

A

Because Jesus is the sinless Son of God, His death made new life possible.

The funeral service that was never held

Q

What did Jesus' resurrection prove?

A

The resurrection proves that Jesus has power over sin and and death and can give me new life.

"I have no tears," Mary of Magdala thought to herself as she lay tossing in the dark. "Jesus is dead and there is nothing I can do to bring Him back. What will happen to me now? What will happen to all of us?"

It had been nearly three days since the cruel crucifixion and hasty burial of Jesus. His friends were still numb from the shock. It had all happened so fast. There hadn't been time to prepare His body properly before putting it in the tomb. That detail would have to wait till dawn, when the Sabbath was over and work could resume.

Memories raced through Mary's mind. How awful life had been before she met Jesus. The demons that controlled her mind and body had almost destroyed her. Then Jesus came. He cast out the demons and gave her new hope—new life. "At least I can do this for Him," she thought as she began to plan the proper burial that she and the others would give their dead Master as soon as it was light . . .

◆ TAKE A LOOK / Matthew 27:57-61; 28:1-9

Death is permanent and painful—*permanent* for the victim it strikes and *painful* for the saddened families and friends it leaves behind.

Put yourself in the "sandals" of Mary Magdalene. Imagine how heartbroken you would have been at the Crucifixion . . . how bleak your future would have looked . . . how little you would have slept. But then, to your amazement and joy, something happened to change all that—something almost too wonderful and too good to be true. Read about it in Matthew 27:57-61; 28:1-9.

▲ TAKE A STEP

"Were you there when He rose up from the grave?" Instead of marking the end of Jesus' life, His death and resurrection became the guarantee of new life—life that cannot be cut off by death. The resurrection of Jesus proved that He has power over sin and death—power to give new life to all who believe in Him.

"He is not here; he has risen" (Matthew 28:6).

That's why the angel's triumphant announcement is more than a 1st-century headline. It's 20th-century good news for you to give your world.

Mary Magdalene would have completed this sentence one way; how would you complete it? "Before I learned about the empty tomb, my life was sad because _____ ; but now that I know Jesus is risen, my life is joyful because _____ ."

*P*eter was nearly out of breath. Fishing on the Sea of Galilee was one thing, but running a footrace against young John was something else. Yet, when news is as exciting as what Peter had just heard, you don't mind getting a little tired in order to find out for yourself if it is really true.

And the reports from Mary Magdalene and the other women were exciting. Jesus was alive! But when you've denied your Lord not once . . . or twice . . . but three times, you don't take anything for granted. So Peter started running, going straight to the tomb to see if the stone was indeed rolled away . . . if the body really was gone . . . and if Jesus truly was alive from the dead.

◆ **TAKE A LOOK / Luke 24:1-12; Matthew 28:16-20**
After the Crucifixion, Peter and the other disciples were afraid and hid (John 20:19). But when the women came from the tomb with the glad report, "He is risen!", their *fear* gave way to *faith*. These humble, uneducated men and women became bold proclaimers of the good news. They were so eager to tell the world about their risen Savior that they would later be known as people who "turned the world upside-down."

Discover what made the difference in their lives by reading the first 12 verses of Luke chapter 24, and the last 5 verses of Matthew 28.

▲ **TAKE A STEP**
New life for doubting, denying disciples. New life for you. New life for your world. It's all possible because of the resurrection of Jesus Christ!

While hanging on the cross, Jesus exclaimed, "It is finished"—and it was. Jesus' death had paid sin's awful price. But now there was an unfinished task—the job of spreading this tremendous news of new life to those who hadn't heard. Just before He returned to heaven, Jesus assembled His disciples and gave them this command:

"Go and make disciples of all nations, baptizing them . . . and teaching them. . . . And surely I will be with you always, to the very end of the age" (Matthew 28:19-20).

The angel said, "GO . . . and tell . . . " (Matthew 28:7). Jesus said, "GO . . . " (Matthew 28:19). As a family decide to whom you will GO to TELL that "Jesus is alive!" Make plans now to share the good news of the Resurrection, and ask God to give you an opportunity to do just that.

Good news travels fast when you share it

Q

What should I do with this new life?

A

New life is too good to keep to yourself; tell someone about it!

PRAYER

*I*t was a lonely time in Jenna's life. After her father died, her mother was left with five children to care for, and Jenna was sent to live with Aunt Di and Uncle Jay. And it was there Jenna first heard about God's love. Soon she was praying every day that her mother would learn about God's love too.

One day, Aunt Di noticed Jenna standing quietly in the kitchen. "Jenna, is anything wrong? Do you feel all right?"

"I'm fine, Auntie. I was just asking God to let Mama learn about Him so she could be in His family too. And He told me not to worry—Mama would learn about Him this summer."

Aunt Di seemed surprised. "And what did you say?"

"I just said 'Thank You' because I know it's true."

◆ THINKING ABOUT PRAYER

Like Aunt Di, you may not be quite sure what to think about Jenna's prayer for her mother, especially the part when Jenna said God had spoken to her. Aunt Di had been standing right there, and all she heard was the sound of chicken frying on the stove.

Jenna's story is true. She was only 10 years old when she began to pray for her mother. Prayer to her was not simply a subject to be studied, but **a vital two-way conversation with her heavenly Father.** She was following this command:

● KEY VERSE ON PRAYER

Pray continually; give thanks in all circumstances, for this is God's will for you in Christ Jesus (1 Thessalonians 5:17-18).

"Thank goodness for Your twenty-four-hour hotline."

▲ TAKE A STEP

Learning about prayer this week will encourage us to obey that command and talk with God more often.

Three months after Jenna's prayer, her mother—who lived 500 miles away—invited Jesus into her life. Can you think of an answer to prayer that God has given you or your family recently?

There's no better way to learn about prayer than to learn what Jesus taught His disciples. Read Matthew 6:5-13. If your family doesn't already know the Lord's Prayer, learn it together this week!

Ready to say your prayers?" asked Mrs. Bennett as she bent to kiss eight-year-old Dean goodnight.

"I guess so," he mumbled. Kneeling by the bed, Dean recited hurriedly, "God bless Mommy and Daddy and Grandpa and Grandma, and please keep Chip warm in his doghouse. Amen."

Almost before Mrs. Bennett could blink, Dean was back in bed with the covers pulled over him.

"Dean," his mother asked, "who's your best friend?"

"Randy, I guess."

"Well, how do you think Randy would feel if you said the same thing to him every time you saw him? Would he like that?"

"Naw, that would be boring." Dean paused. "Oh . . . I see what you mean. It's like I say the same thing in my prayers every night, and maybe God gets bored. Hey, Mom, I heard a good story at school today. Do you think God would like to hear it?"

◆ TAKE A LOOK / Psalm 13

What did you talk about the last time you talked with God? Did you talk to Him as you would a close friend? Or did you sound more like you were ordering a meal at a restaurant?

King David understood that prayer is like conversation: two people sharing the things that are important to them. David didn't always ask for something when he prayed. Sometimes he just shared his feelings and fears, his happy moments and anxious thoughts. And he always remembered to praise God. As you read one of David's prayers in Psalm 13, try to imagine what was going on in his life that caused him to say what he said.

▲ TAKE A STEP

How many friends would you have if all you ever said to them was "Do this for me or get that for me"? David's love for God grew as he prayed his feelings, not just his requests. Because David talked with God about *all* the details of his life, he practiced the truth behind this week's key verse:

Pray continually (1 Thessalonians 5:17).

When you begin to think of prayer as talking with your Father in heaven, it will help you make prayer as interesting as a conversation with your best friend. What would you tell God if He were sitting beside you right now? "God, I just want you to know that . . ."

Try it! He's listening.

Now I lay me down to sleep

Q

Is prayer more than asking for things?

A

Prayer is conversation with the God of the universe.

But we pray another way at our house

S harla was from a country where people of her race were treated badly. A miracle had brought her to America for three months of special training. Now, with only two weeks left, all her money was gone. She had nothing left to buy the gifts she wanted to take back to her husband, children, and a few friends.

When the training time was over, a classmate took Sharla home to meet her family. Over breakfast the next morning, she handed Sharla an envelope. "It's for you to buy gifts to take back home for your family."

Tears welled up in Sharla's eyes as she opened the envelope and discovered three crisp new $50 bills. Suddenly, Sharla stood up and began to pray aloud in her native language. No one else in the room could understand a word she was saying, but the look on her face and the tears in her eyes said it all!

Q

Is there a "right" way to pray?

◆ **TAKE A LOOK / 1 Samuel 1:9-20**

Sometimes we are quick to judge those who don't do things exactly the way we do. That goes for prayer as well. It might have seemed "out of the ordinary" for Sharla to stand up during breakfast and pray, but there was nothing wrong about it.

The Bible tells us of people who prayed in many different ways, locations, and languages. Here is a verse that says a lot about praying:

Pray in the Spirit on all occasions with all kinds of prayers and requests (Ephesians 6:18).

A

Prayer can be done in many ways and many places.

One person who did exactly that was Hannah, a childless wife whose greatest wish was to be a mother. Even though she was in the Lord's temple, she did some "out of the ordinary" praying. Read about her prayer and God's answer in 1 Samuel 1:9-20.

▲ **TAKE A STEP**

You can pray sitting, standing, lying down, or kneeling. You can pray out loud, silently, with song, or with written words. You can pray prayers of praise, thanks, petition, confession, and worship. You can pray any time, any place, and for any reason.

Just as there's room for all kinds of people in the family of God, there's also room for all kinds of prayers. If your family normally prays at bedtime, try praying first thing in the morning instead. If you're a person who tends to pray "on the run," set aside 10 minutes in a quiet place just to talk to your heavenly Father. You can pray in many ways and many places, but the important thing is—PRAY!

***T**his would be an evening John and his girlfriend Dianne would never forget! Dianne's father had made reservations for them at the Diplomat, the downtown restaurant where he often took business clients. But before they left, Dad gave them instructions.*

"Feel free to order anything you want from the menu. And when they bring the check for the meal, just sign my name on the back."

"That's all I have to do?" asked John in amazement.

"That's all! They know who I am, and whenever they see my name, it's as if I had ordered the meal myself. Have a good time!"

◆ TAKE A LOOK / James 4:1-3

John was told to use the name of his girlfriend's father as his "passport" to an exciting evening. It wasn't the words themselves that had the power, but the person behind the words.

But those words couldn't be used for just anything. John couldn't say, "I think I'll buy a car or a new suit." The signature had to be used according to the will of the one who gave John the authority to use his name.

In the same way, praying in Jesus' name is asking for something Jesus would want—something that brings praise to God. It isn't a magic formula for getting what you want. It's an invitation to ask for something God wants.

"I will do whatever you ask in my name, so that the Son may bring glory to the Father" (John 14:13).

Read more about praying in Jesus' name by turning to James 4:1-3.

▲ TAKE A STEP

When you pray, do you wait for God to show you what He wants you to ask for? Are your prayers like band-aids, magic wands, or blank checks?

"Band-aid" prayers try to pray away problems as quickly as possible. "Magic wand" prayers address God as if He were a magic genie who does our every bidding. But "blank check" prayers allow God to fill in the amount (what I need), the date (when I need it), and the payee (the person God uses to answer my prayer).

Close your family devotional time by reading another portion of God's Word written by the Apostle John—1 John 5:14-15. Then use the name of Jesus as your passport to ask for the Father's will.

The name that unlocks prayer's power

Q

What does it mean to pray "in Jesus' name"?

A

Prayer in Jesus' name uses Jesus' authority to ask for God's will.

You never go wrong by taking God at His Word

Of all the things in the whole wide world, five-year-old Ethan Evans really wanted only one: a puppy. All winter long he asked his father repeatedly, "Can we get a puppy?" And always the answer was the same: "Wait till spring, Son. Dogs are easier to train when the weather gets warm."

Saturday dawned warm and bright, and Ethan decided now was a good time to ask once again: "Dad, can we get a puppy?" Mr. Evans, working intently on some new shelves for the kitchen, answered without thinking, "Sure, sure, we'll get a puppy."

Later, Ethan's father noticed his son working busily in the back yard. "What's he doing out there now?" he asked his wife.

"Getting the doghouse ready," Mrs. Evans replied. "He said you were getting a puppy this afternoon."

"Oh, no, we're not," Mr. Evans protested. Then he paused and looked out the window again. "He believed exactly what I said, didn't he?" Then picking up his jacket, he called to Ethan, "Come on, Son, let's go find us a puppy!"

◆ TAKE A LOOK / Luke 11:5-13

Ethan asked for a specific thing—a puppy. And when his father answered, Ethan believed what his father said. He demonstrated his confidence in his father and even built a doghouse in anticipation of the answer to his frequent requests.

God is in the business of answering prayers. Like the loving Father He is, He cares for us and delights in giving us good gifts.

Every good and perfect gift is from above, coming down from the Father of the heavenly lights (James 1:17).

Read more about your prayer-answering Father in Luke 11:5-13.

▲ TAKE A STEP

Ethan got the puppy he desired for at least three reasons: (1) It was a *specific* request in tune with his father's will; (2) It was a *persistent* request, showing that Ethan was serious about it; and (3) It was an *expectant* request, based on the promises of Ethan's father.

Now take a prayer item from your family's prayer list and ask these questions: "Are we asking specifically? . . . persistently? . . . expectantly? . . . and in line with God's will?" Remember, your heavenly Father is more eager to answer your prayer than you are eager to ask!

Q

Does God always answer prayer?

A

Prayer in tune with God's will is always answered.

PARENT:
A family prayer journal is a wonderful way to record prayer requests and see God at work in the answers He provides.

JOY

*I*f you were rich enough to buy anything in the world and powerful enough to do anything you wanted, would you be truly happy? A Spanish king who ruled more than a thousand years ago was almost that rich and powerful. Here is what he said as he came to the end of his life:

"I have now reigned about 50 years in victory and peace. I have been loved by my subjects, dreaded by my enemies, and respected by my allies. Riches, honor, and power have been mine. I have not lacked any earthly blessing. In this situation I have counted the days of pure and genuine happiness which have been mine: They amount to 14."

◆ THINKING ABOUT JOY

When the king looked back over the 18,250 days he had ruled, he could only remember a total of two weeks that were truly joyful.

Joy is something we associate with happy times in our lives: a new baby, wedding, graduation, promotion, family reunion, retirement. Joy makes us feel like our heart is having a party and all our happy feelings are invited!

But joy is more than happy feelings. A good way to remember what joy really is, is this: True joy is **Jesus Overflowing in You**. Put the first letters of those words together and they spell JOY!

Jesus explained joy to His disciples with these words:

● KEY VERSE ON JOY

"I have told you this so that my joy may be in you and that your joy may be complete" (John 15:11).

▲ TAKE A STEP

Regardless of your age, you can discover more joy in life than a king who ruled for half a century! Quickly make a list of the 14 happiest days in the life of *your* family. Then close your time together by looking up these verses to discover some other occasions of great joy: Job 38:7, Matthew 2:10, Matthew 28:8, and Luke 24:52. Who was the cause of all that joy?

"And to think that I started out as a little bundle of joy."

Joy is more than a one-point victory

The final seconds of the championship game wind down with the home team trailing by a single point. A desperate last-second shot finds the mark. Swish! Instantly, the court swarms with screaming, cheering students. JOY!

The high school senior opens an envelope from the college he hopes to attend. Inside he finds a letter that begins, "We are happy to inform you . . . " JOY!

Two children jump into bed with Mom and Dad on Saturday morning for a game of "toss and tumble" under the covers. JOY!

A young wife answers the phone and hears the words she has waited two years to hear: "This is the adoption agency. We have a baby for you—a seven pound, eight ounce boy." JOY!

Q

What is the source of true and lasting joy?

A

Joy comes from obedience to God's commands.

◆ **TAKE A LOOK / John 15:9-11**

Joy comes in many shapes and sizes, but the joy Jesus spoke of is a constant supply—a steady flow, not just a series of surprises.

Jesus' life was not always happy. He was sometimes tired and hungry. His friends sometimes failed Him. The crowds made constant demands. And His life was marked by many sad times—the saddest of all being the way He died. But the Bible says that Jesus was anointed "with the oil of joy" (Hebrews 1:9). He experienced joy in every circumstance of His life.

The night before He died, Jesus told His followers how they could have that kind of joy as well. Find John 15 in your Bible. As you read verses 9-11, see if you can discover two reasons why Jesus was a "joy-full" person.

▲ **TAKE A STEP**

Jesus knew what the psalmist meant when he said:

Your statutes [commands] are my heritage forever; they are the joy of my heart (Psalm 119:111).

Joy is linked with obeying God's commands. When children are disobedient and rebellious, there is no room for joy in their hearts. They use all their energy being angry! By contrast, the person who obeys God can be confident and happy, rewarded by joy.

If you're not a joy-full family, you may discover why by discussing: (1) Do we obey God's commands when we find them in the Bible? (2) Do we obey and honor our parents? (3) Do we obey the rules and laws of our school, and country?

*I*t was all Mrs. Hansen could do to pull herself out of bed. "I'm so tired," she thought. "I feel like I haven't slept in a month."

Mrs. Hansen had reason to be weary. Her husband's slow recovery from surgery meant she had to look after him, manage their hardware business, juggle the family schedule, and keep the housework done. The three children helped, but night after night she found herself doing dinner dishes at 9:30—after driving one of the children to an activity or helping with homework.

When 13-year-old Neil came into the kitchen fuming, it was the last straw. "Mom, my corduroy jeans have been dirty for a week, and I don't have any clean socks, and. . . ." Mrs. Hansen burst into tears, while her startled children looked on.

◆ **TAKE A LOOK / Acts 16:16-31**

The stresses and strains in the Hansen family were no different from those many families experience: illness, financial trouble, family conflict, job pressures, and more things to do than there are hours in the day to do them.

The Apostle Paul knew from firsthand experience how circumstances can wear a person down, both physically and spiritually. Yet he also knew the secret of finding joy in the midst of misery. Even when he was near the end of his life and locked in a Roman prison cell, Paul could write:

Rejoice in the Lord always. I will say it again: Rejoice! (Philippians 4:4).

To discover how Paul was able to "rejoice always," read about another of his times in jail. There's a key to joy hanging in Acts 16:16-31. Can you find it?

▲ **TAKE A STEP**

Beaten. Imprisoned. In chains. In many ways things looked bleak for Paul and Silas. But no dungeon was deep enough, no night black enough, to block out the light of God's love. Paul and Silas knew that God was in control, so they overflowed with joy by singing hymns of praise at midnight!

What Scripture song or hymn of praise would you have sung if you had been with them in that dungeon? Find a hymnbook right now, or pick a song you know from memory, and sing it as a family. Then discuss how those encouraging stanzas can become a "candle of joy" when dark circumstances surround your family.

Joy is more than eight hours of sleep

Q

How can I be joyful in all circumstances?

A

Joy comes alive when I praise the Lord.

PARENT: Music is one way to express "the joy of the heart." Set aside an evening to listen to joyful music with your child.

To double your joy, give it away

Nine-year-old Robyn could hardly contain her excitement. She had worked so hard on her mother's present. It was a clay vase, baked in the kiln and painted bright blue—her mother's favorite color. Even the wrapping and the card were specially made with her mother in mind.

When Mrs. Coleman opened the gift, it was hard to tell who was more pleased—Robyn or her mother. "Oh, Robyn, it's a beautiful vase, and it's my favorite color. You made it by yourself, didn't you? Well, it's lovely. I know just where I'll put it." She hugged Robyn.

But Robyn's older brother Bill was jealous of their excitement. With a few cruel words, he made his feelings known. "Aw, Mom's just saying that to make you feel good. It looks like a piece of junk to me."

Q

How is joy related to giving?

◆ **TAKE A LOOK / James 1:18; Ephesians 2:8-9**

Giving and receiving gifts is one of the best ways to spread joy. It really is "more blessed to give than to receive" (Acts 20:35)—to know that a gift you have prepared with love is accepted, liked, and appreciated by the person you gave it to.

But like Robyn's ceramic vase, joy must be handled carefully. It is easy to shatter another person's joy by making him think his gift is not good or by refusing to accept it.

God, the giver of "every good and perfect gift" (James 1:17), has prepared a gift with you in mind—a gift designed to meet your needs. Read about God's priceless gift in James 1:18; Ephesians 2:8-9; and Romans 6:23.

A

Joy comes when I accept God's free gift of everlasting life.

▲ **TAKE A STEP**

God's gift is nothing less than salvation—new life in Jesus! Like any gift, it can be *accepted* or *rejected*. Like any gift, it can bring joy both to the *Giver* and the *recipient*.

The Bible doesn't tell much about what is going on in heaven right now, but here is a verse that gives us a clue:

"There [is] . . . rejoicing in heaven over one sinner who repents" (Luke 15:7).

Do you remember the date when you accepted God's gift of eternal life in His Son Jesus? If you do, mark it on your family calendar with these words: "On this date, angels rejoiced in heaven because ___(your name)___ accepted God's free gift." If you have not received that free gift, why not do so right now and mark today's date as "Joy in Heaven" day!

*S*even-year-old Jason had been waiting at the airport
with his mother for what seemed to be forever.
Impatiently he pressed his face against the cold window and studied each plane that rolled by.

"That one, Mom?" he would ask.

"No, Jason, not that one. But it will be here soon."

At last a voice came over the loudspeaker. "Flight
142 from Chicago is now arriving at Gate 12." A quick
glance at his mother was all Jason needed to know that
his father was on that plane.

As the passengers got off, Jason craned his neck for
the first glimpse of his father. "Boy, grown-ups sure
move slow," he thought to himself. But at last, the wait
was over. With a whoop Jason announced to the world,
"There he is. There's my dad!" And everyone within
hearing distance smiled.

◆ TAKE A LOOK / 1 Peter 1:3-9

Jason's joy was complete when he was reunited
with his father. The time apart had been hard, but
it had made everyone in the family realize how
much they loved each other and how wonderful it
was to be a family.

Being separated from someone you love is
never easy, but the reunion can make it all worthwhile. This is true of other painful circumstances as
well. The joy comes—not because the experience is
pleasant—but because you know God is at work.

*Consider it pure joy, my brothers, whenever
you face trials of many kinds (James 1:2).*

See if you can discover why we can be joyful
and triumphant in the midst of trials by reading
1 Peter 1:3-9. (Hint: Watch for the word *rejoice* and
look for the "this" that makes it possible!)

▲ TAKE A STEP

"In this you greatly rejoice"—that God has
given us new life through Christ's resurrection. We
have a wonderful reunion to look forward to in
heaven. And with that as our comfort, we can face
each new day in His strength because He lives.

Close your time together by reading (or singing, if you know the melody) the joyful third
stanza of "When We All Get to Heaven":

Let us then be true and faithful,
Trusting, serving every day;
Just one glimpse of Him in glory
Will the toils of life repay.

Life is worth living because Jesus lives!

Joy to the world, the Lord is come

Q

What will
be the
most joyful
day in
history?

A

The most
joyful day
will be
when Jesus
returns.

GENTLENESS

*T*his would be the first birthday Penny had ever celebrated without Grandma and Grandpa being there. But their letter from England said that a gift was on the way! Sure enough, on the day before her birthday, a box arrived, stamped "FRAGILE—HANDLE WITH CARE."

"Mom, please let me open it now," Penny pleaded. "I've never had a present like this. Please, Mom, please . . ."

That night Penny's parents let her open that special package. Carefully she opened the top of the box. Slowly she pulled out the styrofoam packing pieces. Gently she lifted out a dainty porcelain figurine. After several minutes of excitement, she turned it over and found the figure's name—Penny—printed beneath the manufacturer's seal.

◆ THINKING ABOUT GENTLENESS

The next day Penny found a safe place to display her new "Penny," a place where the figurine wouldn't be bumped by a careless elbow or toppled by a frisky kitten. Its need for gentle handling didn't end when the package was opened.

Like Penny's figurine, people's feelings are often fragile, in need of gentle treatment. Even though we live in a world that is often harsh and unfeeling, God intends that we be sensitive to the feelings of others. He has given us this command to obey:

● KEY VERSE ON GENTLENESS

Let your gentleness be evident to all. The Lord is near (Philippians 4:5).

▲ LOOKING AHEAD

Gentleness, the quality of **treating others with kindness and care**, is the T.L.C. (tender loving care) everyone loves to receive.

How many things can you think of around your house that, like Penny's porcelain figurine, need to be handled with care? Don't forget to add your family members to that list! Then begin your week on gentleness by reading Isaiah 40:10-11. What very familiar Psalm do these verses bring to mind?

"Go to sleep, or she'll sing it again."

P lease, Daddy, just for a few nights—until Winky gets used to being here. I'm sure he won't cry if you put his bed in my room."

"Sandy, I've told you no for the last time," her father replied sternly. "You cannot take the dog to your room. He'll be fine here in the kitchen, and after a few more nights he won't cry anymore. Now scoot! It's already past your bedtime."

The next morning when Mr. Timmons turned on the kitchen light, he was startled by what he saw. There was Sandy with her head on a pillow and wrapped in a blanket from her bed, sleeping soundly beside the puppy's box.

Waking to face her father, Sandy quickly began to apologize: "I didn't mean to go to sleep, Daddy. I thought if I sang to Winky, it would help him through the night. I guess I was the one who fell asleep."

◆ **TAKE A LOOK / John 19:17-27**

Not everyone can truthfully say, "I'm a gentle person." But one Man did make that claim, and then lived a life of gentleness to show He meant what He said!

Jesus Christ was the most gentle Person who ever lived. Kindly, patiently, tenderly, He spent His days helping hurting people. He told them, "Learn from me, for I am gentle and humble in heart, and you will find rest for your souls" (Matthew 11:29). Even when He was treated cruelly, Jesus returned nothing but gentleness. Read John 19:17-27 right now to see the Man from Galilee at His "gentle best." How many gentle actions can you find in those 11 short verses?

▲ **TAKE A STEP**

Gentleness is a quality God wants to build into your life. It is a fruit that grows when the Holy Spirit is at work within you.

The fruit of the Spirit is . . . gentleness (Galatians 5:22-23).

Do you have any fruit trees in your yard? If so, then you know fruit grows best on trees that are well-cultivated. The same is true of the fruit of gentleness that God wants to cultivate in your life. Look for opportunities to practice gentleness. Sandy did exactly that by singing Winky a lullaby. Who is one person you can show gentleness to today?

How will you have a gentle attitude toward that person?

Gentle people are made, not born

Q

Where does gentleness come from?

A

Gentleness is a "fruit" that grows when the Holy Spirit is at work in my life.

Gentle people keep in touch

Q

How can I communicate gentleness with a touch?

A

Gentleness in a touch says, "I'm here and I care about you."

PARENT: If you find it difficult to demonstrate affection to your child, perhaps the place to begin is with a gentle touch, a hug, a hand on the shoulder. The bumper sticker asks a good question: "Have you hugged your child today?"

Baby Andrew looked okay to six-year-old Burke. It was hard for the proud big brother to understand that Andrew had been born with a heart that didn't work properly. One day an operation might help, but the doctors weren't sure. Until then, the only thing the family could do was love their baby and treat him tenderly.

Mom and Dad didn't let Burke hold Andrew much, but everyday after school the first thing Burke did was to check on Andrew. Soon Andrew knew when it was time for Burke to come home, and he began to watch for his brother. Burke was quick to sense how the tiny baby was feeling. When Andrew was restless or having difficulty breathing, Burke knew it. With Mom and Dad's help, he would prop Andrew up on a pillow in the middle of the big bed and then talk softly to him, smoothing his hair, rubbing his back, or gently rocking him back and forth.

◆ **TAKE A LOOK**
Mark 5:21-23, 35-43; Matthew 19:13-15

When you are afraid or in pain, a gentle touch can mean so much. It is the best way to say, "I care and I'll do what I can to keep you from hurting."

It's nice to get a long distance telephone call from someone you love, but there's an even better way to "reach out and touch someone." Do you know what it is? Reach out and physically touch them! That's what Jesus did many times in the lives of others. Read about two such instances in Mark 5:21-23, 35-43 and Matthew 19:13-15. Would you like to have been one of the children Jesus touched?

▲ **TAKE A STEP**

Your mother gets up in the night to soothe your fever—even though you're 14 years old. A friend puts his arm around your shoulder just to say, "I understand your disappointment." The dental assistant holds your hand and explains what the dentist is about to do.

Each is an example of the comfort of a gentle touch. They are ways of putting this important verse to work:

Therefore, as God's chosen people, holy and dearly loved, clothe yourselves with . . . gentleness (Colossians 3:12).

Give each member of the family a cotton ball or soft tissue to put in pocket or purse. It's a good way to remind yourself throughout the day that a gentle touch can mean so much!

When a boy from Tammy's class began calling regularly on the phone, 12-year-old Taylor couldn't resist teasing his older sister.

"Well, what did Mr. Wonderful have to say? I'll bet you're hoping he's going to ask you to the Spring Banquet, aren't you? Well, forget it! He only likes you 'cause you help him with algebra."

But instead of the angry reply Taylor expected, Tammy answered calmly, "It really doesn't matter what you think."

The next day Taylor tried again. "Well, Sis, the banquet's next weekend. Time's running out on Cinderella."

But instead of hitting her brother with a pillow—as Taylor expected—Tammy responded, "It's really not your problem, Taylor. I know you're trying to make me mad, but forget it."

"What's she trying to do?" Taylor frowned. "Teasing her isn't nearly as much fun as it used to be."

◆ TAKE A LOOK / Job 2:3-10

By her soft response to Taylor's teasing, Tammy was practicing gentleness, helping a tense situation from getting worse by using the right words in the right tone of voice. She was learning that

A gentle answer turns away wrath, but a harsh word stirs up anger (Proverbs 15:1).

In the Old Testament Job turned anger away with a gentle word. Job was a very wealthy and godly man, but suddenly he lost *all* he had: wealth, health, family, and friends. All this was too much for Job's wife, who became angry with her husband—not only about his misfortune, but also about the way he was accepting it. Read Job's gentle answer to his angry wife in Job 2:3-10.

▲ TAKE A STEP

Sticks and stones may break my bones,
But words can never hurt me.

That little rhyme sounds good, but there is just one problem: *It isn't true!* Words can hurt—and often do—when they are used as weapons. Angry words spoken in response to angry words usually hurt people in the process.

Taylor could learn an important lesson from his sister about using his tongue to put out fires, rather than to start new ones. After reading Psalm 34:1-3, could you tell him at least one reason why God has given us a tongue in the first place?

Gentle people don't wound with harsh words

Q

How can I communicate gentleness with my voice?

A

A gentle word turns away anger.

Gentle-ness— the eyes have it

Q

How can I communicate gentleness with my eyes?

A

A gentle look says, "I love you and I want to help."

PARENT:
One good way to discover what your young child is reading in your eyes is by examining the facial expressions used most often in his or her pictures. Does the child draw happy faces . . . sad faces . . . angry faces? Observe carefully!

Since the time Toby was in kindergarten, his teachers had told his parents what the problem was: "He simply won't tell us when he has difficulty understanding or when he needs help with his work." But no one seemed to know how to help Toby solve his problem.

No one, that is, until Toby met Mrs. Carpenter, his fourth-grade teacher. And suddenly he began to blossom. His work improved, and for the first time he began to make friends with some of the other boys and girls.

One day Toby came home in such a happy mood that his mother decided to investigate: "Toby, why do you like Mrs. Carpenter so much?"

Toby thought for a minute and replied, "She's the first teacher I ever had who didn't yell at me. Mom, she's so kind, her eyes don't even get angry!"

◆ **TAKE A LOOK / Psalm 31:9**

Have you ever seen two people in love? Even their eyes reveal the feelings they share for each other. One verse from the Song of Solomon says it all:

You have stolen my heart with one glance of your eyes (Song of Solomon 4:9).

Already this week you've learned that gentleness—**treating others with kindness and care**— can be expressed by a tender touch or a soft tone of voice. Look up the following verses to see what the Bible says about the message you communicate with your eyes as well:

What the Bible says . . . about what my eyes are saying:

Psalm 31:9_____
Psalm 36:1-2 _____
Psalm 101:5_____
Psalm 141:8 _____
Proverbs 21:4_____

▲ **TAKE A STEP**

Your eyes can say as clearly as your tongue, "I want to help you" or "I want to hurt you." Prove that to yourself right now. Turn to the person next to you and, just by using your eyes (no words), say to that person, "I love you very much." Did your partner get the message? Now tell that same person —again without a word—"I don't like you one bit!"

Did the message come through clearly again? Discuss as a family the most common messages you give and receive with your eyes.

GOD

*A*aa-choo!"

"Cover your mouth when you sneeze, Bethany. One cold around this house is enough," said Mrs. Thomas.

Six-year-old Bethany got a tissue from the bathroom. She stopped to look in the mirror at her runny nose and red eyes.

"Hey Mom, how come you can 'catch' a cold, but you can't 'catch' freckles?"

"Because, Bethany, a cold is 'communicable.' You can give it to someone else. But freckles are 'incommunicable.' They are something you either have or don't have based on your type of skin."

"Oh," said Bethany with a look of disappointment on her face. "I was hoping I'd get freckles like Ben."

◆ THINKING ABOUT GOD

Did you know there are certain characteristics of God that Christians can catch and pass on to others? Things like love, kindness, and patience are God's communicable attributes.

But there are other incommunicable traits which God—and God alone—possesses. Only God is **omnipotent** (all-powerful), **omniscient** (all-knowing), **omnipresent** (everywhere at once), and **immutable** (unchanging).

▲ TAKE A STEP

Don't let those big words frighten you.

King David knew he could never completely understand God, and neither will we. But thinking about what God was like helped David love God all the more.

Make David's prayer of praise the closing prayer of your family today as you thank God for His *omni* attributes:

● KEY VERSE ON GOD

Yours, O LORD, is the greatness and the power and the glory and the majesty and the splendor, for everything in heaven and earth is yours (1 Chronicles 29:11).

"How does God know everything? Is He a silicon chip?"

Can God make a rock so big He can't pick it up?

Q

Is there anything God can't do?

A

God's omnipotence means that He can do anything that is true to His character.

A fter passing out the math test, Mr. Sullivan sat reading at his desk, unaware of the cheating in the class.

Hayes, too, paid little attention to what was happening around him until he felt a tug on his elbow, and Gloria motioned for him to uncover his paper. He stiffened his arm and said, "I can't."

"Sure you can," Gloria whispered. "It's easy—just move your arm." Hayes covered his paper more carefully and continued working.

After class Gloria came over. "Why'd you say you couldn't let me copy your paper, Hayes? All you had to do was move your arm. Nobody would've known."

"No, I really couldn't, Gloria. I'm trying to please God by doing the right thing, and you and I both know cheating isn't right. I just couldn't do it, that's all."

◆ TAKE A LOOK / Job 40:1-2, 6-14; 42:1-3

Gloria didn't understand Hayes's beliefs about cheating. She knew that if he moved his arm, he *could* uncover his paper. But she didn't realize that because he was determined not to cheat, he *couldn't* move his arm.

Some people are similarly confused about God. The Bible refers to Him as *the Almighty* (the One who is all-powerful and can do everything), but that doesn't mean He *will do* just anything. For example, God will not make 2 + 2 equal 5, or draw a square circle, or cheat when it's convenient. God is perfect in every way and will not do *anything* that is against His nature.

How powerful is God? Let's ask Job (the same one whose life gave us the saying, "the patience of Job"), and his personal testimony about God's omnipotence is found in Job 40:1-2, 6-14; 42:1-3.

▲ TAKE A STEP

What decision did Job make about God's power? *I know that you can do all things; no plan of yours can be thwarted. . . . Surely I spoke of things I did not understand, things too wonderful for me to know (Job 42:2-3).*

Like Job, none of us completely understands God's power. But that shouldn't keep us from living in step with the part of God's plan we do understand. Hayes did that by keeping his paper covered; Job did it by trusting God, even when he couldn't find a reason for his suffering and pain. What is one way *you* can do the same thing today?

*T*here was good news and bad news at the Shaw residence. The good news? After waiting many weeks, they had moved at last into their new house. And the bad news? Thirteen-year-old Jamie had a report due tomorrow for his health and safety class—and the set of encyclopedias was still packed somewhere in the many boxes and crates!

After much looking, Jamie uncovered Volume I, the "A" volume, and breathed a big sigh of relief. He had chosen AIDS—acquired immune deficiency syndrome—as his topic! But his relief was short-lived.

"Hey, Mom, there's nothing in this encyclopedia at all about AIDS. How come?"

"I guess they didn't know much about it when that encyclopedia was written, Jamie."

◆ TAKE A LOOK / Matthew 10:29-30

Chances are, even if Jamie's encyclopedia had listed his topic, the information would have been outdated. Facts about diseases are being discovered so rapidly that they become outdated almost before they can be printed!

In spite of the information explosion that is going on, there is one thing you can be sure of: No discovery will ever be made that takes God by surprise. He is omniscient—all knowing. Look up the following verses, and complete each statement:

God sees when _____ (Matthew 10:29-30).
God knows _____ (Acts 1:24).
God watches both the ____ and _____ (Proverbs 15:3).
God knows _____! (Hebrews 4:13 and 1 John 3:20).

▲ TAKE A STEP

Some of the hottest selling games have been about trivia, thousands of little-known facts you can use to amaze your friends. But the knowledge God has is never trivial or purposeless.

Nothing in all creation is hidden from God's sight. Everything is uncovered and laid bare before the eyes of him to whom we must give account (Hebrews 4:13).

God knows everything: the good and the bad . . . the beginning and the end . . . what *could* happen, *should* happen, and *did* happen. So when things happen to you which are hard to understand, turn to your omniscient God. If you could ask Him one question right now, what would it be?

God's knowledge is never out of date

Does God really know everything?

God's omniscience means that He knows the purpose for everything that happens in my life.

If You're there, God, please hold my hand

F our-year-old Elizabeth didn't like the new house. It was big, strange, and sometimes frightening—especially the open stairwell going down to the bedrooms in the basement. Unless the light in the hallway was on, Elizabeth wouldn't go to her room alone.

Both her mother and father talked to her about it. "There's nothing to be frightened of," they said. "You're a big girl now. You can reach the light switch yourself."

But nothing seemed to help.

After a week of Elizabeth's refusals, her father thought he had the answer. "Elizabeth, remember what you learned in Sunday school? God is everywhere. You don't need to be afraid."

"But Daddy," she replied, "I don't want God to be everywhere. I want Him here to hold my hand."

Q

Is God really everywhere at the same time?

A

God's omnipresence means that I am never out of His care.

◆ **TAKE A LOOK / Psalm 139:1-12**

Elizabeth wanted a real hand to hold as she walked down the dark hall, but learning about the attribute of God that we call His omnipresence could help her overcome her fear. *Omnipresence* means that God is not limited by time or space. He can be everywhere at the same time.

The Psalmist David had many scary moments as he tended his father's sheep, faced the anger of giants, and later ruled the nation of Israel. Like Elizabeth, he could find comfort in the omnipresence of his God, who was with him even in the "valley of the shadow of death" (Psalm 23:4).

Take turns reading a verse at a time from one of the most comforting passages in the Bible— Psalm 139:1-12.

▲ **TAKE A STEP**

Another spokesman for God wrote these words about the omnipresence of God:

"Can anyone hide in secret places so that I cannot see him?" declares the Lord. "Do not I fill heaven and earth?" declares the Lord (Jeremiah 23:24).

The answer, of course, is no to the first question, and yes to the second. There is no place to hide from God.

In Psalm 139:7-12, David uses the pattern, "If I _____ , God is _____ ." See how many other ways you can complete that sentence. For example, "If we go on a vacation to Canada, God is right there with us every mile of the way." As you think about your daily routine, let each family member suggest other ways to declare God's omnipresence.

*I*t wasn't the homework assignment in English 301 that caused Marylou so much trouble. It was Mr. Baxter's habit of changing his mind. Already he had changed the seating arrangement twice and the classroom procedure once. Now he was revising his grading system.

"Whew, I feel like I'm on a roller coaster," a student remarked after class one day.

"Yeah, only this is no amusement park," another student sighed. "Those grades go on our record. I wish he'd make up his mind about what he wants to do."

"Well, cheer up," Marylou joked, "it could be worse. He could be teaching driver's education, and then you'd never know if a red light meant 'Stop' or 'Go'!"

◆ **TAKE A LOOK** / **Malachi 2:17–3:7, 16-17**
This week we've been learning about God's "omni" attributes: omnipotence, omniscience, and omnipresence. But no single attribute of God is more important than any another. God always acts consistently with all of His attributes all the time. He always has been and always will be the same. He cannot change. In a word, He is *immutable.*

Malachi, the last book of the Old Testament, was written about 400 years before Jesus was born. God's people, the Jews, had changed in their love for God, but God had not changed in His love for them. As you read Malachi 2:17–3:7, 16-17, see if you can spot a warning, a promise, and a description of our unchanging God.

▲ **TAKE A STEP**
Marylou and her friends were frustrated and confused because their teacher kept changing the rules. A similar confusion occurs when society tries to ignore God's standards of right and wrong.

For God's standards of right and wrong to change, God Himself would have to change. And He has clearly declared:

*I the L*ORD *do not change (Malachi 3:6).*

God's immutability, His changeless personality, means that what was wrong yesterday (or in the time of Malachi) is still wrong today. Discuss as a family how this fact can help you make decisions that are pleasing to God, whether at school, work, or play. Regardless of what others say, how can you be sure you are doing what is right in God's opinion—the only opinion that really matters?

Don't look now, but somebody changed the rules

Q

Why is it important to know that God doesn't change?

A

God's immutability means that right and wrong do not change.

PARENT: *Using Galatians 5:19-21 and Romans 1:18-32, discuss with your older child the kind of behavior God condemns.*

CREATIVITY

*D*uane could hardly stand to look at a blank sheet of paper or a bare wall. He loved colors and shapes, and soon after Grandpa gave him a set of colored pencils (not the kind you buy in the drugstore but "real" ones from the art supply store), nearly every wall in the house was decorated with Duane's art.

Mom used little magnets to hold some of his pictures on the refrigerator door. Dad taped three others over his workbench. Duane hung his own personal favorite on his bulletin board.

Now that it was spring and the world was overflowing with color, Duane's pencils were busier than ever! As he handed his mother a drawing of her flower garden, she looked lovingly at her eight-year-old son. "Duane," she asked in amazement, "how do you do it? Your pictures are just beautiful!"

"It's easy, Mom," he replied. "I just draw what's in my head."

◆ THINKING ABOUT CREATIVITY

Only God can create *something* out of *nothing*. But because human beings bear a special likeness to God, we too have the God-given ability to be creative—**to imagine and invent new things.** Not everyone has *artistic* talent (like Duane), but almost everyone has some *creative* ability. You'll discover why in this Bible verse:

● KEY VERSE ON CREATIVITY

God created man in his own image (Genesis 1:27).

▲ TAKE A STEP

Perhaps when you think of creative people, you think of musicians, poets, and painters. But if God has given you a mind with imagination, then you, too, have everything you need to be creative!

"Until today's geography test, Sir, I never realized just how much earth You did create."

Have Mom or Dad (or whoever leads your family time) read ahead to be sure you have the few items you'll need in order to get the most out of this week's study. Then start your week on creativity by reading Isaiah 64:8. Discuss ways God is molding and shaping your life in the same way that a potter molds and shapes his clay.

"I do not like it, Sam-I-Am.
I do not like green eggs and ham!"

What do you think of when you think about fun with colors? Most people think about painting or drawing. But for Sam-I-Am, one of the heroes in Dr. Seuss's book Green Eggs and Ham, colors made him think of food.

To better appreciate the wonderful variety of color in the foods God has given us, why not let each person make a "Sam-I-Am Spaghetti Salad" for dinner tonight.

For a family of four, divide these ingredients equally on double thickness paper plates (the more ingredients, the better!): 1 small can drained pineapple chunks, 1 small jar maraschino cherries, 2 bananas, a kiwi fruit, 1/2 cup blueberries, shredded coconut. (Save the blueberry and cherry juice for coloring). Start with 1/4 cup per person cooked, drained spaghetti noodles. Let each person season his spaghetti with sugar, cinnamon, and nutmeg. Dye the banana slices and shredded coconut with the blueberry or cherry juice. Arrange all the fruit chunks on the spaghetti, and ENJOY!

◆ TAKE A LOOK / Exodus 31:1-6

Color itself is a gift from our Creator God—something we enjoy all the time, though we seldom think about it. And in Old Testament times God instructed His people to build a "work of art"—a place where they could worship Him in the beauty of holiness.

After the Israelites left Egypt, God gave Moses detailed instructions for building the tabernacle (also called the tent of meeting). As you read Exodus 31:1-6, notice why artists were needed and what an important role color played in the magnificent tent.

▲ TAKE A STEP

Every detail of the tabernacle—from its shape and size to its color and materials—was rich with symbolism about God. And it was the creative skills of the artists and builders that turned the plan into a beautiful building where God would be worshiped.

Those artists used their God-given talents exactly as this verse commands:

Whatever you do, work at it with all your heart, as working for the Lord, not for men (Colossians 3:23).

By the way, what is your favorite color? Is it a color you would have seen in the finished tabernacle (Exodus 25:1-5)?

Aren't you glad it's not a black-and-white world?

Q

What can I learn from the colors all around me?

A

Creativity with color reflects the variety and beauty of God's creation.

What shape is your world in?

*H*ere's a fun family quiz. Have each person answer yes or no to these three questions:
   1. Did you ever (or do you now) own a security blanket or teddy bear?   YES NO
   2. Did you ever (or do you now) have a favorite chair that you like to sit in while watching television? YES NO
   3. Did you ever (or do you now) own a pair of pants or shoes that are worn out and should be discarded, but you keep them because they "feel so good"? YES NO

◆ TAKE A LOOK / 1 Kings 6:14-15, 18-30
   Though we sometimes take pleasure, comfort, and security for granted, familiar shapes and textures (like those of security blankets, teddy bears, favorite chairs, and comfortable shoes) play an important part in our lives.
   To remind yourself of this, try your creativity with a "Texture Treasure Hunt." Give each family member a sheet of paper and a pencil or crayon. Set a timer for four minutes, and see how many different designs you can make on your paper in that length of time by laying it over a rough texture (such as a screen door, stucco wall, linoleum floor, face of a push-button telephone) and rubbing on the paper with your crayon or pencil.
   About 400 years after Moses and his craftsmen built the tabernacle, a second beautiful place of worship was erected—this one appropriately called Solomon's Temple. As you read 1 Kings 6:14-15, 18-30, count the number of things that were carved into shapes and textures.

Q

What can I learn from shapes and textures?

A

Creativity with shapes and textures helps me think about God's works and deeds.

▲ TAKE A STEP
   Visit a museum and you will quickly find that most of the objects preserved from the past are the creative expressions of men and women who lived long ago—their music, architecture, paintings, sculpture, and literature. King David, a great artist in his own right, expressed one purpose of creativity this way:
   I will meditate on all your works and consider all your mighty deeds (Psalm 77:12)
   One way to meditate on God's works is with the help of artists who show God's creation from a fresh perspective. Why not make plans now to attend a play, visit a museum, picnic at an outdoor performance of a symphony orchestra, visit a local artist, or browse in an arts festival this weekend. Have fun!

You don't have to be a poet or a politician to use lots of words. All you have to be is a teenager with a telephone!

Think of words as keys that unlock your mind and heart, allowing your thoughts and feelings to reach out to the minds of others. Helen Keller, who could neither see nor hear for almost her entire life, said that without words it is impossible to think. Because words are so powerful, they need to be used carefully.

Do you remember the popular game called "Password"? It's a good way to build your vocabulary and improve the way you use words. One person writes down a word, then tries to get his or her partner to say that word in response to one-word clues. With four people, divide up into two teams, show the Password to one person from each team, and alternate back and forth in giving clues until one team guesses the Password.

◆ **TAKE A LOOK**
Genesis 2:19-20; Matthew 12:33-37

When God created Adam, one of the first jobs He gave him involved words. Do you remember it?

God told Adam to name all the animals— every living creature on earth! Livestock, birds, and beasts—they all received their names from Adam's creative mind (Genesis 2:19-20).

When God gave Adam the ability to form thoughts and feelings into words (both spoken and written), He was giving the human race and every individual in it a powerful tool for good—and evil. Read what Jesus had to say about the words you speak in Matthew 12:33-37.

▲ **TAKE A STEP**

The way you use words is important. You can encourage someone who is sad . . . or discourage someone who is happy; build up a person's self-esteem . . . or tear it down; honor God's name . . . or use it profanely. It all depends on the words you choose. But the right word used in the right way?

A word aptly spoken is like apples of gold in settings of silver (Proverbs 25:11).

In other words, a well-chosen word is like a valuable and beautiful piece of jewelry. As you close your time together, identify a word or phrase that has been heard around your house recently but has no place being there; also choose another word or phrase that needs to become a part of your family's daily vocabulary (such as "I'm sorry . . . thank you . . . I love you").

Words unlock the world around me

Q

Why is it important to be creative with words?

A

Creativity with words can encourage and strengthen others.

Music hath power to soothe the six year old

Q

Why is it important to be creative with music?

A

Creativity with music brings praise to my Creator God.

PARENT: Sample your family's taste for different kinds of music by visiting your public library and checking out an album of symphonies, waltzes, polkas, or concertos.

Warm up for fun with music today by saying the "Musical Alphabet." Each family member in turn tries to think of a musical instrument that begins with the next letter of the alphabet: (A)ccordion, (B)anjo, (C)oronet, etc. (X is easy, but watch out. Don't get the Q or Z!)

Now play a couple of songs from a tape your whole family enjoys. (Or if you're a daring family, choose songs you can sing a cappella.) Sitting behind one another in a circle on the floor, "play" the song on the back of the person in front of you. Move your fingers, palms, fists, and wrists to convey the rhythm, volume, tone, and meaning of the music. Be sure to switch on the second song so each person can be both an "instrument" and a "musician." (It's a great way to get a back rub!)

◆ TAKE A LOOK / Psalm 145:3-7, 10-13

Music is everywhere. In shopping malls and waiting rooms, restaurants and sports arenas, churches and schools, and even when your telephone call is put on hold, chances are good you'll hear a tune!

Music enriches our lives every day. One of the greatest musicians who ever lived was the shepherd-turned-king, David. You'll find his name on many of the 150 songs in the Book of Psalms. Though we read these songs today, they were originally written to be sung. Turn to Psalm 145:3-7, 10-13 and read a few verses by this musical genius who loved God with all his heart. Perhaps you'd like to try composing a tune to fit the words of one of these verses.

▲ TAKE A STEP

Because we are made in God's image, we have the ability to be creative in many different ways. But whether we create as an artist, architect, musician, or sculptor, the goal is the same:

So that all men may know of [God's] mighty acts and the glorious splendor of [His] kingdom (Psalm 145:12)

In Psalm 145, David answers the question, "Why is it important for me to use the creative talents God has given me?" Ten different words show what happens when you allow your creativity to grow. Use each of the ten to complete this sentence: "When I use my creative talents, I exalt (praise, extol, commend, tell of . . .) my great Creator God."

COURAGE

*T*he history of the world is marked by moments of courage.
• 500 years ago a monk named Martin Luther bravely faced the church of his day with a list of 95 thoughtful questions. His courage led to the beginning of the Protestant Reformation.
• 200 years ago American patriots wrote the Declaration of Independence, knowing it would mean a life-or-death struggle with the mighty empire of Great Britain.
• 100 years ago President Lincoln faced the prospect of civil war as he courageously signed the proclamation which freed countless slaves.
COURAGE. What comes to mind when *you* hear that word?

◆ THINKING ABOUT COURAGE

Often we think of courage as heroic *deeds*. But first and foremost it is the attitude of heroic *people*: the bystander who jumps into the icy river to save a child . . . the girl who, though unable to move from the neck down, lives a full life while confined to a wheelchair . . . the boy who overcomes a speech impediment to become president of his class.

Courage is something even ordinary people in ordinary places can have! And that's encouraging, because the Bible tells us . . .

● KEY VERSE ON COURAGE

Be on your guard; stand firm in the faith; be men of courage; be strong (1 Corinthians 16:13).

▲ TAKE A STEP

This week we want to learn about courage—**the ability to confidently face our inward fears and outward enemies.**

Take turns sharing your story of "The Most Courageous Person I Know." Then read Psalm 18:1-3. David wrote those words when he was fleeing for his life because King Saul was trying to kill him. Make a list of the words David uses to describe God. How does knowing that your heavenly Father is the kind of God David describes help *you* to have courage?

◀ DENTIST

"Quit reciting the 23rd Psalm."

Hold my hand and we're halfway there

Five-year-old Bradley had just passed his beginner's swimming test, and with all the confidence in the world he dived into the water from the low diving board. What wonderful fun! "Can I jump off the high dive now?" he asked his instructor.

"All right, Bradley, but be careful."

Eagerly he climbed up the ladder of the high dive, walked out to the end of the board, and stood. And stood. And stood. From below he heard the calm voice of his swimming instructor: "Bradley, you can do it. It's not as far as it looks. If you decide to jump, I'll be right here to help you. You'll be fine."

Encouraged by the teacher he had learned to trust, Bradley gathered his courage and JUMPED!

What does courage involve?

◆ **TAKE A LOOK / Joshua 1:1-9**

Unlike Bradley, you might not need courage to jump off a diving board—especially if you've done it many times before. Instead, you may need courage to give that speech in history class, to speak up for someone who is being treated unfairly, to share your faith in Christ. Courage involves facing the things that frighten you.

When Joshua became the leader of the Israelites after the death of Moses, he was given a scary assignment: lead the Israelites to conquer the land which God had promised them. The enemy was well armed. The land was vast and uncharted. If ever a general needed courage, Joshua was the one! Read the words which God used to encourage the new leader of His people in Joshua 1:1-9.

Courage involves facing my problems, confident that God will be with me.

▲ **TAKE A STEP**

Just as Bradley drew courage from hearing the voice of his swimming instructor, so Joshua's courage came from hearing and believing the promises of his trustworthy God:

Do not be terrified; do not be discouraged, for the LORD your God will be with you wherever you go (Joshua 1:9).

Can you think of anything you have to do today that might make you afraid or discouraged? Remember, you're not alone! God has promised to be with you wherever you go. And that means in all the events of ordinary days as well as when something unusual upsets you. Hold hands in a circle as you pray for one another and the challenges you will face today at home, school, or work. Aren't you glad God will be right there with you!

Mr. Franklin wasn't the worst teacher in the world. Still, only a few of the kids seemed to learn much chemistry from him. He was always trying to keep order in the classroom, but a number of unruly students constantly made his life miserable.

As a senior, Hank needed this chemistry course to graduate. Day after day he grew angrier with his classmates who goofed off, slouched into class tardy, and distracted others by mocking the teacher behind his back. "But what can I do?" Hank wondered.

The next day, Hank went to the principal's office and explained the situation. When he finished, the principal replied: "Hank, thank you for coming to me. You did the right thing."

◆ TAKE A LOOK / Esther 4:6-16

The disrespectful students weren't just wasting time. They were robbing students like Hank of a chance to learn. By reporting this behavior, Hank risked facing the anger of his classmates.

Throughout history, people have often faced choices similar to Hank's: to go with the crowd and do nothing, or to take an unpopular and sometimes painful stand for the right. Esther, queen of Persia, knew if she entered the king's presence without first being called, she could face execution. But to remain silent meant the certain death of her countrymen. Should she remain silent and hope for the best, or approach the king and face the worst? Read the account of her courageous decision in Esther 4:6-16.

▲ TAKE A STEP

Esther was where she was in order to do what God wanted her to do. Mordecai's words gave Esther the courage she needed to enter the king's presence and begin a daring plan:

"Who knows but that you have come to royal position for such a time as this?" (Esther 4:14).

And her response showed that she was willing to take a stand for what was *right*, even if it turned out all *wrong*.

What do you suppose Hank was thinking as he wrestled with the decision about going to the principal's office? What price did he have to be willing to pay if he did the courageous thing? Close by discussing a tough choice you have faced. What decision did you make?

It's no accident that I'm in this predicament

Q

How can I have courage to stand for what's right?

A

Courage to stand for what's right comes from knowing God has put me where I am.

PARENT:
Help your child find the courage to overcome a fear he or she has been battling (such as fear of darkness, heights, public speaking, or being away from home).

Don't look now, but I think we're sur- rounded

J enny liked to live in the country. And the best thing about it was staying with Grandma until Mom and Dad got home from work. Grandma's house was so close, Jenny could see it from her front porch. It was fun walking the hillside path between home and Grandma's.

In the daylight Jenny never worried about stumbling over a log, getting scratched by a prickly bush, or stepping on a snake. But during the winter months—when it got dark early—Jenny thought about all those things.

Each evening Jenny would ask, "Grandma, will you walk home with me?" And each night Grandma would reply, "No, but I'll keep my door open and watch until you're safe inside." And Grandma always did!

◆ TAKE A LOOK / 2 Chronicles 32:1-8

Years later, when Jenny herself was a mother, she recalled how scared she had been to walk along that path after dark. She also remembered how comforting it had been just knowing that Grandmother was there watching.

King Hezekiah and the people of Judah had every reason to be afraid. They were threatened by the armies of Assyria—then the most powerful nation in the world. Surrounding countries had been captured or destroyed already. Now Jerusalem was facing an enormous army ready to attack.

Hezekiah knew his troops were no match for the Assyrians. How could the king instill courage in his countrymen in the face of such a threat? Read 2 Chronicles 32:1-8 to find out what Hezekiah did. Then read verses 20-22 to learn the outcome of "The Battle That Was Never Fought."

▲ TAKE A STEP

In times of danger, words of encouragement can give *ordinary* people *extraordinary* courage—if those words are about our extraordinary God.

Hezekiah's words reminded his people where their real strength lay—in the Lord of hosts (literally, "the Lord of armies"). Take a few minutes right now to have each family member make a copy of today's key verse. (Index cards are excellent for this purpose.) Put the card in your pocket, purse, lunchbox, or briefcase. Before another day has passed, you'll probably have plenty of opportunities to read the verse again and take it to heart.

With us is the LORD our God to help us and to fight our battles (2 Chronicles 32:8).

Q

How can I help others to have courage?

A

Courage comes when I remind others of God's strength.

One evening Mrs. Stevenson noticed Stanley blowing bubbles with a large wad of gum. "Stanley, we've told you before . . ." Then she paused and looked at him thoughtfully. "Where did you get the gum anyway? You didn't have any money when we went to the store this afternoon, and I know I didn't buy it for you."

"I guess I just picked it up and forgot to pay for it."

"Stanley, if you didn't pay for it, then you stole it."

"Aw, Mom, what's the big deal? It's a big store. They'll never miss one crummy pack of gum."

"That's not the point, Stanley. What you did was wrong. Get your jacket. We're going back to the store."

"But Mom, what can I do now? The gum's gone and I haven't got any money to pay the store back."

◆ TAKE A LOOK / Ezra 9:1-3; 10:1-6

God expects His people to take sin seriously—to confess wrong actions promptly and, as much as possible, make things right. And that kind of obedience takes a lot of courage!

Ezra was the leader of a group of Jews who were returning from Babylon to rebuild the city of Jerusalem. Both he and the people wanted to live by the law God had given them many years before, but some of the people had committed a sin which needed to be set right.

As you read about this difficult situation in Ezra 9:1-3 and 10:1-6, put yourself in Ezra's place. Why might you need extra courage to do what needed to be done to set things right once again?

▲ TAKE A STEP

The Jewish people had disobeyed God's specific command by marrying foreign wives—women who followed false gods and encouraged their husbands and children to do the same. Their leader Ezra knew that dealing with this problem would not be easy. But ignoring the problem would have been far worse.

So Ezra tackled the unpleasant task with the same attitude Paul expressed in one of his letters:

I eagerly expect and hope that I will in no way be ashamed, but will have sufficient courage so . . . Christ will be exalted in my body, whether by life or by death (Philippians 1:20).

Telling your parents when you've done something wrong isn't easy. But if Stanley had done that, how might his parents have helped him learn the same lesson in a less painful way?

The hardest three words to say: "I was wrong"

Q

Why does obeying God's Word take courage?

A

Courage is needed to confess a wrong and set things right.

PARENT: Don't forget to practice the principles of confession and restitution when your dog chews up the neighbor's doormat or the cashier gives you too much change. Your actions speak louder than your words.

JAMES

Have you ever seen a TV advertisement like this?
The camera zooms in on a sparkling piece of jewelry as the announcer says: "Nothing sets off the beauty of a woman like the brilliance of diamonds. And now, the beauty of sparkling 'diamels' can be yours at tremendous savings. Never again will the opportunity to own this exquisite jewelry come your way. Send check or money order for $19.95 to P.O. Box 1234, or call the number you see on the screen. Don't wait! Send for yours today."

Diamonds or glass . . . gold or brass . . . butter or margarine. How can you tell the genuine item from the cheap imitation?

◆ THINKING ABOUT JAMES

In each case, you need to find a "test for genuineness"—something that sets apart the *real* from the *imitation*. Genuine diamonds don't break; glass imitations do. Gold doesn't tarnish; brass does. Genuine articles pass the test; imitations don't. Not everyone who claims to be a Christian actually is one. But how do you tell the *real* Christians from the *pretend* ones? You can't just say, "Will the real Christian please stand up . . ." But you can apply the "James Test for Genuine Faith"!

● KEY VERSE FROM JAMES

As the body without the spirit is dead, so faith without deeds is dead" (James 2:26).

▲ TAKE A STEP

The evidence of living, breathing faith in God is good deeds. Have one family member lie on the floor and "play dead" while the others look for as many signs of life as they can find (pulse, breathing, flickering eyelids). Can you find at least 10 evidences of life in your pretend corpse? Can you find 10 or more signs of a living faith in your own life?

James 5:17-18 discusses the faith of Elijah. Review his story in 1 Kings 17-18. What actions demonstrated his faith?

"No wonder people in China are starving. This is their food!"

George Müller's desire was to prove that God is a "father to the fatherless" (Psalm 68:5). Müller's congregation laughed, his best friend discouraged him, but he was determined to help the orphans of Great Britain. He would do it by prayer, asking only God for the money!

During his lifetime, Mr. Müller built five orphanages and proved God's love to thousands of orphans. When Mr. Müller prayed about the children's needs, God answered in wonderful and often unexpected ways.

Once while Mr. Müller was praying for kitchen utensils, a knock came at the door and there stood a man with kitchen supplies. Another time when the children had no milk, a milk wagon broke down outside the orphanage. The milk was given to the children.

During his 93 years, Müller was determined to believe the promises and obey the commands of God.

◆ TAKE A LOOK / James 1:22-27

The orphans of George Müller's day were usually cared for in asylums with criminals and the insane. When Mr. Müller learned of this, he knew that being obedient to God's Word meant doing something about that situation.

One of the commands Mr. Müller may have read is found in the Scripture reading for today. As you read James 1:22-27, see if you can find the verse that may have led George Müller to his life's work.

▲ TAKE A STEP

God's faithfulness in answering George Müller's prayers has inspired many Christians to *pray* for the needs of others. But Mr. Müller's faithfulness in his determination to *provide* for orphans should be equally challenging. He knew that if a person's faith is real, he or she will obey God's command by helping the less fortunate.

Religion that God our Father accepts as pure and faultless is this:

to look after orphans and widows in their distress and to keep oneself from being polluted by the world (James 1:27).

"I don't want to get involved" is an expression you will often hear today—but not from the lips of those whose *deeds* for God match their *faith* in God. Are you willing to get involved? Plan today to invite a widow over to your house for a meal, plan an outing with a fatherless family, visit a children's home, or even look into becoming a foster family.

Not every Orphan Annie has a Daddy War-bucks

Q

Why help the widows and orphans?

A

The Book of James teaches me that a living faith means helping people who hurt.

Don't tell me about God's love, show me

Q

How should I treat the poor?

A

The Book of James teaches me to treat the rich and poor with love and compassion.

PARENT:
Does your child know the difference between an orphan and a foster child . . . a divorcee and a widow . . . a natural parent and a step-parent? Defining terms will open up avenues of discussion with your child.

A pawnbroker by day and a street preacher by night, William Booth walked the cobblestones of London in the mid-1800s. Urchins playing in the gutters shouted, "Hey, preacher—catch," and a rock struck his chest.

"What is wrong?" Mr. Booth wondered. Why didn't the poor people of London listen to the wonderful message he was preaching? Why did they have so little respect for God and His Word?

Finally, Mr. Booth found the answer. The people attending his meetings were too hungry, too cold, and too poor to pay attention to his message. In addition to hearing about God's love, they needed to see it in action.

And so William Booth organized what is today the Salvation Army—a major force in fighting poverty, hunger, and disease in Jesus' name. Because of Mr. Booth's willingness to match words with deeds, millions of people have heard the good news of Jesus in a way no mere sermon could ever communicate.

◆ TAKE A LOOK / James 2:1-12

If you've never been cold, hungry, or without a place to sleep, then you probably have noticed the Salvation Army only at Christmastime. In malls and shopping centers across the country, their brass bands, bell-ringers, and red kettles call you to remember the poor. But for some people the Salvation Army's shelters and soup kitchens are a lifeline. For the homeless and poor in some of the world's largest cities, men and women of the Salvation Army are among the few who care.

You may never need the help of the Salvation Army, but you do need to answer today's question: "How should I treat the poor?" The answer is as near as James 2:1-12!

▲ TAKE A STEP

It's easy to think that someone who is less *fortunate* is also less *important*. But that is definitely not what God thinks. James gives this strong warning:

If you show favoritism, you sin and are convicted by the law as lawbreakers (James 2:9).

William Booth showed the reality of his faith in God by reaching out to the poor. Rather than show favoritism to those who wore nice clothes, Mr. Booth went out of his way to be kind to those who were wearing shabby clothes. Can you think of one way to show that same kind of love to a poor person your family knows? Even an "army" of three or four persons can share a lot of love in Jesus' name!

L eTourneau College in Texas. The Christian village of Tournata in Liberia, West Africa. The Christian colony of Tournavista in Peru. The LeTourneau Foundation that sponsors Christian and educational programs. These all exist because one man, R. G. LeTourneau, knew the money he made selling construction equipment didn't really belong to him. It belonged to God.

A millionaire many times over, Mr. LeTourneau saw money as a way to reach people with the gospel. He didn't hoard it or use it selfishly. "What counts," he said, "is not how much money you give to God, but how much of God's money you keep for yourself!"

◆ **TAKE A LOOK / James 5:1-6**
There is a right way to *make* money and a right way to *spend* money. Mr. LeTourneau believed that all of his money belonged to God. His job was simply to manage it wisely in order to make more of it available for spreading the good news about Jesus.

Though the quarters in your piggy bank may not compare with the millions of R. G. LeTourneau, you are faced with the same questions: "How much will I keep for myself? How much will I give to my church? How much will I use to help others?" James 5:1-6 describes people who neglect the poor and spend all their money on themselves. As you read, decide who you'd rather be like—Mr. LeTourneau or the "Unhappy Hoarders" of James 5.

▲ **TAKE A STEP**
Luxury: an extravagant excess; having more than you need
Indulgence: giving in to your own desires
It's important to remember that James isn't saying it is sinful to be rich. Nor is he saying that you should never buy something you want. He *is* saying it's sinful to spend your money *only* for luxuries and indulgences. God has a special blessing for those who could buy *luxuries,* but who instead give their money to meet the *necessities* of others.

A generous man will himself be blessed, for he shares his food with the poor (Proverbs 22:9).

Now's the time to plan what you *could* do, *should* do, and *will* do with the money God entrusts to you. Agree on a project you can do, such as sending support to a missionary, helping in a shelter for the homeless, or even teaching someone to read.

You can't take it with you, so send it on ahead

Q
Why should I share what I have with others?

A
The Book of James teaches me that selfishness is sin.

Suffering can make you bitter or better

Q

Why can I face suffering with a happy heart?

A

The Book of James teaches me that suffering joyfully strengthens my life.

She had heard that these villagers didn't like Christians, but she would visit anyway. After all, it was only a short journey from her home in Dohnavur (DOE-nah-ver). As she walked down the narrow jungle path, she suddenly felt herself falling, down, down into a pit—a pit dug "where no pit should be."

At the time of her fall at age 63, Amy Carmichael had already worked 35 years in India, rescuing children who were used for immoral purposes in the pagan temples. After her fall, she became an invalid who lived in almost constant pain until her death 20 years later. But suffering didn't stop Amy Carmichael's service for the Lord. Nor did it halt her love for the people of India.

◆ **TAKE A LOOK** / James 1:2-12

That perilous pit in India was designed with Christians in mind, and a missionary became its victim. But looking back over her life, was Amy Carmichael really a *victim* or a *victor*?

Far from being bitter or withdrawn after her "accident," Amy Carmichael used her time in bed to write 15 more books (in addition to the 21 she had written before the accident)—books that have encouraged and strengthened thousands of Christians around the world.

What appeared to be a tragedy turned out to be a triumph! Her story is a living illustration of James 1:2-12. Read those verses right now and see if you don't agree!

▲ **TAKE A STEP**

Amy Carmichael's life was remarkable for two things: the love she showed to the people of India and the suffering she endured. The pain that could have caused her to grow bitter instead deepened her faith in God. James describes that process this way:

Consider it pure joy, my brothers, whenever you face trials of many kinds, because you know that the testing of your faith develops perseverance (James 1:2).

What is your first response when painful circumstances come your way? Do they become for you a path to *bitterness* or a path to *better-ness*? Let these words of Amy Carmichael help you decide how to face your trials today:

Hold us in quiet through the age-long minute
While You are silent and the wind is shrill:
Can the boat sink while You, dear Lord, are in it?
Can the heart faint that waiteth on Your will?

SIN

B arry glanced at the clock. If he wanted that money, he needed to get to the pawn shop before it closed.

Barry had found his dad's ring in the garage—the one his dad misplaced weeks ago and had given up for lost. Surely there was no way for Dad to know Barry had found—and sold—the ring. And Barry's car needed tires so badly. Maybe this was God's way of supplying the $200 he needed.

But Barry couldn't get a verse of Scripture out of his mind: "Thou shalt not steal." The battle raged as the minutes slipped by. At last, Barry made up his mind. Slipping the ring into his pocket, he picked up his car keys and headed for the pawn shop.

◆ THINKING ABOUT SIN

When God created Adam and Eve, they were perfect. They lived in a perfect world and enjoyed a perfect relationship with their Creator. God gave them one law, one rule—"Don't eat of the tree of the knowledge of good and evil." He told them what would happen if they did: "When you eat of it, you will surely die."

But Adam and Eve did break God's law. They chose their own way and **disobeyed God.** In a similar way, Barry chose to disobey God's law concerning stealing. Whenever human beings fall short of meeting the standards God has set, the disobedience is called **sin.**

● KEY VERSE ON SIN

For all have sinned and fall short of the glory of God (Romans 3:23).

▲ TAKE A STEP

Since the day sin entered the world, everyone descended from Adam has been born sinful, including you.

In Psalm 51:1-13 David shows the problems and guilt sin causes. After you read this passage, share with the other members of your family a time when you—like Barry—battled with a decision to do right or wrong.

"He has your social security number. That's how God knows when you commit a sin."

How do you get a "10" in the game of life?

I don't understand how they score gymnastic events," Lydia confided to her friend Ginger as they watched a preview of the Summer Olympics on TV. "Everybody looks so super! I can't tell who's better unless somebody falls off one of those bars. How do the judges know who's best?"

"Well, it's not like a race where the fastest person wins," Ginger replied. "Gymnastics is measured by how well each move is made—how the feet and hands move, how the body arches, how difficult the moves are, how the landings are done. Because you don't know what to look for, you might not see any mistakes, but the judges know what's perfect—it's all written down—and they watch to see how close each athlete comes to that standard."

Q

What is sin?

A

Sin is missing the mark of God's perfect holiness.

◆ **TAKE A LOOK / Romans 5:18-20**

All gymnasts know the standard for a perfect performance. Though thousands never come near it, every gymnast always aims for that target.

Life is not an event in Olympic gymnastics, but in some ways the two are similar. Our God is holy and perfect. He cannot allow sin in His presence. And just as most gymnasts fall far short of reaching that Olympic standard, *all* human beings fall short of reaching the standard God has set for us. No one—except Jesus Christ—has lived a life without sin (Romans 3:23).

See if you can find four words or phrases that mean the same as *sin* as you read Romans 3:23; Romans 5:18-20; 1 John 3:4.

▲ **TAKE A STEP**

God hates sin because sin is . . .
- falling short of His glory, or missing the mark
- trespassing, or taking over God's rights in your life
- disobedience, or breaking God's commandments
- lawlessness, or not keeping God's law

Colossians 1:21 describes sin and its effects this way:

You were alienated [separated] from God and were enemies in your minds because of your evil behavior (Colossians 1:21).

If a judge had been grading your life over the past 24 hours, and 10 was the perfect score for sinlessness, what score would you get? This week you'll learn about God's remedy for all who fall short of His perfect standard.

"**D**ad, did you ever have Black History Week when you were in school?" Kip asked.

"No, Kip, we never did. Why do you ask?"

"I was thinking about that film we saw last Wednesday night at church—you know, the one on abortion—and it reminded me of something I learned during 'Black History Week.' Back before the Civil War in a case called the Dred Scott decision, the Supreme Court said that black people could be 'owned' just like property. It was wrong, Dad—really unfair—and the courts finally overturned it, but not before a lot of people were hurt."

"What made you think of that, Kip?" his father asked.

"Well, the Supreme Court said that abortion was okay, too, so now it's legal. But isn't that just like the Dred Scott decision? I mean, passing a law that says something is right doesn't make it right . . . does it?"

◆ TAKE A LOOK / Psalm 78:5-8

Kip had grown up believing that all laws were fair and good. Most are, and we should be thankful for them and carefully obey them. But when he studied the Dred Scott decision of 1856 and the *Roe vs. Wade* case of 1973, Kip realized that a thing can be *legal* in the eyes of the courts but still be *sinful* in the eyes of God.

The entire Old Testament shows how God blessed His people when they obeyed Him, and judged them when they sinned. Asaph condenses Israel's history into a single song: Psalm 78. Sometime today you might like to read all 72 verses. But for now, read verses 5-8, 10, 17-18, 37, 56-59.

▲ TAKE A STEP

How can you know if an activity (such as abortion, or lying, or taking drugs, or disobeying your parents) is sinful? Should you go by what others say about it? By who is doing it? By how you feel about it? Or by what God says about it?

God's Word, the Bible, provides the unchanging standard of right and wrong. That's why knowing God's Word will keep you from sin.

I have hidden your word in my heart that I might not sin against you (Psalm 119:11).

"Right is right, even if everyone is against it, and wrong is wrong, even if everyone is for it." In your own words, tell the person sitting next to you why you agree or disagree.

Making it legal doesn't always make it right

Q

Who decides what is sinful?

A

Sin is defined by our unchanging God in His unchanging Word.

PARENT:
Your child needs to know the behavior God calls "sinful." With a dictionary handy, read together Galatians 5:19-21 and be sure your child understands each word.

There's nothing as slippery as a secret sin

Everyone on the swim team had a new gym bag—everyone, that is, except Lacey. She hadn't saved enough money to buy one.

Then one day Lacey found a nearly new gym bag on the locker room floor—with nothing in it and no one's name on it. "I could write my name on this one and no one would even know," she thought. And so she did. But the very next day, Amy Wells—whose locker was next to Lacey's—opened her locker door and exclaimed, "Hey, my bag's missing! I was sure I left it here last night. Lacey, have you seen it?"

Lacey continued to dress slowly as she answered, "Not me. Maybe the custodian picked it up."

But that night in bed, Lacey was miserable. She'd stolen something that wasn't hers and then lied to cover it up. She never intended things to turn out this way, but what could she do now?

◆ **TAKE A LOOK / 2 Samuel 11:5-17**

Lacey discovered that she couldn't enjoy the bag she had taken because she was too busy trying to hide the fact that she had stolen it.

Beginning with Adam and Eve, people have tried to hide their sins—from God, from others, and even from themselves. King David learned firsthand how slippery a "secret" sin can be. Once, when he should have been on the battlefield, David stayed in Jerusalem. While walking on the balcony of his palace, he saw a beautiful woman who was someone else's wife. One slippery sin led to another—lust, adultery, lying, murder. Read about David's attempted cover-up in 2 Samuel 11:5-17.

▲ **TAKE A STEP**

Whether you're a king like David or an ordinary person like Lacey, you cannot commit a truly secret sin. Even if no one else on earth sees what you have done, God sees—and knows. There is nowhere you can go to hide from Him. The best thing to do is what King David did: Confess your sin and turn away from it.

Against you, you only, have I sinned and done what is evil in your sight (Psalm 51:4).

Lacey discovered the hard way how one sin can lead to another. She also needs to learn how repentance can lead to asking forgiveness and making restitution to the one offended. If you were Lacey, how would you go about undoing the damage done to Amy?

Q

What should I do when I have sinned?

A

Sin should be confessed and given up, never covered up.

*H*e paid a debt He did not owe,
  I owed a debt I could not pay—
I needed Someone to take my sins away.
And now I sing a brand new song.
Amazing Grace all day long,
  Christ Jesus paid the debt
That I could never pay.

Those words mean a lot to Marty now. For seven summers he had come to camp, waiting impatiently for morning Bible study to be over so the sports, crafts, and games could begin. But this year, for the first time, Marty is beginning to understand the true meaning of these verses: "All have sinned . . . the wages of sin is death . . . God made [Jesus] who had no sin to be sin for us."

Now it is the last evening of camp. As he sits by the bonfire, Marty reviews in his mind all that he has learned about sin. And he's thankful that Jesus paid the price for sin by His death on the cross.

◆ TAKE A LOOK / Romans 5:12-19

Marty is learning that sin is the transgression (breaking) of God's law (1 John 3:4). The wages (penalty) of sin is under that death penalty. God is a just, fair God. More than any earthly judge, He must uphold His unchanging laws. He cannot set His own rules aside and say sin doesn't matter. The death penalty must be paid—in blood.

Without the shedding of blood there is no forgiveness (Hebrews 9:22).

Justification is one of the words the Bible uses to tell us what God did about our sin problem. A judge uses this word to say that as far as the law is concerned, all the penalties have been paid and you have a clean slate. Notice what the Apostle Paul has to say about that important truth in Romans 5:12-19.

▲ TAKE A STEP

As we've seen this week, sin is serious business. If you were standing before the Judge of the universe right now, and He were to ask you, "Have you paid your sin debt?" what would you tell Him? If you've agreed with God about your sin, realized that you cannot pay your own debt, and accepted what Jesus did when He died on the cross, you can say with assurance, "Yes, Jesus paid it all for me!"

The debt that I owed, my Savior paid

Q

What did God do about sin?

A

God sent Jesus to pay the penalty for sin.

PARENT: Sin at its root is separation from God and other people. Discuss with your child how sin causes separation in human relationships and how confession helps to heal those broken bonds.

MEDITATION

*W*endy *paused between bites of her apple. "Mom, we did something kinda strange in school today."*

"What was it. Wendy?" Mrs. Wells asked curiously.

"Well, it sounds silly, but first Miss Carter had us all sit in a circle," Wendy *explained as she sat down on the kitchen floor. "Then she showed us a special way to cross our arms and legs, close our eyes, and say a funny, humming sound over and over. She said we were meditating, but she didn't tell us what was supposed to happen. Some of the kids giggled, but I felt kinda funny. I thought maybe it was a new way to pray."*

◆◆ THINKING ABOUT MEDITATION

When Mrs. Wells heard about the lesson in meditation, she was concerned—and with good reason. She recognized that Wendy's teacher had shown the third-grade class a yoga position and taught them to repeat a "mantra," a chant designed to empty a person's mind and put him in touch with the universe. TM (transcendental meditation) is at the heart of many Eastern religions. But it is a dangerous practice, and definitely *not* what the Bible is talking about when it commands us to **focus our minds and hearts on God and His law day and night.**

● KEY VERSE ON MEDITATION

May the words of my mouth and the meditation of my heart be pleasing in your sight, O LORD, my Rock and my Redeemer (Psalm 19:14).

"Couple of times a day, mom likes us to have a few minutes of prayer and meditation, not to mention peace and quiet."

▲ TAKE A STEP

Look up the word *ruminate* in your family dictionary and read the definition. That word will provide a key in understanding the kind of meditation God wants us to practice every day.

Now read Psalm 119:97-104 and count the many benefits the psalmist received from meditation. How many of these benefits would you like in your own life? They can be yours—when you take time each day to "chew" on God's Word.

L isa was barely off the bus before she excitedly began sharing the events of the last two weeks.

"Oh, Mom, I had a wonderful time at camp. It was good to see everybody again after a year—and I made so many new friends!"

But on the way home she became more serious.

"Mom, do you remember a girl I met last year named Alicia? Well, I was looking forward to seeing her again, but she wasn't there. A couple of girls from her church told me that Alicia has anorexia nervosa. One girl said Alicia starved herself for so long, now she can't digest her food anymore. Mom, do you think that can really happen?"

◆ **TAKE A LOOK / Joshua 1:1-9**

Until some unwelcome flu bug or virus upsets your tummy, you probably don't think much about your amazing digestive system. Working night and day with no vacation, it absorbs the nutrients from the food you eat and puts them in the blood stream for distribution to every cell in your body.

As Alicia and her family learned, the digestive process is vital for life. If it shuts down, the body will slowly starve. God's Word is the believer's spiritual food, necessary for spiritual health and vitality. Like physical food, it must be taken in, digested, and absorbed. Meditation is one part of that "spiritual digestion" process.

After Moses died, God appointed a new commander-in-chief to lead the people—General Joshua. God told Joshua exactly how to be successful in his demanding new job. As you read Joshua 1:1-9, notice *when* Joshua was to meditate and *why*.

▲ **TAKE A STEP**

Do not let this Book of the Law depart from your mouth; meditate on it day and night, so that you may be careful to do everything written in it. Then you will be prosperous and successful (Joshua 1:8).

You might not be a general, but if you're a child of God, you have the same duty as Joshua: to know and do God's Word. Part of that process involves meditation.

Tonight before you go to bed, open your Bible to Exodus 20 (the Ten Commandments) and leave it by your bedside. When you awake in the morning, spend the first two minutes focusing on one verse from God's Law. It will make your day!

Eating is more than a good idea

Q

Why should I meditate?

A

Meditation is not just a good idea but is a command from God.

It's never too late to meditate . . . or too early

A t 4 A.M., the baby awoke—loudly. To keep him from waking the older children, his mother rocked him gently. As she did, she sang some of her favorite hymns and gospel songs that reminded her of God's great love.

Not far away in a quiet hospital ward, an elderly lady was reliving the day's events. She had so hoped the operation would be successful. Sight was precious and she longed to read again. But the doctor's verdict was clear: permanent blindness. Now as she lay alone in the darkness, she thanked God for all the wonderful things she had seen in her 84 years. Then she praised Him for giving her spiritual eyes that could always see Jesus. And the last thought on her mind before she fell asleep was a verse she had learned long ago: "We walk by faith, not by sight."

Q

When should I meditate?

◆ TAKE A LOOK / Psalm 77:1-15

Meditation has been called "the time when our spirit is on tiptoe, and our heart is listening for the voice of God." The young mother and the elderly lady each had a heart in tune with God. One was meditating through song, the other through Scripture. But both had the same object in view: their ever-faithful, never-sleeping God.

Psalm 77 was written by Asaph during one of his sleepless nights! Though you may not find the verb *meditate* in the Bible version you are using, as you read the first 15 verses of Asaph's song, watch for similar words in verses 3, 6, 11, and 12.

A

Meditation can take place anytime, because God never sleeps.

▲ TAKE A STEP

Muse. Remember. Consider. Did you find those words as you read Psalm 77? They are verbs that require an object—something you "muse" about.

The writer of this psalm was in such deep trouble that for a moment he thought God no longer loved him. But then he remembered something he had temporarily forgotten.

I will remember the deeds of the LORD; yes,
I will remember your miracles of long ago
(Psalm 77:11).

Spend the next few minutes playing the "I Remember When" game. Take turns completing the sentence, "I remember when God did something special for our family by _____."
Think back to occasions when He protected you . . . provided for you in a special way . . . brought a baby into your family . . . restored health to a sick family member . . . gave you something you really wanted but couldn't afford.

PARENT: *Prayer is a vital part of meditation. Encourage your child to enjoy regular times of solitude in prayer and praise to God.*

When he woke up, Jason's mind was filled with happiness. For months he had prepared for this day. In only a few short hours, surrounded by family and friends, Jason and his fiancée, Cindy, would be married.

Jason lay there for a moment thinking about Cindy. She might not win a Miss America pageant, but in his eyes she glowed with a special inner beauty. Her love for God was contagious. Her smile, her laugh, the way she put her whole self into every project she tackled—no doubt about it, she was the woman for him!

Nobody was ever bored when Cindy was around. Like Mary Poppins, she could find ways to fill ordinary days with wonderful surprises. Jason grinned. That's what she is, he thought to himself. "She's SUPERCALI-FRAGILISTICEXPIALIDOCIOUS!"

◆ **TAKE A LOOK / Psalm 119:27**
Jason's day was special because his mind was filled with thoughts about a special person. In a similar way, meditation is focusing your mind and heart on God in all His beauty and grandeur.

In the New Testament, the Apostle Paul reminds us:
Whatever is true . . . noble . . . right . . . pure . . . lovely . . . admirable—if anything is excellent or praiseworthy—think about such things (Philippians 4:8).

But how do you do that? The Psalms will tell you. Look up each reference and write what you discover about meditation in the space provided.

According to . . .	God tells me to meditate on
Psalm 48:9	_____
Psalm 119:27	_____
Psalm 119:48	_____
Psalm 119:148	_____
Psalm 143:5	_____

▲ **TAKE A STEP**
Jason found that by focusing on Cindy's wonderful qualities throughout the day, he could enjoy her presence even when they were apart.

You can do the same with your Father in heaven as you pick one of the "meditation projects" from the list above and close your family time by doing just what the verse says to do—meditate on something special about your wonderful God. Try it!

Thinking of you makes each day special

Q
What should I meditate upon?

A
Meditation is focusing upon God's beauty and grandeur.

Pray it, think it, hear it, sing it!

Q
How can I meditate?

A
Meditation involves praying, listening, thinking, and singing about God.

PARENT: For further help in the discipline of meditation, we recommend MEDITATION by Thomas McCormick and Sharon Fish (Inter-Varsity Press, 1983).

Now when Wendy's third-grade class did their yoga-meditations, Wendy sat reading quietly. She knew she was doing the right thing, but she still felt left out.

"Mom," she asked again one afternoon, "Grandpa's a Christian and I've heard him talk about meditation. How does he do it?"

"Why don't you ask him?" her mother replied. And Wendy did!

"Wendy," Grandpa began as he lifted his granddaughter onto his lap, "meditating upon God is not something you learn so much by studying. It's something you learn by doing—like learning to play a musical instrument. When I was a boy, I practiced the violin so I could be a better musician. But I don't meditate so I can be a better meditator. I meditate because I love God and want to know Him better."

Then Grandpa paused. "Why don't I just pretend you're not here and I'll meditate like I do every morning—only I'll talk out loud. Then you'll see what I mean when I say meditation is part praying, part listening, part thinking, and part singing."

◆ **TAKE A LOOK AND A STEP / Jeremiah 17:5-8**

Grandpa took his Bible from the table, closed his eyes, and sat very still. Wendy pretended she was "asleep" too. Then, without opening his eyes, Grandpa said, "Good morning, Father. This is a beautiful day that You've made, and I want to do things Your way today. I want to be an obedient child. I know that Your ways are always the best. So Lord, today lead me each step of the way."

Then Grandpa opened his Bible to Jeremiah 17:5-8 and read it out loud. (Have someone in your family do that right now.) "Hmmm," he said, "let's meditate on what it means to be trees planted by water. You help me out here, Wendy." (Let your family members take Wendy's place as you answer one question at a time.)

"First, have you ever seen a tree by a stream? What was it like? How did Jeremiah describe this tree? Why do you think he said a man who trusts the Lord is like a tree?

"Now, how are you like a tree? Where are you planted? What do you need in order to grow tall and strong spiritually?"

After Grandpa and Wendy finished answering these questions, Grandpa closed his eyes and sang a verse of "The Old Rugged Cross." Wendy joined in enthusiastically, for she had discovered that meditation is a way to worship God.

HUMILITY

*M*indy, is it true? Have you and Greg really broken up?" Cheri grabbed her friend by the arm and demanded an answer.
Mindy nodded and tears welled up in her eyes.

"But I don't understand," Cheri continued. "Greg's a super guy. He's great looking, he'll be starting quarterback this fall, and he's an honor student. Mindy, every girl in the school would love to date him and you broke up with him. Are you nuts or something?"

"You don't understand, Cheri. Greg is nice in a lot of ways, but he's so good at everything he does that he's beginning to expect people to praise him all the time. I broke up because he's so stuck on himself, there's no room in his life for anybody else."

◆ THINKING ABOUT HUMILITY

The football player who scores the winning points and dances around the goalposts to draw attention to himself . . . the student who asks you what you made on your report card so you'll ask him in return . . . the employee who flaunts a raise or promotion.

No doubt about it, proud people stand out in a crowd! But harder to spot are those people who are truly humble—people who don't *demand* praise for their achievements and **won't take credit that should be shared with others.**

● KEY VERSE ON HUMILITY

Clothe yourselves with humility toward one another, because, "God opposes the proud but gives grace to the humble" (1 Peter 5:5).

▲ TAKE A STEP

You can probably name 10 people who, like Greg, are stuck on themselves. But who comes to mind when you think of someone humble—someone quick to give credit where credit is due?

To see a portrait of a truly humble man, read Philippians 2:5-9. What important quality should others be able to see in our lives?

"That should discourage my imitators."

It's hard to be humble when you're perfect

*I*t seemed to Mrs. Maxwell that her daughter's sassy speech was getting worse. She disciplined Michelle again and again, but nothing seemed to stop her daughter's disrespectful mouth.

One evening Michelle opened the refrigerator to pour ice water for herself and two friends. From the den, Mrs. Maxwell asked Michelle to pour her a glass as well, only to hear this sassy reply: "What makes you think I want to pour you a glass of water?"

Quietly Mrs. Maxwell replied, "All right then, don't."

So Michelle didn't. But as she stood there with her friends, her mother came in, took the jug of ice water from the refrigerator, unscrewed the cap, raised the jug, and poured the water all over her daughter's head. Then she set the jug on the counter and said very calmly, "When you've finished mopping the floor, please bring me a glass of water. And don't ever speak to me like that again." And Michelle never did.

Q

Why is humility the opposite of pride?

◆ **TAKE A LOOK / 2 Chronicles 26:3-5, 8, 16-21**

Michelle's proud desire to answer to no one's authority but her own led to disrespect toward her mother. Her *pride* left no room for *humility*—and led to a chilly consequence.

Michelle's pride problem is shared by kings and common people alike. It can be seen both in the young and in the old. Many stories are recorded in the Bible about proud people and their downfall. Read about Uzziah, one of Judah's kings, in 2 Chronicles 26:3-5, 8, 16-21. What did *his* pride lead to?

A

Humility means I submit to the authority God has placed over me.

▲ **TAKE A STEP**

Whether it's a king who tries to do the work of a priest or a teen who is disrespectful, pride in all its forms is rebellion against God. Humility, on the other hand, recognizes that God works through the authorities He places over us.

"God opposes the proud but gives grace to the humble." Submit yourselves, then, to God. Resist the devil, and he will flee from you (James 4:6-7).

Cold water dumped on your head or leprosy attacking your skin are two ways to discover you have a "pride problem." But why learn a lesson in pride the hard way? James 4:7 contains two commands: *Submit* to God, and *resist* the devil. If Michelle had taken that verse to heart, how might she have learned her lesson the easy way?

*T*onight the graduating seniors are being honored for outstanding achievement and service to their school. In addition to scholarships, three trophies will be awarded—one to the student with the highest grade point average, one to the best all-around student, and the third to a student chosen by the faculty for his or her contribution to school and community.

It was always exciting to see who won the first two trophies, although almost everyone knew in advance who would receive them. However, the third trophy was different. As the winner walked forward to receive the trophy, fellow students found themselves remembering all sorts of quiet ways that person had made an impact for good at the school.

◆ **TAKE A LOOK / Numbers 12:1-14**
Everyone has a hero—someone we admire for his or her achievements. But there are unsung heroes as well—people who are seldom in the public eye.

Moses learned both roles firsthand. Born a slave in the land of Egypt, he was adopted by the royal family of Pharaoh, given the best education, and at age 40 was in line for the throne—and national attention.

But God had other plans. Instead of becoming a king, Moses became a shepherd in an obscure desert. Forty years in the deserts of Midian taught Moses hard lessons in humility before he was ready to be the leader and deliverer of God's people.

But not everyone was happy with Moses' rise to leadership. Aaron and Miriam, Moses' brother and sister, became jealous and began to talk behind his back. Read about it in Numbers 12:1-14.

▲ **TAKE A STEP**
The key verses for Day One and Day Two each contain the same phrase. God opposes the proud and rewards the humble. You've already seen where pride can lead (remember Uzziah, Aaron, and Miriam?). But why is humility a better path?

[God] guides the humble in what is right and teaches them his way (Psalm 25:9).

You won't always get a trophy for being humble, but you can always expect a blessing—for yourself and those you serve. Select two family members to play the parts of Miriam and Aaron. Instead of jealously gossiping, how *should* they have talked about their brother Moses?

They don't give trophies for humility

Why is humility better than pride?

A

Humility leads to God's blessing.

PARENT:
Pride comes naturally; humility takes practice. Look for everyday situations that illustrate our interdependence on one another and our dependence upon God. Share your insight with your child.

Winners don't always come in first

*T*he preliminary judging was over and only five contestants remained. Very soon now "Miss Taylor County" would be crowned.

Lindy was sure she would win. "Mom," she exclaimed as she dressed for the final competition, "something's wrong with those judges if I don't win. A few of the girls are pretty talented, but I'm sure I'm the best overall. I'm the only true blond, and this dress we found is perfect. I just know I'll win. I have to win!"

In the next dressing room, Amanda was beaming from ear to ear as she hugged her mother. "Well, Mom, this is it. No matter what happens, it's sure been fun. All the girls look so pretty in their formals, and I've never seen so much talent! I'm sure whoever wins will be a great representative at the state contest."

Q

How do I demonstrate humility toward others?

A

Humility involves putting others ahead of myself.

◆ TAKE A LOOK / Luke 14:7-14

If you were judging that particular beauty contest on the basis of *attitude* rather than *appearance*, who would get your vote?

The difference between Lindy and Amanda is the difference between pride and humility. Lindy's pride caused her to overrate her abilities. Amanda's humility enabled her to make a fair assessment of herself and the other girls.

Jesus had some important things to say about humility. In Luke 14:7-14 He warns about the danger of pushing and shoving to sit in the "seat of honor" at a banquet. Take turns reading one verse at a time from that important passage.

▲ TAKE A STEP

Lindy's pride could easily have caused her great embarrassment in front of her family and the other contestants. Amanda's humility left room for her to be honored without becoming proud. The girls illustrate the truth of what Jesus told the Pharisees:

"Everyone who exalts himself will be humbled, and he who humbles himself will be exalted" (Luke 14:11).

Think of the times when you like to be first—in the cafeteria line, the checkout at the grocery store, the shower each morning, the front seat of the car, the parking space nearest the door at work. How can you demonstrate a Christlike (and Amanda-like) attitude of humility in each of these places?

E ver since Mrs. Brown had gone back to work, the laundry had gotten totally out of hand. Dirty clothes overflowed the hamper and spilled onto the floor. Clean clothes piled up waiting to be pressed. Every Saturday morning Mrs. Brown battled her way through load after load of laundry, wondering how four people could use so many T-shirts and towels, skirts, blouses, jeans, and socks.

But now, with Mr. Brown's complete approval, a new lighten-the-load-for-mom plan was underway. Both teenagers were presented with their own laundry basket, operating instructions for the washer and dryer, and a quick course on sorting clothes.

Fifteen-year-old Nathan was having no part of it. "Nobody else's mom makes her kid do this," he said angrily. "I'd rather wear dirty clothes all the time than do her work."

◆ TAKE A LOOK / John 13:1-7, 12-16

Nathan enjoyed wearing clean clothes, eating nice meals, and living in a neatly kept home. But he had a lot to learn about gratitude, service, and humility. Like the 12 proud men who were Jesus' disciples (and who argued about who was the greatest of the 12), Nathan needed this reminder:

"If anyone wants to be first, he must be the very last, and the servant of all" (Mark 9:35).

Before His death, Jesus set the example of how to put the needs of others before your own. Read the account of His "humility in action" in John 13:1-7, 12-16.

▲ TAKE A STEP

During Jesus' time, washing the dusty feet of visitors was the job of a slave, not the master of the house. By His action Jesus showed that love in action is serving others. And right *actions* flow best from right *attitudes*.

In our opening story, Nathan didn't want to serve his mother by helping with the laundry. Laundry's not the only "heavy load" around the average home. Other dirty jobs include taking out the garbage, cleaning the bathroom, changing diapers, washing dishes, cleaning the oven.

Become a "humble servant" this weekend by cheerfully "doing the dirty work" on behalf of another family member. Pick a chore that needs doing and tell Mom or Dad how you plan to lighten the load by helping out. You'll be glad you did!

Real teenagers don't do laundry . . . or do they?

Q

How do I develop the attitude of humility?

A

Humility is a servant's heart in action.

PARENT: Discuss with your child how he can rejoice over personal achievements (such as sports or academics) and still be humble. Encourage him or her to praise the achievements of classmates.

MONEY

S *everal months earlier Larry had overheard his parents give up their plans for an anniversary trip in January.*

"But anniversaries are supposed to be special," thought Larry. "I know, I'll save my money and buy them something nice."

And now that dream was about to come true. Even the long line at the checkout counter couldn't dampen Larry's excitement about the clock radio he had chosen for his parents.

"That'll be $41.75," announced the clerk impatiently. Larry smiled, reached into his bulging pockets . . . and $45 in quarters, dimes, and nickels poured onto the counter. Three months' savings!

But the clerk wasn't at all pleased. "You can't pay with that," he muttered. "It would hold up the line for me to count it now. Come back when you have paper money. Next, please."

◆ THINKING ABOUT MONEY

Larry was learning the hard way that money matters. It matters to you, to others, to God, to everyone.

Money can be defined as **anything of value that people agree to exchange with one another for goods and services.** Sheep and cattle, gold and silver, pearls and diamonds, printed paper and shiny coins—someone somewhere in the world calls these "money." You might have a lot of money, or only a little. God has said a great deal about money in the Bible, but the most important thing about it is how you *use* what you have.

"We learned a great Bible verse in Sunday school today! Lay not up for yourselves treasures on earth."

● **KEY VERSE ON MONEY**
Honor the LORD with your wealth [money] (Proverbs 3:9).

▲ **TAKE A STEP**
Pull out all the coins and dollar bills in your pockets, wallets, and purses right now. Just for fun, see if your family would have had enough to buy the clock radio Larry had his heart set on!

Then read Proverbs 10:4-5; 14:23; and 22:4 to find three ways to increase your riches.

"Oh, Mom," Angie sighed as she felt the fabric of a beautiful new winter coat, "this is just what I've been wanting. And if we get it now, I'll be able to wear it next year. And look, it's marked down to half price."

"I agree, Angie. It looks like a good buy. And I'm glad you're learning to be aware of the cost and quality of things. But we can't afford it right now. These two sweaters will have to do."

"Mom, if you don't have enough money, why don't you just write a check?" Angie asked innocently.

"Because, honey, that's not how things work. I don't have enough money in the checking account, and writing a bad check is illegal. That would only make things worse! If you truly need that coat, then don't you think God can supply the money we need to buy it at the right time?"

"I guess so. But I wish He'd hurry before someone buys it!"

◆ TAKE A LOOK / 1 Timothy 6:6-10

Some people can afford to buy anything they want; others have trouble paying for the necessities of life. Most of us are somewhere in-between— able to buy the necessities, but not as many of the extras as we would like.

Of those three types of people, which do you think the Bible says is "rich"? The answer will surprise you, for all three groups may stumble into the pitfalls of the rich.

As we learned, the key is not the amount of money you have, but rather the *attitude* you have toward your money, regardless of the amount.

"A man's life does not consist in the abundance of his possessions" (Luke 12:15).

One of the best places to learn the right attitude toward money is in the passage you will read today—1 Timothy 6:6-10.

▲ TAKE A STEP

A truly rich person is not the one who makes the most money, but rather the one who uses the money God provides in ways that please Him.

Angie confused a *need* with a *want*. She thought she needed that particular coat. But there was an easy way to tell that it *wasn't a need* right then. How could she tell? Philippians 4:19 will help!

Close your family time by discussing the next purchase you plan to make. Use what you've learned to decide if it's a need or a want.

There is something money can't buy— poverty!

How much money is enough?

I have enough money when my needs, not my wants, are met.

Common sense about dollars and cents

"Well, Mom, I'm ready to buy the pig," Alan stated matter-of-factly as he bit into an apple.

"You're ready to do WHAT?" his mother responded in disbelief.

"I'm ready to buy the pig. You remember—you told me last summer I could have a miniature pig if I'd work real hard and pay for it myself. Well, I cut lawns all summer and threw newspapers all fall, and now I've saved up enough money."

"But Alan, pets like that are expensive . . . and you don't know anything about raising a pig."

"It's okay, Mom. I've found a pet shop that has some for sale. They're already a year old so the owner will sell them cheap. The pig can sleep in Shep's old doghouse. Mom, I'm so excited. Can we get it Saturday?"

Q

What is a good way to get money?

A

Money can be earned by honest, hard work.

PARENT:
How are allowances handled in your family? Now might be a good time to discuss why you do (or do not) give them, and what you expect in return.

◆ **TAKE A LOOK / 2 Thessalonians 3:6-15**

Alan planned, worked, and saved to buy the pet he wanted. In a similar way, earning the money to buy the things we need and want is a concern in most families.

There are only about four things you can do with money: You can earn it, spend it, save it, and give it away. Most of us like the spending part. But the Bible gives wise advice about handling money in all four ways.

The Old Testament Book of Proverbs has a wealth of counsel about earning money by hard work (10:4), planning your work (21:5), and avoiding laziness (20:4). The New Testament also has much to say about the role of work in our lives.

Read 2 Thessalonians 3:6-15 to see if you can discover the verse that links the work we do with the things we need. How does God often supply our daily needs?

▲ **TAKE A STEP**

"If a man will not work, he shall not eat" (2 Thessalonians 3:10).

People need a chance to earn, by their own hard work, things they want or need. This is God's most common way of supplying our basic needs.

Alan set a goal and then worked hard to reach it. Perhaps now is a good time for your family to set a financial goal and come up with a list of jobs (excluding ordinary chores) which the children can do to help reach that goal. (One word of caution: Parents, be sure to heed the counsel of 1 Timothy 5:18!)

*S*tanding with her mother in the grocery store check-out line, Gretchen noticed a familiar face nearby.

"Mom," she whispered, "see that man over there? That's Mr. Franklin—the man our Sunday school class took food to last Thanksgiving."

Glancing to her right, Mrs. Page watched as the elderly man pulled a few wrinkled bills from the pocket of his thin trousers. She noticed he had no coat suitable for the cold, rainy January day. As she wondered about offering him a ride, her thought was interrupted by another urgent tug at her sleeve.

"Mom," Gretchen whispered in a puzzled tone, "why would Mr. Franklin be buying dog food? I know he doesn't have a dog!"

◆ TAKE A LOOK
1 Timothy 6:17-19; Proverbs 28:27

Perhaps you've never seen someone as poor as Mr. Franklin buy dog food to eat in order to save a few dollars. Maybe you've never had a classmate who had trouble concentrating because she didn't get a nutritious breakfast. You've probably only heard about about people so poor that they rummage through garbage cans to find food. But people really do live like that. Some of them may be as near as your city or your neighborhood.

If you work hard to earn money, you'll want to spend part of that money on the things you need and want—and rightly so. But don't spend so much on yourself that you overlook another way to spend it—a way you'll discover by reading 1 Timothy 6:17-19 and Proverbs 28:27.

▲ TAKE A STEP

Rather than use your money *selfishly*, you can honor the Lord with your wealth by using it *selflessly*. Just open your eyes, your heart, and your pocketbook to others around you who are in need.

He who is kind to the poor lends to the LORD,
and he will reward him for what he has done
(Proverbs 19:17)

Discuss how your family can honor the Lord by giving to the poor. A special gift to a mission fund or favorite charity, a basket of food delivered to a needy family, an unexpected gift for an underprivileged child—these are just some of the ways you can use your money in a selfless way. As a family decide what kind of gift you will give and to whom. Set a date to complete the project.

To enrich your life, give some-thing away

Q

What is the right way to spend money?

A

I spend money wisely when I spend to meet my needs and the needs of others.

Store your treasure in the world's safest place

Q

What is the best way to save for the future?

A

Treasure on earth is temporary; treasure in heaven is eternal.

PARENT: *You can protect the financial investments you've made for your family by making a will and keeping it up to date. It's your responsibility.*

"**D**ad, I wish you and Mom could have seen the house where I baby-sat tonight," Gail exclaimed. "It was like a palace! The stuff they own must have cost a fortune."

"What kinds of things, Gail?"

"Oh, the furniture for one thing. A grand piano. Antiques. Oriental rugs. Mrs. Davidson told me that just one of those rugs was worth as much as a small house. Maybe she was kidding, but I don't think so. And they've got display cases . . . and paintings like a museum . . . and stained-glass windows. I guess the Davidsons are just about the richest people in town."

◆ TAKE A LOOK / Matthew 6:19-24

The Davidsons are indeed very wealthy people. But in the light of eternity, there is a much safer place to keep your money than in houses, furniture, paintings, and fine rugs.

Savings accounts, stocks, art collections, jewelry, wall safes, real estate—none of these is a permanently secure place to put your money. But if you are truly interested in saving for the future, there is one foolproof place you should consider. Read about it in Matthew 6:19-24.

▲ TAKE A STEP

"Store up for yourselves treasures in heaven, where moth and rust do not destroy, and where thieves do not break in and steal" (Matthew 6:20).

The Davidsons are rich by *earthly* standards. But given a little time, the moths, rust, and thieves could easily destroy all their earthly treasures.

By contrast, Jesus urges you to store up treasure in *heaven*. Why? Because when life is over, all you'll have is what you have invested in that couldn't be . . .

. . . eaten by termites or moths (unlike houses and clothes)

. . . destroyed by rust (unlike cars or bicycles)

. . . stolen by thieves (unlike TVs or toys)

When you get right down to it, the only investments that will pay eternal dividends are those involving people. By concentrating on people rather than possessions, your family can be richer than the Davidsons in treasure that truly counts—treasure that will last eternally.

Think about how you spend your money, how you use your time, and how you relate to other people. Are you laying up treasures in heaven?

READING

*T*he others turned in amazement, for the voice (which had told the story) was Sam's.

" 'Don't stop!' said Merry.

" 'That's all I know,' stammered Sam, blushing. 'I learned it from Mr. Bilbo when I was a lad. He used to tell me tales like that, knowing how I was always one for hearing about Elves. It was Mr. Bilbo who taught me my letters. He was mighty book-learned, was dear old Mr. Bilbo. And he wrote poetry. He wrote what I have just said. . . . There was a lot more,' said Sam, 'all about Mordor. I didn't learn that part, it gave me the shivers. I never thought I should be going that way myself.'

" 'Going to Mordor!' cried Pippin. 'I hope it won't come to that!' "

From The Fellowship of the Ring by J.R.R. Tolkien. Copyright © 1965 by J.R.R. Tolkien. Reprinted by permission of the Houghton Mifflin Company.

◆ THINKING ABOUT READING

For Sam Gamgee, stories and poems about elves were gates to wonder and trails to adventures he never expected to experience.

Reading is **entering into the experience and knowledge of another through the printed page.** God Himself chose to write a Book telling us how to live life as He intended it. Only by reading the Book God wrote can we begin to understand His thoughts, His plans, and how He wants us to live.

▲ KEY VERSE ON READING

Whatever is true . . .
noble . . . right . . . pure
. . . lovely . . . admirable
. . . think about such
things (Philippians 4:8).

● TAKE A STEP

This week, choose a good book to read aloud as a family. Also, see if you can name a book, short story, or poem you've read that fits each of the categories in Philippians 4:8. For instance, *The Hiding Place* by Corrie Ten Boom— True; *A Christmas Carol* by Charles Dickens—Right; and so on. Choose one of your selections to read as a family.

"This is a pretty good book. It could probably even be made into a three or four part mini-series."

To get ahead, get a book and read it!

Gary, who was saving money for his first car, needed a summer job. As he scanned the ads, one job caught his attention: "Immediate openings for warehouse trainees. Must be dependable and able to follow directions."

"That's me," he thought. "Dependable!"

Soon he was at the parts store filling out a job application. "Name, address, phone . . . nothing to it," he mumbled to himself. "Educational background, character references . . . " He chewed on his pencil. "Why would they want to know all this stuff?"

"All right, Gary," said the store manager, "let's see how well you can follow directions. Here's a list of parts we've just received. Look them up in this catalog and write the inventory control number next to each item."

"No problem, sir," said Gary confidently. And sure enough, in a matter of minutes the job was done.

"Good work, son," the manager said. "The job's yours."

◆ **TAKE A LOOK / Amos 8:11-13**

Think what life would be like if you couldn't read. From traffic signs and textbooks to newspapers and magazines—everything in print would be a "closed book" to you.

Time and again in the Old Testament, God's people forgot about the importance of *reading* the Law of the Lord. And every time they neglected the Word of God, they sinned against God. Eventually they were taken out of their homeland and were scattered abroad—all because they didn't *read* and *heed* God's Law. Read in Amos 8:11-13 about a most unusual famine—not a famine of food or water, but a famine of God's Word.

▲ **TAKE A STEP**

Gary's ability to read not only helped him find a job opening, but it was also one of the main reasons he got the job. By contrast, the Israelites' failure to read cost them their country. Why? Because the people of Israel

rejected [God's] decrees and the covenant he had made with their fathers and the warnings he had given them (2 Kings 17:15).

Try an all-family trip to the library some evening this week. See if you can find (1) a book about space, (2) a biography of a famous inventor, and (3) a picture book of animals. Share with each other occasions that have been easier or more enjoyable because you know how to read.

Q

Why is reading important?

A

Reading is important because it is a skill I will use for a lifetime.

O h boy! Just what I wanted!" Rick exclaimed as he tore the wrapping from a model of the space shuttle.

Shaking the contents out onto the floor, Rick sifted through the pile of fins and rods, plates and panels. Fitting a piece here and gluing a part there, he was soon absorbed in the challenge of his new project.

When his mother called him for dinner, Rick gulped down his food, anxious to get back to his model. But when he returned, Rick noticed something peculiar. The fin sticking out on the side wasn't like the picture on the box. And why did the rear section have a big hole in it? Digging through the wrapping paper on the floor, Rick found the instructions—in a hundred little pieces!

◆ TAKE A LOOK / Psalm 119:9-16

Rick wasn't too pleased with his finished plane. The model—put together without the aid of directions—looked messy and incomplete. But just imagine if a real airline mechanic treated his plane that way. Leaving something as tiny as an "O-ring" out of a jet engine could cause engine failure and a terrible loss of life.

If you've ever wondered, "How can I keep my life from becoming a disaster?" you'll be glad to know the Psalmist David asked that same question. He knew that a happy spiritual life is only possible when you follow the directions God has given in His Word. How do you keep your life from becoming as messed up as Rick's model? You'll find David's answer to that most important question in Psalm 119:9-16.

▲ TAKE A STEP

Question: How can a young person remain pure?
Answer: By living according to God's Word (Psalm 119:9).
Question: How can I keep my life pure?
Answer: By not neglecting God's Word (Psalm 119:16).

Through reading, you can prepare to, live in the physical world around you. And through reading God's Word you can discover the best way to live in the spiritual world around you as well.

End your family time today by sharing something you've recently learned from reading a book. Then share one thing you've learned from the Bible about the spiritual world in which you live.

Q

How can reading help me learn?

A

Reading teaches me about the physical and spiritual worlds around me.

PARENT: Good books that your child might enjoy are listed in Honey For a Child's Heart by Gladys Hunt (Zondervan Publishing House), available at most Christian bookstores.

Please walk a mile in my shoes

Q

How can reading help me in my every-day life?

A

Reading helps me understand God, myself, and others.

I feel just like Heidi," Laura thought to herself as she started down the mountain trail. Like the little girl in the book Heidi, Laura had a grandfather with a cabin in the mountains.

Every other summer that Laura had come to the cabin, both of her grandparents were there. But Grandma had died during the winter and now Grandfather was alone. Laura sensed his loneliness, and like Heidi, she wanted him to know laughter and happiness once again.

"Listen to this, Grandpa," Laura said later that night as she played a melody on her harmonica.

"Wait a minute," Grandpa replied as he reached up to the mantle and brought down a clay ocarina, an instrument shaped like a sweet potato. "See if you recognize this little tune."

"That's 'Eidelweiss'!" Laura exclaimed. "We can play it together. Oh, won't that be fun, Grandpa?"

◆ **TAKE A LOOK / Esther 6:1-10**

Laura was glad that she had read about Heidi's grandfather. What she had learned helped her understand and respond to her own grandfather's loneliness.

The Bible tells of an Old Testament king who couldn't sleep one night. But instead of picking up a book as Laura often did, he called for someone to read a book to him. You'll find this unusual account of "The King's Bedtime Story" in Esther 6:1-10.

▲ **TAKE A STEP**

As King Xerxes listened to his servants reading the "book of the chronicles," he discovered an overlooked act of bravery. This led to Mordecai being *honored*, Haman being *hanged*, and Haman's wicked plot being *uncovered*.

The Book of Esther shows God at work behind the scenes to protect His people. You, like Esther, have only one life to live. But by reading good books, you can enter into the lives of many other people—presidents and princesses, athletes and artists, missionaries and medical doctors. Of course, the one book you won't want to overlook is the Bible, where you can read about Jesus,

The Word [who] became flesh and made his dwelling among us (John 1:14).

Think about all the people you have met in books you've read. Have any helped you better understand your own or another person's feelings?

R usty wasn't too excited about the end of summer vacation and the start of second grade. To encourage him, his mother sat down with him to examine his new workbooks.

When they came to the arithmetic workbook, Rusty opened it and carefully read the title. Then he came to a long list of names: "Duncan, Capps, Dolciani; Quast, and Zweng."

His mother wasn't sure her young son knew the significance of those names (the authors and editors of the book), so she asked, "Rusty, who do you suppose those people are?"

After a few moments of thought, Rusty's face lit up. "I know! They're all people who make yo-yos and donuts. Right, Mom?"

◆ TAKE A LOOK / Revelation 20:11-15

In that list of unfamiliar names, the only one Rusty recognized was *Duncan*. He immediately associated that name with yo-yos and doughnuts of the same name. That often happens with names in books. Nearly everyone knows the characters in the classic children's story *The Tale of Peter Rabbit*. (In case you've forgotten, they're Flopsie, Mopsie, Cottontail, and Peter!) But do you remember the author? Or the publisher? Or the printer?

Revelation is the last book in the Bible. Some parts of Revelation are difficult to understand, but today you'll be reading a passage that talks about books—and everyone knows what those are! As you read Revelation 20:11-15, make a list of the different books it mentions. Watch for the book that, like Rusty's arithmetic book, contains a list of names.

▲ TAKE A STEP

Reading is one of the most important skills you will ever learn. But not all books are equally important. One very important book is the Book of Life, the book that contains the names of every person who is a part of God's family. Why is it such an important book? Because

"If anyone's name was not found written in the book of life, he was thrown into the lake of fire" (Revelation 20:15).

When you realize you are a sinner, believe in your heart that Jesus died for your sins, and repent (change your mind concerning your sins), your name is written in the Book of Life. Is your name written there?

Take a look in the Book (of Life)

Q

What is one book everyone should want his name in?

A

I want my name in the Book of Life.

PARENT:
To lead your child in a simple gospel presentation, follow the "Roman Road," reading in sequence Romans 3:23; 6:23; 5:8; 10:9-10, followed by the invitation of Revelation 3:20.

FAITHFULNESS

*S*oon after Joe and Lena were married, an auto accident left Lena with permanent brain damage. For the rest of her life she was like a little child, requiring constant care.

At first, Joe's friends urged him to put Lena in a home for disabled people, or even to divorce her. *"She really won't know the difference,"* some said. *"And besides, what kind of life would you have looking after her? She's not the girl you married."*

But Joe knew their advice was wrong. For 17 years he kept the marriage vows he had made to Lena: *" . . . for better or for worse, in sickness and in health, in joy and in sorrow . . . "*

Now, standing beside Lena's freshly dug grave, Joe knew he had done the right thing. He had been faithful *"till death do us part."*

◆ THINKING ABOUT FAITHFULNESS

We hear more today about *unfaithfulness* than faithfulness. Newspapers report broken treaties between nations, broken contracts between companies, broken vows between marriage partners. Life is littered with broken promises and great personal hurts.

But even though human beings break faith with one another, God remains faithful to us. He has given us His Word and His unconditional love. He continues to keep His promises, even when we—like Joe's wife—are no longer capable of keeping ours.

● KEY VERSE ON FAITHFULNESS

For the LORD is good and his love endures forever; his faithfulness continues through all generations (Psalm 100:5).

▲ TAKE A STEP

Faithfulness, or **steadily doing the good things you promised someone you would do,** is a rare quality in many people today.

Reread today's Key Verse, then see how many ways you can complete this sentence: "I know God is faithful because . . . "

"I don't know how they could tell they were going to live happily ever after, dear. I just know there was no prenuptial agreement."

*A*re we ever going to get a new car?" Sharon whined irritably as the family climbed into their 10-year-old station wagon. "Everybody in the neighborhood has a new car except us. It's just too embarrassing."

"Yeah," Buddy chimed in, "and the Mortons just put up a new fiberglass basketball goal."

"You both better do some thinking about thankfulness before you say another word," their mother said sternly.

Silently both children thought about their mother's warning. Dad worked hard to provide the things they really needed, and many of the extras too. And whenever Sharon or Buddy had a problem, they could count on Dad to be there—something that wasn't true of many of their friends' fathers.

Suddenly basketball goals and new cars didn't seem quite as important, compared to a father's faithfulness. As Sharon reached over the front seat to give her dad a hug, she told him so!

◆ TAKE A LOOK / Psalm 89

When they thought about it, Sharon and Buddy realized how they took their father's faithfulness for granted. His whole life—the work he did day after day, the things he bought, the money he saved each month—was for their benefit. And when he made a promise to them, he kept it. He wanted his family to be able to count on him.

God, too, wants His children to rely on Him because He is

The LORD . . . the compassionate and gracious God, slow to anger, abounding in love and faithfulness, maintaining love to thousands, and forgiving wickedness, rebellion and sin (Exodus 34:6-7).

Psalm 89 begins with a celebration of God's faithfulness, but when you reach the end of the psalm you see that things weren't going too well for the writer. Begin by reading the end of the psalm (verses 46 and 49). Then read the beginning (verses 1-5 and 8). Finally read the very last verse (52).

▲ TAKE A STEP

You can tell a lot about a person by the promises he makes (or breaks). In Exodus 34:6-7 you learned that God is "abounding in . . . faithfulness." Do you . . . always . . . usually . . . sometimes . . . seldom . . . never . . . keep your promises? Pick the word which best describes you; then see if other family members agree.

"I'm a man of my word— most of the time . . . "

What does it mean to be faithful?

Faithfulness means others can count on me to keep my word.

A "forever" promise lasts a long, long time

Q

How is God faithful?

A

God shows His faithfulness by always keeping His promises.

A stillness fell over the audience when the bride and groom turned to face each other. As the minister read line by line, the nervous young groom repeated his vows to his bride.

"I, Edward, take you, Rose, to be my wedded wife, to have and to hold from this day forward, for better or for worse, for richer or for poorer, in sickness and in health, in joy and in sorrow, to love and to cherish till death do us part. And I do promise and covenant before God and these witnesses to be your loving and faithful husband."

◆ **TAKE A LOOK / Hebrews 13:5**

Did you know that your life is affected by the vows or pledges that someone has made?

Perhaps you begin each school day with these words: "I pledge allegiance to the flag . . . " Or you vow your loyalty to the ideals of a club or organization. If your mom or dad has ever served on a jury, they were asked to take an oath of honesty. Doctors take the Hippocratic oath. Government officials are sworn into office with an oath to uphold the laws of the land.

Look up the following verses to see what God has vowed to do:

In this verse . . .	God made this promise!
Genesis 8:22	
Genesis 17:5, 8	
Isaiah 7:14	
John 3:36	
John 14:3	
John 15:7	
1 Thessalonians 4:15-17	
Hebrews 13:5	

▲ **TAKE A STEP**

Vows aren't hard to write . . . or even recite. Anyone can *make* a promise. A faithful person *keeps* a promise.

God is one such Person. When He says "I will," it's as good as done! That's why the psalmist could say with confidence,

He will cover you with his feathers, and under his wings you will find refuge; his faithfulness will be your shield and rampart (Psalm 91:4).

Rampart isn't a word you hear often these days (except in the "Star Spangled Banner"). Look up the definition in a dictionary. See if family members can think of three ways God has been a rampart in situations at school, work, or play.

S ix-year-old Rhonda didn't understand the divorce. Her mother tried to explain, and her father talked to her about her "new mother." But it was all still quite confusing. Rhonda's life suddenly changed, and there were many times when she felt very sad.

Time passed, and Rhonda saw her father less and less. She and her mother moved into an apartment. Her mom found a job, but even with the money her father sent each month there was barely enough to pay the bills.

A year later, there were more changes. The checks arrived later and later until they finally stopped altogether. Rhonda watched as her mother dried her tears, and then she asked, "Mommy, does this mean Daddy doesn't love us anymore?"

◆ TAKE A LOOK / Job 2:11-13

Faithfulness is *steadily doing what you promised someone you would do.* But sometimes, like Rhonda and her mother, you find that someone you counted on has been unfaithful to you. What should you do then?

Rhonda felt that she was unloved. Others going through a family crisis may feel angry, rebellious, bitter—or all three. But whatever you feel when someone lets you down, it helps to remember you have friends who care.

When Job lost most of his family, all of his possessions, and his health, he had plenty of reasons to question God's faithfulness. But at that critical moment Job was joined by three friends. As you read Job 2:11-13, notice how those friends eased Job's burden—without even saying a word!

▲ TAKE A STEP

When someone you trust lets you down, you may feel that God has let you down too. That's when a Christian friend can be a help, reminding you that God is always faithful. David, whose once-trusted allies turned against him, wrote this:

He sends from heaven and saves me, rebuking those who hotly pursue me; God sends his love and his faithfulness (Psalm 57:3).

If you are experiencing a difficulty or if you've been hurt by another's unfaithfulness, find someone to listen. Why not invite your Sunday school teacher or a close family friend from your church over for an evening. Friendship at its best means an arm to lean on in time of need.

He'll lift you up when others let you down

Q

What should I do when someone is unfaithful to me?

A

When someone is unfaithful to me, a listening friend may remind me of God's faithfulness.

Faithfulness is as faithfulness does

*A*s a senior, Mick was trying to explain to his father the first D he'd ever made—a D in sociology.

"You see, Dad," he said, "our semester grade depended on this one project that was supposed to make us understand responsibility. A guy and a girl had to draw names and pair off as partners. Then we had to spin a wheel to select an annual income as a 'married couple.' We had to set up a budget and keep a journal showing how we would live off it.

"But it got really dumb when the teacher gave each couple a hard-boiled egg that was supposed to represent a kid. The egg had to be carried by one of us for 24 hours a day for a week. We had to write how we solved all the problems with the 'kid.' Well, first of all, my partner was Valerie. We can't stand each other. Neither one of us wanted to baby-sit a hard-boiled egg. So we didn't keep a journal. That's why I made the D."

How can I be more faithful to God and others?

My faithfulness grows when I obey God's commands.

PARENT:
Do you have a plan for rewarding faithfulness in your child by giving added privileges? Does your child know about it?

◆ **TAKE A LOOK / Acts 9:10-19**

Mick made a D for just one reason—he didn't faithfully follow the teacher's instructions.

Ananias was an early believer in the New Testament church. And he, like Mick and Valerie, was given an unusual assignment. Though he lived in Damascus, Ananias had heard the terrible reports about a man named Saul who was persecuting the believers in Jerusalem. He knew Saul would soon come to Damascus to make life miserable for the Christians there too. When Jesus told Ananias to go to Saul and restore his sight, Ananias had a choice to make—a choice that involved faithfulness. Read about Ananias's "blind obedience" in Acts 9:10-19.

▲ **TAKE A STEP**

Compared to facing a hard-boiled persecutor of Christians, carrying a hard-boiled egg for a week would have seemed simple to Ananias!

But Ananias understood that obeying God was part of being faithful to God. Perhaps he recalled this verse from the Book of Proverbs:

My son, . . . keep my commands in your heart.
. . . Let love and faithfulness never leave you; bind them around your neck, write them on the tablet of your heart (Proverbs 3:1, 3).

Explain to the family a recent school project in which you *did* follow the teacher's instructions. What grade did you receive? What grade *might* you have gotten if you had done your project the way Mick and Valerie did theirs?

HEAVEN

S wing low, sweet chariot, coming for to carry me home,
Swing low, sweet chariot, coming for to carry me home.
I looked over Jordan and what did I see,
Coming for to carry me home?
A band of angels coming after me, / Coming for to carry me home.

◆ THINKING ABOUT HEAVEN

Have you ever wondered what heaven will be like?

The slaves who sang about angels "coming for to carry me home" thought about heaven a lot! They looked forward to going there—to lay their burdens "down by the riverside."

A group of American seventh graders who thought about heaven had these questions: "Will we wear clothes in heaven?" "Will my dog be there?" "Will there be computers and skateboards?"

Half a world away in a war-torn Middle Eastern country, young Muslim boys also think about heaven. Each boy wears a small metal or plastic key around his neck. As they hold hands and search for mine fields in the desert sand, they overcome their fear of dying with thoughts that the key will open the door to heaven.

● TAKE A STEP

Heaven is **the place God Himself has designed for His children to spend eternity.** It will be both beautiful and exciting, but the Bible makes it clear that a plastic key won't open the door of heaven.

▲ KEY VERSE ON HEAVEN

"In my Father's house are many rooms; . . . I am going there to prepare a place for you . . . I will come back and take you to be with me" (John 14:2-3).

Heaven is a *real* place. . . a *prepared* place . . . a *pleasant* place . . . *God's* place. Can you match each of those four facts with a phrase from John 14:2-3?

"Of course He's still up. They don't make you go to bed in heaven."

Heaven is the best place

"**W**hoopee!" Darrell yelled as he watched the big moving van drive slowly up the street. "They're here, Mom. They're here!"

Three months earlier, Darrell's father had announced that the family would be moving from Connecticut to California. Both of Darrell's parents had lived in California when they were children, and grandparents, aunts, uncles and cousins were still there. Darrell couldn't think of a more wonderful place to live.

But the move didn't happen right away. Mom and Darrell had to stay in Connecticut to finish the school year and sell the house. Dad went ahead to find a new house. "But I'll be back to get you," he promised, "and we'll drive across the country together. It'll be a great vacation and well worth the wait."

Now that long-awaited moment had arrived. "Boy," Darrell thought to himself, "this will be the trip of a lifetime. Maybe the waiting wasn't so bad after all."

Q
What is heaven?

◆ **TAKE A LOOK / John 14:1-3; Revelation 21:3-5**

Darrell knew that when his father got to California he would find the best place for the family to live. Dad would consider everybody's needs. He would remember that Darrell needed space for his fish tanks and that he wanted to be near a soccer field. Dad would think about his wife's love of horses and would look for a place near a stable. He would think about buying a house near a church that would help the entire family to grow spiritually. Darrell's father could be trusted to find the very best place for the family.

A
Heaven is the eternal home Jesus is preparing for me.

Did you know that Jesus is preparing a place for you right now? A house with many rooms—with one exactly right for you! And when He returns to earth, it will be "moving day." Reread Jesus' comforting promise in John 14:1-3. Then turn to Revelation 21:3-5 to discover one thing that will be in heaven, and four things that won't.

PARENT:
Every family will experience the loss of friends and loved ones. At those times, the comforting words of Revelation 21:4 can become especially precious, both to you and your children.

▲ **TAKE A STEP**

There will be no tears, mourning, death, or pain in heaven. And just as Darrell's family was looking forward to being together again, heaven will be wonderful because God Himself is there.

"Now the dwelling of God is with men, and he will live with them" (Revelation 21:3).

If you could build your dream home, what would it look like? Tell the other members of the family. Just imagine, heaven will be even more wonderful than that!

A gray caterpillar with brown spots crawls along a tree trunk in search of its next meal. A few hours later it begins to look for a sheltered place among the leaves. Soon the caterpillar is firmly attached to a branch of the tree, tightly enclosed in the brown cocoon which will be its home for the next several months.

In the spring the chrysalis slowly begins to shake. If you listen carefully, you might even hear a scratching noise inside! Eventually the tough cocoon splits open, and a damp, velvety creature emerges. For awhile it hangs upside-down, drying its wings. Then suddenly the wings open, catch the breeze, and a beautiful butterfly lifts gracefully into the air.

◆ TAKE A LOOK / 1 Corinthians 15:50-56

Almost everyone has seen a caterpillar and a butterfly. But few have watched the stages in between, the metamorphosis that transforms a drab caterpillar into a butterfly.

The body God has given you is suited to this earth. In it you can breathe, eat, run and play. In fact, you might think of your body as your "earth suit."

Just as the astronauts need a spacesuit in order to live and work in space, so you need a "heaven suit" to be properly prepared for heaven. The body you now have will grow old and finally die. But yesterday you learned there is no death in heaven. That means you—like the caterpillar—need a metamorphosis, a body fitted for heaven.

The Apostle Paul tells us about that new body in 1 Corinthians 15:50-56. It's a body you'll want to read about. And it's a body you'll want to own!

▲ TAKE A STEP

In your refrigerator you may find things labeled "perishable." That means they will spoil in time. But not your heavenly body! It will never wear out, grow old, or get bumps and bruises. It will be *imperishable* (indestructible) and *immortal* (eternal).

That metamorphosis is possible only if Jesus Christ is your Savior. You are a new person when He is in your life.

If anyone is in Christ, he is a new creation: the old has gone, the new has come! (2 Corinthians 5:17).

Give everyone a piece of paper and a pencil. Then draw a picture of both a caterpillar and a butterfly. Which creature would you rather be?

You can fly, but that cocoon's gotta go!

Q

What kind of body will I have in heaven?

A

In heaven my resurrected body won't wear out or grow old.

PARENT: *Jesus used many concepts to illustrate salvation: new birth (John 3), living water (John 4), lost and found items (Luke 15). Learn to share these with your child.*

But what if I don't like playing a harp?

Q

What will I
do in
heaven?

A

Heaven is
where I'll
see my
Lord face
to face and
will serve
Him
forever.

A t last Kate had made it to Disneyworld. All her life she had dreamed of this—the endless rides and fun and good things to eat. Now it seemed like a dream come true!

"I think I'm in heaven!" she exclaimed to her friend Peggy. "There's so much to see and do. Where shall we go first? Look, there's the Matterhorn. And oh, there's Pirates of the Caribbean. Judy said that was her favorite ride."

"But I want to start with the slower rides and work up," Peggy protested. "Let's try the Ferris wheel first."

Kate sighed. "Well, okay. But first let's get some cotton candy." They started toward the refreshment stand when Peggy suddenly pointed. "Look—Snow White and the Seven Dwarfs!" And off she went in another direction.

Kate thought to herself, "This trip will still be fun, but it's sure not heaven! At least there you can do what you please."

Was Kate right? Is heaven like a Disneyworld for Christians?

◆ TAKE A LOOK / Revelation 22:1-6

Some people think heaven is one long vacation; others think we'll have work to do there. Some think we'll listen to sermons all the time; others are afraid they'll have to learn to play the harp or sing all the time. And everyone hopes heaven won't be boring!

The Bible doesn't tell us much about what we'll be doing in heaven, but the few sneak previews it gives are exciting! God has planned a wonderful surprise for His entire family. He's kept most of the details secret, but here is just a hint:

The throne of God and of the Lamb will be in the city, and his servants will serve him. They will see his face (Revelation 22:3-4).

In fact, Revelation 22:1-6 tells us three things for certain that we will be doing in heaven. Can you find them? We will _____ God (verse 3); we will _____ God's face (verse 4); and we will _____ with the Lord forever and ever (verse 5).

▲ TAKE A STEP

Most of the things we do today, and especially at a place like Disneyworld, are centered around us. In heaven the focus of attention will always be on *Jesus Christ.* That's what makes heaven different. Every thought, action, and feeling is focused on serving Him. Heaven is a happy place!

Bryson had always been fascinated by the big family Bible at his grandparents' house.

On the day Bryson turned five, Grandpa showed him the place in the center of the Bible where his name was written—on the Brantley "family tree" as the son of Richard and Marjorie Brantley. "Born February 18, 1982, you were!" announced Grandpa. He went on to explain how he kept a record of all births, deaths, and marriages in that treasured family Bible.

"But I like to write something else there too," Grandpa explained. "When someone in the family receives Jesus as Savior, I know his or her name is written in the Lamb's Book of Life. I like to write that date in the family Bible too."

Bryson had never forgotten that conversation. And today he couldn't wait to see his grandfather.

"Grandpa, Grandpa, guess what!" he called as he ran into the house. "I accepted Jesus as my Savior. My name's in His book, and I want you to write it in your book too!"

◆ **TAKE A LOOK / Revelation 21:22-26**

For Bryson it was an exciting moment when Grandpa carefully lettered in the family Bible: "Bryson Brantley received Jesus as Savior and became a member of God's family, July 10, 1990."

In your city, county, state, and nation, there are government offices that keep track of vital records: births, deaths, marriages, school transcripts, military service records, social security benefits. But none is more important than the heavenly "Department of Vital Records" you'll read about today in Revelation 21:22-26.

▲ **TAKE A STEP**

God records in the Lamb's Book of Life the names of those born into His family. There you'll find the names of men and women, boys and girls in every century who have confidently trusted in Jesus Christ as their Savior. They are

"children born not of natural descent . . . but born of God" (John 1:13).

Your earthly birthday is on file in the county where you were born. But have you ever had a "second birth" that's recorded in the Lamb's Book of Life? Until you do, you're missing out on the best birthday ever!

When the roll is called in heaven, I'll be there

Who will be in heaven?

Heaven is for those whose names are in the Lamb's Book of Life.

PARENT:
A family Bible in a translation your family enjoys can become a real incentive to daily Bible reading and a treasured heirloom.

GOOD NEWS

*G*ood news comes in many shapes and sizes.
- For 16-year-old Carl: "Dad, Mom, I got it! I got my driver's license!"
- For 12-year-old Simon: "We won! We won! Hey, everybody, our team's going to the playoffs!"
- For 22-year-old Debbie: "Oh, Dad, Lyle's asked me to marry him! That's why he came to talk to you last night, isn't it?"
- For 6-year-old Gwen: "Grandma, the baby's here! I've got a little brother!"
- For hard-working Mr. Shaw: "Sweetheart, wear your best dress tonight. I got a promotion, and we're celebrating!"

◆ THINKING ABOUT GOOD NEWS

Good news is exclamation points and cheers, bells and brass bands. It's an exciting, **memorable event that brings you joy and makes a change in your life.**

Sometimes good news for one person is bad news for another. When a teen gets a driver's license, that's *good news*. When Dad gets the bill for the insurance, that's *bad news*. But one piece of news is Good News for everyone. It's the fact that Jesus has paid for sin and made it possible for us to live with God forever. It's the message that changes lives.

● KEY VERSE ON GOOD NEWS

I am not ashamed of the gospel [good news], because it is the power of God for the salvation of everyone who believes (Romans 1:16).

SUNDAY SCHOOL CLASSROOMS ←

"Today we studied Matthew, the first of a four-part series."

▲ TAKE A STEP

Your version of the Bible might use "good news" in place of the word *gospel*. But whichever word or phrase you find, it means the same thing—God's Good News has the power to change lives.

What is the best piece of good news you've received in the last week? After you share the exciting information with your family, read together the familiar words of John 3:16. Why do you think this Bible verse is often called the "Good News in a nutshell"?

Mr. and Mrs. Rodman sat tensely in the bright light of the hospital waiting room. Two hours ago they'd gotten a phone call: "Your son has been in an accident. He's been taken to County Hospital. Please come immediately."

"Multiple internal injuries," the doctor had told them. "We'll do all we can, but his condition is very serious." And so the Rodmans prayed . . . and waited.

At last, in the early morning hours, the surgeon came into the room. His hunched shoulders showed how tired he was, but a relieved smile told a happier story. "I've got good news," he announced. "Your son had a close call, and he'll have a long, slow recovery. But he's going to make it!"

◆ TAKE A LOOK / 1 Corinthians 15:1-6

Good news is what everybody hopes to hear in a life-and-death situation. And when the news comes at last, it is often accompanied by excitement, joy, and tears of relief.

Before becoming Christians, we too were in a life-and-death situation. We were separated from God by sin and deserved His judgment. Like the Rodman's son, our condition was hopeless. But then came the Good News: God provided life for us through Jesus Christ His Son, whose death on the cross paid for our sins.

This Good News is described in the first six verses of 1 Corinthians 15—news you won't want to miss—and news you'll want to share with others!

▲ TAKE A STEP

God's remedy for sin doesn't depend on new scientific discoveries or new theories about human behavior. God's Good News is always the same—

Christ died for our sins according to the Scriptures, . . . he was buried, . . . he was raised on the third day according to the Scriptures, and he appeared (1 Corinthians 15:3-5).

After the Rodmans spoke with the surgeon, they relaxed. They believed the good news about their son. In the same way, God wants you to hear, believe, and relax in the good news about His Son Jesus. Write the word G-O-S-P-E-L vertically on a sheet of paper. Then read John 3:16 from the King James Version. Write down the first word you encounter that starts with those successive letters: G-od . . . O-nly . . . S-on . . . etc. When you're finished, you'll have the Good News in a nutshell!

No news is bad news when you need good news

Q

What is God's Good News?

A

God's Good News is that Jesus died for our sins and rose again, according to the Scriptures.

Don't look now, but I'm some-body new

Q

What happens when I believe God's Good News?

A

God's Good News changes my life when I believe it.

No one enjoyed midsummer football practice. The heat and hard work were always bad enough. But even worse than the temperature and tired muscles was Mr. Devlin—the varsity coach.

Most of the players thought of him as an over-grown bully, and his foul language and mean temper seemed to prove it. Coach Devlin never had an encour-aging word for anyone. When the team nicknamed him "Coach Devil," they meant it.

But three days into summer practice, the players were talking among themselves—about Coach Devlin! "Hey, Lee, what's gotten into Coach Devlin?" Willis asked as the boys finished a hard practice. "He's going to lose his bad reputation if he's not careful. He's really acting different."

"Yeah, I noticed it too," Lee replied, shaking his head. "He's not cussing or screaming. And he's even telling the new guys how much they're improving. I wonder what's gotten into him?"

◆ **TAKE A LOOK** / Luke 19:1-10

People will try almost anything to change something they don't like about themselves. Diet, exercise, hair transplants, even plastic surgery can change your physical appearance. But changing your behavior and attitudes? That's much more difficult. It takes the power of God at work in you, the power Jesus came to earth to give you.

"The Son of Man came to seek and to save what was lost" (Luke 19:10).

Zacchaeus was a short man who was easily "lost in the crowd." But being short of stature wasn't his only problem. As a wealthy tax collector who had cheated many people, he was also short on friends and self-respect. Zacchaeus needed to change from the inside out, as you'll discover by reading Luke 19:1-10.

▲ **TAKE A STEP**

Zacchaeus had made his living by cheating; now, he wanted to repay the people he had cheated four times as much as he had taken from them! Not only did the Good News of Jesus change Zacchaeus; it overflowed into the lives of others as well.

When you receive Jesus as Savior, your life may not change as dramatically as Zacchaeus's did. But according to 2 Corinthians 5:17, it will change! Think of one thing that has changed since Jesus came into your heart. How has the change in you made a difference in your family?

J ust before the six o'clock newscast, the reporter relived the tragic story he would soon share with hundreds of viewers.

He had been at the scene all afternoon, watching the firefighters search through the ruined elementary school. At last count eight children were still missing.

"They were in the music room," one student had told him. "It's really hard to hear the alarm back there. Besides, kids pull those alarm switches all the time. It was probably too late by the time they realized this alarm was for real."

◆ **TAKE A LOOK / Romans 10:9-15**
Fire drills and false alarms happen more often than real fires. But when there is a fire, it's important to hear the alarm and to know the escape route. Fire marshals make frequent inspections to insure that alarms and fire extinguishers work, and that escape routes are clearly marked. Without such safety precautions, lives like those of the eight children in the school fire might be lost.

The danger of sin is not just a false alarm. People *will* perish unless they know the way to safety. Romans 10:9-15 is a reminder that many people still need to hear a clear word of warning, and that God wants *you* to "sound the alarm."

▲ **TAKE A STEP**
Scene One: Your family is driving through a quiet neighborhood when you see a house on fire. You know there are people asleep inside whose very lives are in danger. What would you do?

Scene Two: You wake up one night and smell smoke in your house. Somewhere there is a fire burning, and your family is in great peril. Now what would you do?

Scene Three: You meet a person who doesn't know about God's love or sin's danger or Jesus' death and resurrection. You have two minutes to tell that person anything you want to. What would you say? (Hint: Here is a verse you might want to use.)

Jesus answered, "I am the way and the truth and the life. No one comes to the Father except through me" (John 14:6).

In our opening story, eight children lost their lives because they didn't hear the alarm in time. Can you think of one person you can warn about the danger of sin before it's too late?

You can't beat the heat if you don't hear the beep

Q

Why should I share God's Good News?

A

God's Good News contains a warning everyone needs to hear.

When others ask, I'm ready to answer

Summer school was the last place Perry expected to get into a discussion about the Bible—but that was exactly what happened.

His teacher had told the class that the Bible was no different from mythology—just an interesting book of fables and fiction. Later, at lunch with his friend Cliff, the issue came up again.

"I've never read the Bible, but I think Mr. Jones is right," Cliff stated. "The Bible's no different from the writings of Confucius or Mohammed."

"But Confucius and Mohammed were ordinary men. The Bible is inspired by God," Perry countered. "Every word is true."

"Jesus was only a man like everyone else. Why should I base my life on a 2,000-year-old book?"

"Well," Perry replied, "I think you should examine all the historical facts before you make a decision."

Q

How can I share God's Good News?

A

To share God's Good News I must always be ready.

PARENT: A book to help your older child prepare for witnessing opportunities is How To Be Your Own Selfish Pig by Susan Schaeffer Macauley.

◆ **TAKE A LOOK / 1 Peter 3:13-16**

Before He ascended back to heaven, Jesus said: *"Go into all the world and preach the good news to all creation"* (Mark 16:15).

One of the disciples who received that command was Peter, the same Peter who denied Jesus three times. Peter knew firsthand that fear can keep a Christian from standing up for Jesus in a tense situation. But Peter learned from that experience, and later wrote the words you will read in 1 Peter 3:13-16. There you'll discover how to share the Good News of Jesus fearlessly with your classmates and neighbors.

▲ **TAKE A STEP**

When Perry signed up for Mythology 301, he didn't dream it would be an opportunity to share Christ with his classmates. But when the discussion about mythology turned into a discussion about Jesus, Perry was ready! Notice the steps that led to an effective witness.

Perry and Cliff were in a situation of *common interest;*

Cliff was *curious* about the person of Christ;

Perry was able to answer Cliff's *questions* without condemning Cliff's *views;* and

Perry knew enough about his Bible to tell Cliff the *claims of Christ* and why He is different from Confucius and Mohammed.

If you had been in Perry's place, would you have been ready to give a reason for the hope that you have?

PATIENCE

*H*ere are some humorous—and anonymous—quotations about patience. Which member of your family do you think of when you hear each of the following?

"Dear God, give me patience. And I want it right now!"

"The key to everything is patience. You get the chicken by hatching the egg, not by smashing it."

"Patience is something I admire in the driver behind me, but not in the driver ahead of me."

"Patience is what enabled the snail to reach Noah's ark."

"Patience is the ability to count down before blasting off."

◆ THINKING ABOUT PATIENCE

Cities build highways and subways to move people faster. Stores install laser equipment to speed the checkout process. Fast-food restaurants turn out burgers faster than you can say, "Give it to me quick!"

People who live in the "fast lane" don't like to wait. But patience is certainly a quality God wants His children to have. To build patience, God gives us many opportunities to respond to delays with a joyful spirit. He allows trying circumstances, difficult relationships, and even temptations to enter our lives so that we can develop patience. The key verse shows us that patience is **a quality the Holy Spirit produces in us.**

● KEY VERSE ON PATIENCE

But the fruit of the Spirit is love, joy, peace, patience, kindness, goodness, faithfulness, gentleness and self-control (Galatians 5:22-23).

▲ TAKE A STEP

When things don't happen on schedule, it's easy to become angry, upset, frustrated—even fearful.

On a scale of 1 to 10 (1 for low, 10 for high), who is the most patient person at your house? Find out! Have each person write down a number from 1 to 10 for every family member. Reward "Mr./Mrs./Miss Most Patient" with an extra dessert!

"I guess we can't expect her to have the patience of Job. This *is* a public school."

Shortcuts can lead to long delays

Q

Why should I be patient?

A

Patience is not just a good idea; it is a command from God.

Tina's father was taking her to a national park near their home. As they drove down the interstate highway, a car with huge tires and a loud muffler roared up close behind them. Tina's father maintained his speed, but the "tailgater" soon grew impatient. With a sharp jerk, he steered his car into the left lane, accelerated, and pulled past Tina and her father. Tina just stared.

"That man's not a very good driver, is he, Daddy?" Tina asked.

"No, he's not, Tina. Looks like he's headed for trouble."

Squinting into the late afternoon sun, they both watched as the car sped down the highway, weaving in and out among slower cars.

Suddenly, the speeding driver miscalculated and swerved out of control. Tina and her father both gasped at the same time.

"Wow! Did you see that, Daddy? He cut in too soon —that yellow car is really spinning. Look, it's skidding off onto the shoulder. Oh, Daddy, he's turning over . . . "

◆ **TAKE A LOOK / Romans 12:12**

Like many impatient people, the driver who caused that accident simply wanted to have a good time, to see how fast he could go, to count the cars he could leave behind. He was not considering the safety and comfort of others around him.

Being patient is not merely a nice idea. God's children are *commanded* to be patient. And every time we find that command in the Bible, it is surrounded by other commands which show us how to consider the needs of others. As you look up and read the following four verses, see if you can also find in each verse two *other* commands for the person intent on practicing patience:

According to these verses patience also includes:

Romans 12:12 _____

2 Corinthians 6:6 _____

1 Thessalonians 5:14 _____

James 5:8 _____

▲ **TAKE A STEP**

You should have discovered that patience includes joyful hope, faithful prayer, purity, understanding, kindness, warning, encouraging, helping, and standing firm. Read 1 Corinthians 13:4, and look for a one-word summary for patience. Patience is ___(what?)___ in action!

How could Dad give Jerry another chance?" Jim wondered. "It's just not fair. I've never disgraced him by winding up in jail for stealing. But what thanks do I get?"

Jim wasn't happy. Their dad had paid Jerry's bail bond, welcomed him home, and was helping him find another job.

"Dad, Jerry doesn't deserve the things you've done for him," Jim said angrily at dinner one night. "Why didn't you let him pay for his own mistakes? That's the only way he'll ever learn."

"You're wrong, Jim," his father answered gently. "When Jerry accepted the Lord in that jail cell, it was for real. God forgave Jerry and I do too. He needs my help and support to start over. Yours too, if you'll give it."

◆ TAKE A LOOK / 2 Peter 3:4-9

Like Jim, perhaps you feel your parents' patience is always directed to other children in your family. But if the truth were known, most parents try to be fair and patient with *all* their children.

So too, God is patient with His children. An angel might ask Him, "Why have You put up with those sinful human beings all this time?" God's answer would be, "Because I love them."

The Apostle Peter once wrote a letter to a group of scattered, persecuted Christians who were asking similar questions: "Why does God wait? Are His promises really trustworthy?" Read the comforting answer God revealed to Peter in 2 Peter 3:4-9.

▲ TAKE A STEP

Some people doubt that God is "for real" because they don't see Him judging sin in the same way He did in the days of Sodom and Gomorrah. Peter says this kind of thinking is wrong—and dangerous. People who believe this way are forgetting how God destroyed the earth with a flood. And if they don't believe He destroyed it the first time, they won't believe He will destroy it a second time.

Yet, people who believe God's Word know that *our Lord's patience means salvation (2 Peter 3:15).* God hasn't delayed because He doesn't care; rather, He has withheld judgment because He cares so much!

Think of someone you have had to put up with for a long time. Now use that person's name to complete this thought: "It will all be worthwhile if _(who?)_ finally does _(what?)_ ."

Patience points to the path of repentance

Q

What does God's patience mean to me?

A

Patience on God's part gives sinful people time to repent.

PARENT:
Practice patience by listening to your child. Giving your undivided attention— even if only for brief moments— tells your child, "You're not an interruption; you're important to me."

Please be patient —God is not finished with me yet!

Daniel Martin, a high school senior, had worked and saved all summer to buy a class ring. Now three of his friends were inviting him to join them for one last camping trip to the beach. But no matter how he figured it, there wasn't enough money for both.

"The beach will be there long after you graduate, son," Mr. Martin counseled. "But I'm not going to tell you what to do. It's your money, and your decision."

So Daniel decided—to go to the beach. And he had a great week of swimming, sailing, and sunning. "Best vacation ever," he told his parents. "Worth every cent."

Several months later, Daniel wasn't so sure. The class rings had arrived. While many of his classmates examined their lasting reminder of high school days, Daniel felt left out. Had that trip really been worth it?

◆ **TAKE A LOOK**
Ephesians 4:2-3; Colossians 3:12-13

Mr. Martin gave his son the freedom to make a choice. Though the choice Daniel made was not his father's choice, Mr. Martin never said, "I told you so!" when Daniel was later disappointed.

Perhaps you feel impatient with the faults of someone you love. "He ought to know better!" may be the words on your lips. In Ephesians 4:2-3 and Colossians 3:12-13, the Apostle Paul uses a phrase that means the same as patience. See if you can find it while someone reads those verses aloud.

▲ **TAKE A STEP**

Patience gives others room to learn from their mistakes by family and friends "bearing with them." Perhaps you have seen a badge with the letters "P.B.P.G.I.N.F.W.M.Y." and wondered what it meant. The title of this page will give you the answer!

As you read in Ephesians, being patient is one way to *make every effort to keep the unity of the Spirit through the bond of peace (Ephesians 4:3).*

Patiently accepting someone's faults or failures lets that person see what went wrong and how to improve.

Beginning with the oldest family member, think of one habit you are sometimes guilty of that others in the family find irritating (such as squeezing the toothpaste in the middle, forgetting to wash the gym clothes, or not turning out the lights). Now turn to the "victim," give him or her a big hug, and repeat in unison, "P.B.P.G.I.N.F.W.M.Y.!"

Q

How can I be patient with others?

A

Patience toward others gives them the chance to grow through their mistakes.

O h, Mom, do you think I'll ever feel well again?" Gayle's mother gave her daughter a hug and lovingly smoothed her hair. "You'll get better eventually, Gayle. Sometimes it just takes a long time with mononucleosis."

"But Mom, some of the kids at school who've had mono were back in a week. I've been out six weeks already, and I still don't have any energy. Now I'll have to go to summer school. I get tired of just lying here."

"Gayle, I don't know why you're sick, but I do believe God's in control. He can use this illness to help you grow closer to Him, just as easily as He could use days of perfect health."

"When you put it like that, Mom, I know you're right. But it's still hard to be a 'patient patient.' "

◆ TAKE A LOOK
Genesis 16:1-2, 15-16; 21:1-2, 8-14

Gayle had no choice about getting sick, but she did have a choice about how she would respond to being sick. She could be patient and face her time in bed with a joyful spirit. Or she could be impatient and bitter.

In the Old Testament, God promised an elderly couple named Abram and Sarai that they would have a son. But as the years passed and no son was born, the couple decided to take matters into their own hands. Read about the "Impetuous Solution of Two Impatient Parents" in Genesis 16:1-2, 15-16. Then turn ahead to Genesis 21:1-2, 8-14 to discover what happened 16 years later—right on schedule in God's timetable.

▲ TAKE A STEP

Abram needed patience to wait for God's timing. You need patience to wait for God's timing regarding growing up, learning to drive, dating, finding a job—perhaps even going to college.

The Psalmist David, who often had to wait for God to work out His plan, wrote these words:

Be still before the LORD and wait patiently for him (Psalm 37:7).

What Abram and David did in the Old Testament, you (and Gayle) need to do today: Practice patience in order to show that you are trusting God to work out His plan. If you were Gayle, facing still more time in bed, what would you do to make the most of that time? Have each member of the family state one way he or she would encourage Gayle.

I'd be more patient if it weren't for these problems

Q

How can I be patient in difficult circumstances?

A

Patience in hard circumstances is possible when I trust God to do His will in His timing.

MEMORY

*H*aralan Popov, a pastor imprisoned by the communists for 13 years, tells this story in his book Tortured for His Faith.

"One day," he said, "I noticed that Stoil, the man whose bed was next to mine, was tearing a page out of a little book in order to roll a cigarette. To my astonishment I saw that it was a New Testament. I had not seen a Scripture portion for five years!

" 'Where did you get it?' I asked.

" 'When we were transferred here from the first barracks, I found it in a trash can,' Stoil answered.

" 'Stoil, please give me that book.'

" 'No, I need it,' he answered firmly.

" 'Stoil, I will give you all the money I have for that book.'

"His eyes brightened. 'Here, pastor, take it.' Then I held it! God's Word! I wept before the men, and they turned their heads so as not to embarrass me."

◆ THINKING ABOUT SCRIPTURE MEMORY

Pastor Popov knew the prison guards would eventually find the little Bible and destroy it. But while he had it, he was determined to memorize as much as possible. And he did—47 chapters in all!

For Pastor Popov memorizing Scripture was important because it was **putting God's Word in his heart where no one can take it away.** Psalm 119:11 gives another reason to memorize Scripture.

"I *am* studying my Bible verses."

● KEY VERSE ON SCRIPTURE MEMORY

I have hidden your word in my heart that I might not sin against you (Psalm 119:11).

▲ TAKE A STEP

Read Psalm 1:1-3. What promise do you find there that is related to God's Word (law)? Perhaps you're thinking to yourself, "But I've got a terrible memory and a good forgetter." By week's end, you'll have learned a verse of Scripture without even trying. Really! (By the way, read this week's Key Verse out loud at least two more times.)

Peter and Chet were playing at the table with four other children in their first-grade class.

"Whose turn is it?" someone asked. Suddenly Peter disappeared under the table. He giggled as he heard someone say, "Hey, you can't leave. It's your turn!" It was fun hiding under the big table—until a foot shot out and kicked him in the mouth.

"That's Chet," Peter thought angrily. "He did that on purpose. Well, I'll get even with him."

"Where is he?" Peter yelled as he scrambled out from under the table. But Chet had already run across the room, whimpering with fear of what might happen to him.

Peter marched over, grabbed Chet's arm, and looked at the smaller boy. "I'm not gonna hit you," he said. "The Bible says not to pay back evil for evil, and God reminded me just in time!"

◆ TAKE A LOOK / Matthew 4:1-11

Maybe you've never been kicked in the teeth as Peter was. But you've probably taken your share of unfair knocks, or been tempted to do something you knew was wrong. And when that happened, you had to choose: "Will I do evil . . . or will I do good?" Having God's Word in your heart will help you make the right choice.

For 40 days Jesus was in the wilderness being tempted by His enemy, Satan. Three times He was tempted to sin, and three times Jesus responded with a Scripture verse He had memorized! As you read Matthew 4:1-11, listen for the phrase "It is written" to alert you to verses Jesus had memorized.

▲ TAKE A STEP

Whether you're in the first grade or in high school, at home or at work, your responses to everyday temptations show what's in your heart. Jesus was able to stand firm against Satan's temptations by using God's Word. Peter's response to Chet was corrected just in time by recalling a verse of Scripture he had memorized (Romans 12:17).

The psalmist recognized how God uses His Word to guide our behavior when he prayed:

Direct my footsteps according to your word; let no sin rule over me (Psalm 119:133).

Do you have a plan for hiding God's Word in your heart? (By the way, turn back to page 172 and have each family member read the Key Verse out loud. Don't try to memorize it . . . just read it.)

God reminded me, just in time

Q

Why is Scripture memory important?

A

Scripture memory prepares me to face Satan's temptations.

Never too soon, never too late

Q
When should I start memorizing Scripture?

A
Scripture memory should start when I am young, so that I can draw upon those verses my whole life.

PARENT: The Bible Memory Association is an organization with a memory plan for every age. Their address is P.O. Box 12000, Ringgold, LA 71068-2000.

Bible Emphasis Week at church had inspired the Bakers to start a Scripture-memory program.

"Okay, troops," Dad said as they finished dessert, "how did the first week of memorizing go?"

"I had a chance to use my verses to help my friend Jan," 13-year-old Denise responded.

"Great," Dad replied. "Which verses did you use?"

Denise cleared her throat and quoted Ephesians 6:1-3.

"You did that so well, Denise. Let's all say the verses we've learned. We'll start with you Don, then Mom, then Amelia, then me."

Finally it was four-year-old Amelia's turn. She chanted her verse in a sing-song voice: "We're all little sheep who've gone away, Isaiah 53:6."

"Why are they laughing?" she wondered when everybody chuckled. "I did good."

◆ **TAKE A LOOK / 2 Timothy 3:15; 1 Timothy 4:12**

Amelia didn't get the words of her verse exactly right, but when she reviewed it with her mother each day, she learned its meaning.

The Apostle Paul had a young friend, Timothy, whose mother and grandmother taught him the Old Testament Scriptures. Read 2 Timothy 3:15 to learn how old Timothy was when he began learning God's Word. Then turn to 1 Timothy 4:12 and read Paul's instruction to Timothy years later when he became a leader in the church.

▲ **TAKE A STEP**

Timothy began learning God's Word as a child. He grew to be a mature believer while he was quite young.

At different stages of life your body needs different kinds of food—at first only milk, next mushy cereal, then strained meats, vegetables, and fruits. Finally, you can eat anything, like pizza, popcorn, and apple pie. But you still need to eat balanced meals. In a similar way your spiritual life also needs proper nourishment—no matter how old you are.

Like newborn babies, crave pure spiritual milk, so that by it you may grow up in your salvation, now that you have tasted that the Lord is good (1 Peter 2:2-3).

Memorizing Scripture is part of that balanced diet you need to grow spiritually. (Have a spiritual "snack" right now by reading aloud—you guessed it—the Key Verse on page 172.)

Blair had always enjoyed sports. But never in his 14 years had he shown such dedication, determination, and willpower.

Every day he ran eight miles with his wrestling team and then went through an intensive workout of situps, pushups, and weightlifting. In a few short weeks, strong muscles developed where none had been before.

Even more amazing was his willingness to eat almost nothing but lettuce. His dad worried that this would stunt his growth, and his mom finally laid down the law: "One more day without proper meals and you're off the team."

But Blair's determination held. "One more day and I'll make my weight. Then I can eat."

And the discipline paid off. At the end of the season Blair placed third in his weight class at the county meet and received the trophy for "Most Improved Wrestler."

◆ **TAKE A LOOK / Proverbs 2:1-11**

Blair's hard work and near-starvation diet weren't at all fun. But the stronger muscles and the excitement of pinning his opponent in the wrestling matches made the weeks of training worth it all.

Like body-building, there's no formula for memorizing Scripture. It takes discipline, practice, and perseverance. But the reward is worth more than any earthly trophy. In Proverbs 2:1-11, Solomon likens Bible study to the hunt for hidden treasure. It's worth your time to read those verses!

▲ **TAKE A STEP**
- "Understanding the fear of the LORD" (verse 5)
- "Finding the knowledge of God" (verse 5)
- "Understanding what is right and just and fair" (verse 9)
- Protected by "discretion and wisdom" (vv. 11-12)

The four Scripture portions define benefits of knowing God's Word. But the person who wants those rewards must first be willing to go through the workout.

Verses 1-4 describe the "training program." There are eight "exercises," each introduced by the word *if*. And when you're all done, verse 5 shows the result of such diligent efforts at Scripture memory (watch for the word *then*). How many of those eight exercises can you find in the next two minutes?

My son, . . . accept my words and store up my commands within you (Proverbs 2:1).

Winning is fun when the workouts are done

Q

What if I don't enjoy memorizing Scripture?

A

Scripture memory is hard work, but the rewards are worth the effort.

Say it, sing it, see it, show it, know it!

Q

How can I improve my ability to memorize Scripture?

A

Scripture memory is easy and fun when I use mnemonic devices.

PARENT: Another organization with a fine Scripture-memory program (called the "Topical Memory System") is The Navigators, P.O. Box 6000, Colorado Springs, CO 80934.

When all the papers were handed out, Mrs. Mitchell's fourth-grade class settled down to take the test—50 words to put in alphabetical order and 20 minutes to do it. Now the only sounds in the room were shifting feet, shuffling chairs, scratching pencils, and music.

Music? Mrs. Mitchell cocked her head and listened carefully. Following her ears she moved quietly around the room. The sound seemed to be coming from a blonde head bent low over her paper.

"Diana," Mrs. Mitchell whispered as she leaned down, "what are you singing?"

Diana looked up and blushed. "Oh, I'm sorry, Mrs. Mitchell. I didn't mean to bother anyone. I'm just humming the ABC song. Sometimes I use it to remember how to keep the letters in the right order!"

◆ TAKE A LOOK
Deuteronomy 6:6-9; Numbers 15:37-41

Diana had memorized the alphabet by linking the letters to the tune of a song. Any formula or rhyme like that which is used to help us remember something is called a "mnemonic" (ni'mon'-ik) device. For example, the sentence, "HOMES on a great lake," is a memory aid to help you remember the names of the five Great Lakes (Huron, Ontario, Michigan, Erie, Superior). The first letter of each lake spells HOMES.

Memory aids aren't a recent invention. In Old Testament times, before it was possible for everyone to have his own copy of God's law, mnemonic devices were used to help the people of God remember the Word of God. Read about two of those memory aids in Deuteronomy 6:6-9 and Numbers 15:37-41.

▲ TAKE A STEP

Wearing tassels on your clothes may seem an odd way to learn Scripture, but here are some other methods you may want to try:

1. Learn a verse phrase by phrase.
2. Write the verse in longhand several times.
3. Make a puzzle of the verse by writing each word on a separate piece of paper, scrambling the words, and then putting them back in order.
4. Write the first letters of each word in the verse. For example, I H H Y W I M H T I M N S A Y (Psalm 119:11) stands for this week's Key Verse.

I have hidden your word in my heart that I might not sin against you" (Psalm 119:11).

FORGIVENESS

*I*n the years after World War II, people accepted Corrie ten Boom's message of God's love and forgiveness. Her words rang true because Corrie herself had suffered during the war. Her father had died in prison and her sister in a German concentration camp.

Years later, after Corrie had spoken to a group in Munich, Germany, a smiling man stretched out his hand to greet her. Corrie froze as she recognized him. It was a guard from the camp where her sister had died. How could she shake hands with this torturer, this murderer? Corrie thought she had forgiven her captors, but when her enemy stood there in person, hatred welled up inside her. Silently she prayed: "Lord, forgive me; I cannot forgive."

As she prayed, her hatred melted away. Slowly she extended her hand to her former enemy. As the man grasped it, he exclaimed, "It is wonderful that Jesus forgives our sins, just as you say."

◆ THINKING ABOUT FORGIVENESS

As Corrie ten Boom discovered, forgiveness—**treating someone as if he or she had never hurt you**—is sometimes very, very hard. But none of us gets through life without being hurt by someone we trusted. And very few people—if any—get through life without hurting someone else. So it is very important to understand that forgiving and being forgiven are two sides of the same coin.

● KEY VERSE ON FORGIVENESS

"For if you forgive men when they sin against you, your heavenly Father will also forgive you. But if you do not forgive men their sins, your Father will not forgive your sins" (Matthew 6:14-15).

▲ TAKE A STEP

You may never have done something as evil as the guard, or suffered like Corrie ten Boom, but you still need to give—and receive—forgiveness.

Read Acts 6:8-15 and 7:51-60. Where did Stephen get the power to forgive those who stoned him? Where did Corrie ten Boom find courage to forgive the prison guard?

"To err is human, to forgive divine, and well . . . I've done my part."

Revenge evens the score; forgiveness wins the game

Q

Why should I forgive others?

A

Forgiveness of others shows that I understand God's forgiveness of me.

I *'ll get even, you little sneak,"* Sandra yelled at Lynnette as she grabbed the blouse from the hanger.

"Look what Lynnette did to my blouse," Sandra shouted as she stormed into the kitchen and waved the blouse at her mother. *"She didn't even ask to wear it and now just look. This awful ink stain will never come out. See, she's already tried to wash it."*

Mrs. Sanders took the blouse. After close inspection she said calmly, *"I believe you're right. That stain won't come out. What do you think we should do about it?"*

"Make Lynnette pay for it," Sandra declared. *"She's got to learn to respect other people's property. I don't care if she has to do without allowance for 10 weeks."*

"Well," Mrs. Sanders said quietly, *"does this mean you're going to pay for my lost earrings—the ones you wore without asking?"*

◆ TAKE A LOOK / Matthew 18:21-35

Sandra was interested in only two things: her own rights and getting revenge. Her idea of fairness was making Lynnette pay for what she had done. But Sandra hadn't stopped to think about the times when *she* had trampled on the rights of others.

Jesus told the parable of a servant who owed his master a large sum of money—far more than he could pay. When the bill came due, the servant pleaded with his master, who had pity on the man and cancelled the enormous debt. How grateful the servant must have felt. Surely he too would want to show the same kindness to others. But wait . . . that wasn't how he felt at all! Find out what the servant did by reading Matthew 18:21-35.

▲ TAKE A STEP

As the servant discovered, it's dangerous to have (or hold) an unforgiving attitude. Jesus warned His disciples,

"This is how my heavenly Father will treat each of you unless you forgive your brother from your heart" (Matthew 18:35).

Forgiveness means giving up your right to revenge when someone wrongs you. It's being kind even though you may have been treated badly.

Like the servant in the parable and like Sandra in our story, you have a choice between revenge and forgiveness whenever you have been wronged. And Matthew 18:35 suggests a very good reason for choosing forgiveness every time. Tell the person next to you what that reason is!

Seventy times seven equals a little bit of heaven

"*A*w, Sis, I didn't mean to leave the window down; besides, the rain didn't do any permanent damage. Please give me a ride.*"*

Kim shook her head at her younger brother. "No, Paul. You and your friends have no respect for anybody's property but your own. You can just walk from now on!"

Paul knew Kim had reason to be angry. He had invited his friends to sit in her car and listen to tapes. He had rearranged things in the dash pocket and then left the windows open when the thunderstorm hit.

"Sis, I'm really sorry. I shouldn't have let the guys in your car without asking. And I won't do it again. C'mon . . . please?"

◆ TAKE A LOOK / Matthew 18:21-22

"I've had it with you!" "That's the last straw!" "No more!" Keeping score is an important part of baseball, board games, and bowling. But when it comes to forgiving others for the hurts and disappointments they cause you, there's no place for scorekeeping.

Yesterday in the parable of the unforgiving servant you found the answer to the question, "Why should I forgive others?" But perhaps you noticed that Jesus answered a second question as well in that same parable: "How often should I forgive?" Reread Matthew 18:21-22 to find His surprising answer!

▲ TAKE A STEP

The religious teachers of Jesus' day were experts at keeping score. They taught that when it comes to forgiveness, "one . . . two . . . three times and you're out!" When Peter asked Jesus, "How many times shall I forgive?", he probably thought his Lord would think him a generous man for suggesting seven times! But Jesus' answer was far different:

"I tell you, not seven times, but seventy-seven times" (Matthew 18:22).

Some translations read 77 times, others 70 x 7 (=490) times. But either way, the message is clear. You are to forgive and forgive and forgive again. Jesus' answer and the parable that follows it (the one you read yesterday) make it clear that you are to forgive others as often as God forgives you.

Kim had every reason to keep score against her brother. But she knew it was also possible to forgive him. If you were in her shoes, what would you do?

Q

How often should I forgive?

A

Forgiveness must be given as often as it's needed.

The cure for wounds that can't be seen

I t's so unfair," Marcy thought. "I've been elected drill team captain fair and square." But Priscilla, who was also in the competition, had seen Marcy taking a make-up test in the room where the ballot box was kept. When Marcy won, Priscilla started the rumor that Marcy put extra votes for herself in the box.

Now the thrill of winning had turned to disappointment. Marcy's friends on the team were talking about her. Some even doubted her innocence, and she had no way to prove that she had not tampered with the votes.

"She's ruined it all," Marcy said bitterly as she walked home with Jan, her best friend. "I hate her."

"I know you must feel rotten," Jan consoled. "What Priscilla did was really ugly. But if you can't forgive her, pretty soon you'll be as bitter as she is."

Q

What offenses should I forgive?

A

Forgiveness is needed when someone hurts me deeply.

◆ **TAKE A LOOK / Luke 23:13-14, 23, 32-34**

When Dad drops muddy boots in the kitchen, your brother "borrows" your hairbrush to groom the dog, or someone picks up your lunch by accident, a sincere apology and a little understanding will usually heal the hurt.

But what do you do when someone who ought to be *for* you turns *against* you—or as in Marcy's case, deliberately tries to hurt you? The healing will only come when you are willing to forgive.

Jesus Himself experienced the sting of being betrayed and deserted by those who were supposed to be His closest friends. Yet even when His disciples turned against Him, Jesus forgave—a fact you'll see by reading Luke 23:13-14, 23, 32-34.

▲ **TAKE A STEP**

Forgiving another person frees you from the chains of hatred and bitterness. The Bible says:

Get rid of all bitterness, rage and anger, brawling and slander, along with every form of malice. Be kind and compassionate to one another, forgiving each other, just as in Christ God forgave you (Ephesians 4:31-32).

Because we are sinful, we hurt each other from time to time. Dad misses your awards banquet . . . Mom cuts you down in front of your friends . . . a child steals just for the thrill of it. All inflict wounds that can only be healed by forgiveness.

Are you nursing a bitter, unforgiving spirit toward another person today? What better place to talk it out than with the other members of your family!

*T*he phone call had been from the rescue mission. Now, after all these years, Martin Edwards, age 35, knew where his father was. And nothing had changed. What could he possibly tell his own sons about their alcoholic grandfather?

Martin was only five when his father had left home. He could still remember the terror of that night, as his father hit his mother. When Martin tried to help her, his father knocked him against the desk. It wasn't a pleasant memory. In fact, Martin had worked hard to forget it. But somehow he never could. Until today.

"Lord," he prayed, "I know You want me to forgive Dad, so I will. Help me to love him as only You can."

At the mission Martin looked with compassion at the sick old man who was his earthly father. "C'mon, Dad," he said lovingly. "You've got two wonderful grandsons waiting to meet you."

◆ TAKE A LOOK / John 20:19-23

As a child, Martin needed a father's love. Instead, he and his mother were treated harshly and abandoned. Is it really possible to forgive someone for treating you like that? Believe it or not, YES!

Just before His arrest and crucifixion, Jesus surely wanted the support of His disciples. Instead, Judas betrayed Him, Peter denied Him, and the rest deserted Him.

How did Jesus respond to those who betrayed and abandoned Him? Did He look for a way to even the score or turn the tables? Not at all, as you'll discover by reading John 20:19-23.

▲ TAKE A STEP

At the very time Jesus needed His disciples the most, they let Him down, and it hurt deeply. But He also knew that to make a new beginning they needed to be at peace with Him and with themselves. So He forgave them with these words: "Peace be with you!" (John 20:19).

There are some things you can never erase from your memory—and wishing certain things had never happened won't take the hurt away. Forgiveness is not *ignoring* the past; it is *facing up* to the past and choosing to start over with the person who hurt you. Forgiveness remembers the *healing* more than the *hurting*.

Is there a hurt from your past that still waits to be healed? Take it from Martin . . . there's no time like the present to forgive.

I may forgive, but I'll never forget

Q

Does forgiving mean forgetting?

A

Forgiveness helps me remember the past without bitterness.

PARENT:
It's hard to teach your child forgiveness if you yourself have any bitterness or anger toward your own parents. If you need to, make things right as soon as you can.

CHURCH

*T*he roomful of four- and five-year-olds were excitedly following Miss Phillips's motions to the songs and rhymes they were singing.

Lacing her fingers together, she began: "Here's the church." She lifted both index fingers: "And here's the steeple." Next she unfolded her thumbs: "Open the doors." Finally she turned her palms up and wiggled her fingers: "And see all the people."

The children began to shout with delight—everyone, that is, except Alex, the newest member of the class.

Miss Phillips bent to help him twist his little fingers into the "church and steeple." But Alex still frowned when she recited, "Open the doors and see all the people."

"I don't see any people," he said. "Just fingers!"

◆ THINKING ABOUT THE CHURCH

Just as Alex wasn't "seeing" what he was supposed to see in the little rhyme, some people don't see the same thing God sees when they think of the church.

Most people think of a church as a building with a tall steeple, stained glass windows, and hard pews. But the church is much more than a building. The church is **God's group of called-out people.**

● KEY VERSE ON THE CHURCH

But you are a chosen people, a royal priesthood, a holy nation, a people belonging to God, that you may declare the praises of him who called you out of darkness into his wonderful light (1 Peter 2:9).

▲ TAKE A STEP

In the Greek language, the word *church* is an everyday word meaning "an assembly or called-out group."

By the way, do you know where the idea began of putting steeples on church buildings? Do a little family research; also do some research in your Bible to discover how Christ is related to the church. You'll find the answer in Ephesians 5:23-24.

"Here comes the flock, son, not the herd."

You're doomed. Unless you change, you're on a one-way street to jail, the electric chair, and hell."

Those words, spoken by the court psychologist in 1958, didn't impress the defiant 18-year-old leader of the Mau Maus, a dangerous gang in New York City.

Nicky Cruz lived a life of violence. Growing up with parents who called up evil spirits, he had never felt loved. As a young teenager, he joined the Mau Mau gang hoping to find love and acceptance at last. Instead he felt more and more lonely in a nightmare world where he could kill or be killed at any moment.

One night the gang set out to disrupt an evangelistic crusade meeting. Instead, God's light broke into Nicky's dark world as he heard about Jesus' love. Nicky soon became a minister to street people like he had been.

◆ TAKE A LOOK / Ephesians 2:1-8

Outwardly the young Nicky Cruz lived on the streets of New York. Inwardly that same young man lived in the kingdom of sin and death that Satan controls. In that dark kingdom, love and hope are replaced by lawlessness, evil, and hatred—not a pretty picture. But when Nicky Cruz gave his life to Jesus Christ, he was rescued. He became a citizen of another kingdom—God's kingdom—and his loyalty belonged to another King.

Read the description of the kingdom of darkness in Ephesians 2:1-8. Then find another name that describes Satan's kingdom in 1 John 5:19 and John 15:19. (Hint: It's a five-letter word.)

▲ TAKE A STEP

Are you ever afraid of the dark? If so, you have company, for that's a very common fear. Thieves like to do their wicked deeds in the dark. Wild animals stalk their prey in the dark. It is easy to stumble and fall in the dark. But turn on light, and thieves run and hide, wild animals flee, and every step becomes safe and sure.

God's church consists of people who, like Nicky, have been called out of the kingdom of darkness and into the Sonlight!

For he has rescued us from the dominion of darkness and brought us into the kingdom of the Son he loves (Colossians 1:13).

Turn out all the lights in the room. Aren't you glad God's kingdom is full of *light*, not *darkness*? Tell Him so right now!

No need to fight in the kingdom of light

Q

Where is the church called out from?

A

The church is made up of believers in Jesus, those who have come out of the kingdom of darkness and sin.

Not neglected, but loved and accepted

Q

What is the church called out to be?

A

The church is called to be the family of God.

PARENT: Different churches (sometimes even within the same denomination) use various activities in their worship services. If vacation travel permits, expose your family to the richness of worship experiences by attending a service at another church.

ngela and her friend were discussing a movie many of the kids had seen during summer vacation. "I don't think Tarzan could be real," nine-year-old Angela announced. "I'm going to ask my mom." So she did.

"Well, you're right, Angela," her mother responded. "The legend of Tarzan is just that—a legend. But there have been one or two cases of real children who were lost in the jungle and cared for by wild animals. When the children were brought back to civilization, they didn't know how to behave around people. They didn't know the language, the gestures, or the facial expressions we use to communicate because they hadn't been raised by a human family."

"Wow, Mom. Sounds like the family's pretty important. I sure don't want to grow up acting like a gorilla."

◆ **TAKE A LOOK / Romans 8:12-17**

God designed the home for children. It is their special place of safety and acceptance. Home is where children grow up physically, mentally, socially, and spiritually. Studies have shown that babies who are deprived of tender, loving care often die quite young. Those who do grow up, like Tarzan, often have difficulty adjusting to people.

The Bible describes the church as "the household [family] of faith." Every person who receives Jesus as Savior is born into that family—a family in which there are no orphans, nor children "left out in the wild."

You are no longer foreigners and aliens, but fellow citizens with God's people and members of God's household (Ephesians 2:19).

The church is a group of called-out people with God as their heavenly Father. Read about the privileges of being a member of God's family in Romans 8:12-17.

▲ **TAKE A STEP**

Just as children in an earthly family can come to their father at any time with their cares and problems, so each member of God's family can come to Him, call Him *Abba* (the Aramaic word for "Daddy"), and leave their requests with Him.

Just as earthly families provide the nest in which children can be loved and cared for, God's family is the home where Christians can care—and be cared for—in an atmosphere of love.

Name three things your church does that make it seem like a family, rather than a club or business.

*I*t's your turn to do the windows. I did them last week."

"Oh, no, you didn't!" Clay responded angrily. "You did the bathrooms and I did the windows last week."

The Carter teenagers glared at each other—and at the list of chores on the refrigerator door. Both Clay and Cindy had an individual list of chores, but there were several big jobs which weren't assigned to either one. Mom and Dad simply required that those jobs be done before Cindy and Clay could go out on weekends.

"Look, Clay," Cindy said, "remember why Mom made the list like this? She said we'd do a better job and finish quicker if we worked together. But we've never tried it her way. All we've ever done is fuss. Here, you wash inside while I wash outside. That way we'll catch the streaks and be through in no time."

◆ TAKE A LOOK / 1 Corinthians 12:12-27

Cooperation. It's what enables baseball teams to win pennants, surgical teams to perform delicate operations, and families to function as God intends.

Teamwork means pulling together, not apart. As Cindy and Clay discovered, it's the best way to get things done. And it's the way God expects us to work in the fellowship of His church.

Now you are the body of Christ, and each one of you is a part of it (1 Corinthians 12:27).

The Apostle Paul understood that believers are joined together like parts of a human body. They rely upon one another, with Christ as the Head. Think of the way the parts of your own body work together to enable you to work and play as you read 1 Corinthians 12:12-27.

▲ TAKE A STEP

Your church probably has one or more pastors, teachers, nursery workers, elders, deacons, and custodians. That's because no one person can do all the work!

The church is composed of individual people joined together by God to do a big job—the job of sharing the Good News with everyone (Matthew 28:19). Like Clay and Cindy's chores, it's a job that will only get done as we work together.

Tell the person sitting next to you which part of the body you feel like: a mouth (to tell others about the Good News), a hand (to serve those in need), an ear (to listen to the hurts of others), a knee (to be bent in prayer), etc.

Teamwork lightens the heaviest load

Q

What is the church called out to do?

A

The church is many members in one body, working together to spread the Good News.

Here comes the bride, lovely and purified

Q

What is in store for God's called-out people?

A

The church awaits the return of the Bridegroom, Jesus Christ.

PARENT:
Invest in a box of thank-you cards, and send a family greeting to one or more people in your church who minister to your family on a regular basis: pastor, choir director, Sunday school teacher, nursery worker.

*I*n only four short months Vicki would become Steve's wife. With all that was still to be done, Vicki knew the time would fly.

There were bridesmaids' dresses to order, music to select, catering to arrange, and invitations to send. Today Vicki's goal was to find the perfect wedding dress.

In the bridal shop dozens of majestic white gowns dazzled her. The saleslady showed Vicki and her mom dress after dress, pointing out the lace on one, the intricate beadwork on another, the satin fabric of another.

The saleslady froze. *"What's this?"* she murmured as she carefully examined what looked like a lovely dress. *"This dress is soiled . . . and there is a small tear along one seam. We can't sell this. We would never ask a bride-to-be even to try on a flawed gown. For our brides, everything must be perfect."*

◆ TAKE A LOOK
Ephesians 5:25-27; Revelation 19:6-9

Many traditions are associated with weddings, but one of the most meaningful is that of the wedding gown. Its beautiful design and costly fabric represent the priceless treasure that the bride is to be to her husband; its spotless elegance highlights her purity and beauty.

This week we've talked about God's family, the church. As the body of Christ, its members work together to take the gospel into the world. As the bride of Christ, the church has another mission. Discover what God has in store for His church as you read Ephesians 5:25-27 and Revelation 19:6-9.

▲ TAKE A STEP

One day the Bridegroom (Jesus) will come for His bride (the church). In preparation for that day, Christ is building and cleansing His church now, in order

to present her to himself as a radiant church, without stain or wrinkle or any other blemish, but holy and blameless (Ephesians 5:27).

Purity is not a high priority in our nation today. Many movies and television programs, songs and books encourage actions which *pollute* rather than *promote* purity.

The saleslady was so concerned about a soiled wedding gown that she wouldn't allow Vicki to try it on. Read 1 John 1:9 to discover how to deal with the things that soil, stain, or wrinkle your personal and family life as you wait for the Bridegroom's return.

COMMANDMENTS · ·

The heavy rain had overloaded the storm sewers and high winds had littered the road with fallen branches.

"Oh, no—the traffic lights are out," Mr. Fulton said to his daughter Tammy as they drove toward a major intersection. "We'll probably be late getting home."

When traffic signals don't work, drivers are supposed to follow the rule for a four-way stop, taking turns around the intersection. But this time, some didn't follow the rule. Three cars drove through from one side, and anxious drivers on the opposite side angrily honked their horns. Suddenly two cars began to move at once.

"Dad, look! That man in the station wagon doesn't see—"

A loud crash interrupted Tammy. Glass showered the street.

"What a mess," Mr. Fulton sighed. "And all because a few impatient people wouldn't follow the rules."

◆ THINKING ABOUT COMMANDMENTS

Traffic signals and speed limits help motorists travel safely. But when people ignore the laws, confusion and chaos result.

Just as traffic laws protect us on busy highways, God's commandments in the Bible are **His laws which guide us in our relationships with Him and others.** They are the "manufacturer's instructions" to help us live as God intended.

● KEY VERSE ON COMMANDMENTS

"These are the commands, decrees and laws the LORD your God directed me to teach you . . . so that you, your children and their children after them may fear the LORD your God . . . and so that you may enjoy long life." (Deuteronomy 6:1-2).

▲ LOOKING AHEAD

Some people say that that everyone has the right to do his own thing. But God the Creator knows what's best for His creation. His laws for living are summarized in the Ten Commandments.

As an introduction to God's commandments, read Psalm 19:7-14 and list six things God's laws can do for you if you obey them.

"Thou shalt not steal, except for bases."

Who's reigning on the throne of your life?

*L*inda's heart skipped a beat when she saw the price of the dress. It sure would cut into her savings for the missions trip in December, but after all, tonight was her first date with Neil. Making the right impression was worth the sacrifice. Besides, Mom would never have to know how much she'd spent.

Two hours later, as she put on her make-up, Linda glanced at the picture of the fashion model taped to her mirror. Not a bad resemblance, she thought smugly.

The next morning, Linda groaned as the alarm buzzed at 7:30. She slid wearily out of bed and shuffled into the kitchen, "Mom, I'm not feeling so good. I don't think I can make it through church this morning."

◆ TAKE A LOOK
Exodus 20:1-6; Matthew 22:34-38

Like many people today, Linda went about her daily activities with hardly a thought about the things that please God. Sure, she believed in God. She certainly didn't bow down to idols of wood or stone! But she lived her life with God a safe distance away. And in the process, she disobeyed many of God's basic rules for living.

Read Exodus 20:1-6 along with Jesus' summary of these important verses in Matthew 22:34-38. Which commandments did Linda disobey?

▲ TAKE A STEP

In His summary of the commandments, Jesus said:

"Love the Lord your God with all your heart and with all your soul and with all your mind" (Matthew 22:37).

Linda—not the Lord—is on the throne of her life. She is living according to her desires and interests—not God's—because material things are more important to her than spiritual things.

When you spend time with someone, your love for that person increases as you understand his thoughts and feelings. That's true with God, too, because God is a Person.

As a family, make three columns on a sheet of paper. In column 1, list some ways you can get to know God better. In column 2, list ways you and your family can enjoy His creation. In column 3, think of specific things in your family schedule that keep you from doing the things in the first two columns. Pick one activity from the first two columns and add it to your schedule this week!

Q

How can I give God first place in my life?

A

God's commandments help me put Him first in my life.

Golly, Mom, I'm sure glad you made—" But before Deke could finish his sentence his mother interrupted him.

"Deke, I don't know why you've suddenly begun using the Lord's name in vain, but Dad and I will not allow you to disobey one of the Ten Commandments."

Deke looked puzzled. "I didn't use God's name, Mom. A lot of people say 'golly.' "

Mr. Duncan looked up from his paper. "You'd better go get the dictionary, son," he said calmly. "You've got some work to do."

While Deke got the dictionary, Mr. Duncan jotted down a list of words. "Look up golly for us first, Deke."

Quickly Deke read the definition: "An exclamation of surprise, a euphemism for God."

Then he glanced up. "Gol— I mean, wow! That sounds serious. But what's a 'euphemism'?"

◆ **TAKE A LOOK / Exodus 20:7; Philippians 2:9-11**

A euphemism is a word substituted for another word. *Golly* and *gosh* are substitutes for the word *God*. You may also hear the words *gee, jeez, heck,* and *darn* used frequently. (Why not look them up in a dictionary?) Saying words like those is one way people misuse God's name, which breaks God's law:

"*You shall not misuse the name of the* LORD *your God, for the* LORD *will not hold anyone guiltless who misuses his name*" (Exodus 20:7).

God's commandment in Exodus 20:7 states that His holy name must not be used in a meaningless way. In the New Testament, Philippians 2:9-11 gives a very important reason *why* God's name is to be highly respected, and Colossians 3:17 points out *how* you can honor God's name every minute of the day.

▲ **TAKE A STEP**

Saying God's name meaninglessly is only one way people misuse His name. Sometimes people take credit for something He has done, or they use His name in insincere praise. But Colossians 3:17 says that in *word* and *deed* we are to do *all* in the *name* of the Lord Jesus.

Find a book which gives meanings of names. Have each family member look up his or her name and write the meaning on a 3 x 5 card. On the other side write Colossians 3:17. Carry your card today, and frequently ask yourself, "Is what I'm saying and doing right now honoring *God's* name?"

There's just something about that name

Q

How can I keep from misusing God's name?

A

God's commandments help me honor His holy name.

PARENT:
Help your children choose acceptable words to use as exclamations. Start a family "warning system" when one member hears another fall back into a bad habit.

Even moms and dads can use some t.l.c.!

Q

Why should I honor my father and mother?

A

God's commandments teach me to value my parents all my life.

*E*ven though Tim and Marty knew it would only be temporary, they still didn't like having to sleep in the same bedroom. Both boys were accustomed to having plenty of space in their own rooms.

"Hey, get your stuff off my dresser!" Marty exploded at his younger brother. "You can't just take over."

"But this is my room too—now," Tim yelled back, "so I can put my stuff anywhere I want to!"

Just then their mother walked in. "Be quiet, both of you. How do you think Grandma will feel if she hears you bickering? Your father will finish Grandma's room as soon as he can. But until then, this is the best we can do."

Mrs. Stanley put her arms around her two sons. "Grandma has given so much to us over the years. Now we can do something special for her. Let's show her she's welcome and wanted in our home and will have our help as long as she needs it. The best thing you boys can do is finish your homework and then go help your father work on the new room."

◆ TAKE A LOOK
Exodus 20:12; 1 Timothy 5:8; Proverbs 1:8-9

The first four commandments show us how to relate to God Himself. Beginning with the fifth commandment, we learn how God expects us to treat other people.

"Honor your father and your mother, so that you may live long in the land the LORD your God is giving you" (Exodus 20:12).

God commands children to obey their parents. But when you grow old enough to make your own decisions, God still wants you to honor your parents, to respect and care for them. First Timothy 5:8 and Proverbs 1:8-9 will show you ways to do that.

▲ TAKE A STEP
In many parts of the world today three or more generations of the same family live under one roof. But in our country many families are scattered and only get to visit occasionally. As a result, it takes a special effort to honor your parents in ways that please God.

Brainstorm as a family on ways you can honor a parent (or grandparent). What is one thing you can do this week to make life easier or a little bit brighter for that person God has commanded you to respect and care for? Even an unexpected phone call is a special way to say, "We love you!"

"*Oh, look,*" Donna said as she and Betty watched TV together. " '*Lover-boy*' is making his move. He's so obvious, she should see right through him."

"Yeah," Betty laughed, "but unless somebody's foolin' around, this show would be too dull to watch!"

"Betty, I've told you not to watch that program," her mother said quietly as she entered the room and turned off the TV. "So many of those shows try to make adultery look exciting, but God says it's sin. Look around our own neighborhood and see the heartache and misery it causes."

Betty knew her mom was right. Several families on their street had gone through recent affairs and divorces. In Betty's mind the TV fantasy faded, replaced by the real picture of a broken home, a grieving wife, and confused children who don't understand why their daddy lives with a different woman now.

◆ **TAKE A LOOK / Exodus 20:14; Proverbs 6:32; Malachi 2:13-16**

"Times have changed . . . I need to be free . . . God wouldn't want me to be unhappy . . . We didn't expect it to go that far . . . It was just a little affair." Excuses like these are attempts to make adultery seem right. But the seventh commandment says very plainly, "You shall not commit adultery" (Exodus 20:14). Jesus further explained that command when He said:

"I tell you that anyone who looks at a woman lustfully has already committed adultery with her in his heart" (Matthew 5:28).

People commit adultery when their thoughts or actions lead to sexual involvement with someone to whom they are not married.

Good marriages don't happen by accident; they are hard work. In Proverbs 6:32 and Malachi 2:13-16, look for statements about the damage that results when a marriage is invaded by adultery.

▲ **TAKE A STEP**

Marriage is God's invention. It provides the perfect environment for a couple's love to be expressed and for their children to be raised. Adultery is not a romantic fling. Instead, it is the cause of heartache in millions of homes each year.

In Malachi 2:15-16, the Lord repeats the command to "guard yourself in your spirit, and do not break faith." Brainstorm together as a family on ways you can safeguard your home against the idea that adultery is okay.

The grief comes when the glamour goes

Q

Why does God warn against adultery?

A

God's commandments teach me that adultery destroys families.

PARENT: Television allows immoral people—whom you would never let through your front door—to "visit" in your home. Don't take lightly your family's TV viewing habits.

LEARNING

F or once, everybody was at home. Gina was talking on the phone in the kitchen. Dick was doing homework in his room. Mr. and Mrs. Cooper were reading in the living room.

Suddenly Mr. Cooper put his hand on his chest. "Marge," he groaned as he tried to stand up, "I feel pains . . . " Then he slumped forward onto the floor.

"Dick, Gina, come here!" Mrs. Cooper yelled as she sprang to her husband's side. "Something's wrong with Dad."

Within seconds Dick was there, turning his father over, loosening his shirt, and taking his pulse. "Mom, you call the ambulance. Gina, you help me do CPR. Dad's having a heart attack."

Dick's mind flashed back to the CPR course he had taken. There he had practiced on a dummy, but this was real. As Dick began to rhythmically massage his father's chest, he prayed, "Lord, let Dad be okay. Help me remember all the things I learned."

◆ THINKING ABOUT LEARNING

You may never be in such a critical situation, but every day you rely on the knowledge and skills you've already learned.

Some skills like walking and talking are learned almost automatically as part of normal growth. Hundreds of other skills and abilities such as reading, driving, playing an instrument, or enjoying a sport must be consciously learned and practiced.

"Sudso gets out dirt, which is information that could save your life."

▲ TAKE A STEP

Learning is **gaining knowledge and skill through experience or study.** Even the Apostle Paul, the man God used to write almost half of the books of the New Testament, was constantly learning more about God! Read about Paul's zeal to learn in Philippians 3:7-11. Then let this week's key verse show you where that learning leads—to the person of God's Son.

● KEY VERSE ON LEARNING

[Jesus said,] "Everyone who listens to the Father and learns from him comes to me" (John 6:45).

*T*he year was 1582. As the lamps were lit in the cathedral, a clanking chain disturbed 18-year-old Galileo Galilei. Glancing up, he watched the regular motion of a lamp swinging back and forth on its chain. Suddenly he realized that the smaller lamp beside it was swinging faster on a shorter chain.

Questions raced through his mind. No one ever before had questioned Aristotle's teaching that heavy objects fall faster than light ones. But if Aristotle was really right, why didn't heavier lamps swing, or "fall," faster on their chains?

Galileo hurried to his room. He built two identical pendulums and hung a wooden ball and a heavier iron ball from the rafters. Pulling them back the same distance, he let them go at the same time. They swung together, back and forth at the same speed, and stopped at the same time. All these years, Aristotle had been wrong. The speed of a falling body did not depend on its weight!

◆ **TAKE A LOOK / Proverbs 6:6-10**

During Galileo's time, scientific "fact" was based on the teachings of the ancient masters like Aristotle. Galileo made many wonderful discoveries and helped make science more exact by relying on observation and experimentation.

God gave us minds to discover and use the laws of His creation. From the tiniest animals to the stars in space, the world reveals the power of its Creator. Find one example of how you can learn from God's creatures in Proverbs 6:6-10.

▲ **TAKE A STEP**

The Book of Proverbs also gives another reason for learning about God in the things He has made:

So that your trust may be in the LORD, I teach you today, even you (Proverbs 22:19).

When Galileo and other scientists of his time discovered something by observation, they tested that truth to see how it lined up with the truth God had revealed in the Bible.

Around the 1850s, many scientists began teaching that the Bible wasn't true. Their ideas have been widely accepted, and today many textbooks present only man's point of view, not God's.

Examine your science and history books. Do the sections about the origin of the world and of mankind measure up to what God has said in His Word? If not, which account should you trust?

Learn about your Maker in the things He has made

Q

Why do I need to learn?

A

Learning about God's creation shows me God's power.

My mind goes blank without a chalkboard!

"**W**on't he ever learn?" Mrs. Green muttered angrily as she bundled up the garbage sack. For the third time this week Jeremy had forgotten to empty the trash. Unless Mom or Dad reminded him every time, Jeremy would ignore the full trash can and even walk around the neatly tied bags his mother left beside the door.

That evening, Jeremy's parents discussed the problem. "I've tried everything." Mrs. Green told her husband. "I've reminded him nicely, I've talked to him sternly, I've taken away privileges. He just won't learn that taking out the trash is his responsibility. I will not do it for him."

"I may have a solution," Mr. Green said thoughtfully.

The next morning Jeremy woke and took a deep breath. Holding his nose as he looked around, he saw the three bags of garbage his dad had placed beside his bed. It was a lesson he never forgot!

Q

Do I learn only at school?

A

Learning is not limited to books and classrooms, but means the most when it is focused on God.

PARENT:
Libraries, museums, concerts, and short courses in various subjects open new worlds for your child to explore.

◆ **TAKE A LOOK / Ecclesiastes 1:12-17; 12:13-14**

You may associate the idea of learning with going to school and studying textbooks. But as Jeremy discovered, learning can occur in very unusual ways and places. Unlike animals, which function mainly on instinct and have a limited ability to learn, people keep learning from the cradle to the grave.

Solomon, whose wisdom came from God, wrote the Book of Ecclesiastes to explain what he learned when he investigated "everything that is done under heaven" (Ecclesiastes 1:13). He outlines his "study plan" in Ecclesiastes 1:12-14, and the rest of the book shows that good and evil, pleasure and pain, wealth and poverty come to good and bad people alike. Read Solomon's conclusion about life and learning in the last verses of the chapter, Ecclesiastes 12:13-14.

▲ **TAKE A STEP**

Fear God and keep his commandments, for this is the whole duty of man (Ecclesiastes 12:13).

As a family, list all the courses you have been enrolled in during the past year. Include school subjects, scouting projects, music and craft lessons, and classes at church. Have each family member initial the one in which he or she spends the most time. Then put a "star" by the ones that are helping you "fear God and keep his commandments." Use Ecclesiastes 12:14 to help you decide if the lessons you're learning will pass the test of time!

With help from her dad, Trudy was learning algebra. "Why is this so easy for you?" she asked, copying the figures he had just written down. "It doesn't make any sense to me!"

"Oh, Trudy," her dad chuckled, "I've been doing algebra for years. You're still learning the basics."

Just then a phone call came for Trudy, and her father couldn't help overhearing the conversation.

"I'm not going to talk about it, Marcia. It might not be true, and you could really hurt Alice by repeating that story. Listen, I'm kinda busy. Bye now."

As Trudy returned to her work, her father had a twinkle in his eye. "You're the first sophomore I've ever known who refused to take part in juicy gossip. Some people don't learn that lesson in a lifetime. I'd say you're growing up fast, Trudy!"

◆ TAKE A LOOK / 2 Peter 1:3-11

For Trudy, algebra was important. So were her other subjects. But as her dad noticed, Trudy was also learning the importance of following God's commands like the one found in Isaiah 1:17:

Learn to do right! Seek justice, encourage the oppressed. Defend the cause of the fatherless, plead the case of the widow (Isaiah 1:17).

God is interested in how His children develop and grow both physically and spiritually. Read what every child of God needs to learn in 2 Peter 1:3-11.

▲ TAKE A STEP

Many people try to control the direction their lives will take. They schedule their education, career, exercise, recreation—even their retirement. And certainly all of those things are worthwhile goals.

But did you realize that planning your character is just as important in God's sight as planning your career?

There are eight character qualities listed in 2 Peter 1:5-7. Try to find all eight. Write them on index cards or slips of paper, along with a short definition of what each means (for example, "knowledge—facts and principles God wants me to know and use"). For the next two weeks, review the cards each day. On the back, keep track of the ways you are building these qualities into your life.

Some lessons you won't find in a book

Q

What is the most important thing to learn?

A

Learning how to please God is the most important thing I can do.

It's hard to learn when your eyelids droop

"It can't be seven o'clock," 15-year-old Shelley groaned as the alarm buzzed. She pulled the pillow over her head. But within minutes, her mother flicked the light on, cheerfully announcing, "Up and at 'em, sweetheart—time to start the day."

"Mom, I don't feel like going to school. Please let me stay home," Shelley pleaded.

As usual, her mother ignored her. "Hurry down to breakfast or you'll miss the bus."

Barely awake for her first three classes, Shelley was tired and irritable by lunch. That evening, she fell asleep doing homework, but woke up in time for the late-night news. Unable to sleep, she read until 12:30 A.M.

"Oh, no, it can't be seven already," Shelley groaned when the alarm blared in her ear the next morning.

◆ TAKE A LOOK / 1 Corinthians 6:19-20

Learning about the world around you helps you praise God the Creator. You can learn new skills and gain new knowledge no matter what kind of situation you're in, but learning is most beneficial when the goal is to please God and learn His ways. You are to

Be wise about what is good, and innocent about what is evil (Romans 16:19).

However, some things can—and do—hinder the learning process. The Bible certainly doesn't promise that if you eat regular meals, get proper exercise, and sleep eight hours every night, you'll be a genius. But 1 Corinthians 6:19-20 does show that how you treat your body is important.

▲ TAKE A STEP

As you might imagine, Shelley wasn't a super student because her harmful habits weakened her ability to learn. Before you get much further into this school year, try building some helpful habits which will make learning more enjoyable for you.

1. Bulldoze the clutter from your desk each day and start fresh with a clean, well-lit place to study.

2. Banish television except on weekends.

3. Beat the need to cram for exams by studying consistently.

4. Build good relationships with your teachers by showing respect and appreciation.

Add to the list by telling three ways Shelley could have cared for herself better. Learn all you can—and have a great school year!

Q

How can I be a better learner?

A

Learning is easier when I discipline my body and mind.

PARENT:
A young child may need help with bedtimes and study times while teens need protection from overscheduling. Set loving limits with firmness and flexibility.

PEER PRESSURE

S uppose you're driving around with four other kids, when somebody pulls out a bottle of pills, takes one out, and passes it on. Soon the bottle is in the back seat—where you are—and two more kids take pills. Now the bottle is in your hands. What do you say? What do you do?

You know you shouldn't; but you've just heard the guy sitting beside you sneer, "Come on, don't spoil our fun. It won't hurt you just once."

Suddenly your hands are sweating, your heart is pounding, you wish you were anywhere but here. What should you say? What should you do? You feel so embarrassed you begin to think maybe it wouldn't hurt just this once. And so you . . .

What would you do?

◆ THINKING ABOUT PEER PRESSURE

Peer pressure, **the influence of people on people**, plays a large part in what we think and do. The word *peer* really means someone "equal," and often the pressure comes from people in our own age group. Sometimes it's good, sometimes it's bad.

We all like to think we make up our own minds. What really happens is that because we don't want to be different, we feel the pressure to conform to those around us. (For instance, how many kids can you name who refuse—absolutely refuse—to wear name-brand jeans, shirts, and shoes?) But conformity can lead you to do things you know are wrong. The Bible gives this warning.

● KEY VERSE ON PEER PRESSURE

Do not conform any longer to the pattern of this world, but be transformed by the renewing of your mind (Romans 12:2).

▲ TAKE A STEP

Peer pressure is not new. The Old Testament character Job resisted peer pressure by friends who wanted him to change his view of God. Read what God said and did for Job in Job 42:7-12. What do you think Job would have done when he was pressured by his friends?

"Just say no to drugs, but not to spinach."

Are you an original or a carbon copy?

Q

Why is peer pressure so powerful?

A

Peer pressure affects me because of my need to feel loved and accepted.

Silently and near tears, Glenda climbed into the car. As her mother drove away from the school, she asked quietly, "Something's really wrong, isn't it? Can you talk about it?"

"It's so dumb," Glenda said, and the tears began to roll. "I hate being new. This morning Jennifer said in front of everybody, 'Don't you have anything else to wear? You wore those jeans last Friday.' Mom, it was so embarrassing. I wanted to die. All the girls here have tons of clothes."

Mrs. Martin shook her head. "I know it's hard to make do with what you have, but remember, it's what you are, not . . . "

"I know," Glenda interrupted. "It's what you are, not what you wear that counts. But Mom, nobody even wants to know the 'inside me' unless the outside looks like everybody else."

◆ **TAKE A LOOK / Genesis 37:2-11, 26-28**

Because Glenda didn't dress as well as the other girls, she didn't fit comfortably in their group. And the result? Glenda's peers made her feel left out and alone.

Joseph, whose story is found in the first book of the Bible, stood out among his peers—ten older brothers! He too wanted to be accepted, and he too felt pressure to conform. Turn to Genesis 37:2-11, 26-28 and read the story we've entitled, "The Danger of Wearing a Sportscoat When Everyone Else Wears Jeans." As you read, notice the ways Joseph was different from his brothers.

▲ **TAKE A STEP**

Favored by his father and set apart by a richly decorated robe, Joseph really stood out! At age seventeen, he knew his brothers hated him. And how did he handle the pressure? He told them his dreams and made his brothers angrier still!

Joseph was right in not wanting to be like his brothers, but he acted unwisely toward them in that "pressure situation" because:

Whoever corrects a mocker invites insult; whoever rebukes a wicked man incurs abuse (Proverbs 9:7).

Like Joseph and Glenda, you've probably had an experience when your speech, appearance, or behavior made you feel left out. Divide your family members into two groups. After Group 1 shares a peer-pressure situation they have encountered, let Group 2 use Proverbs 9:7 and the story of Joseph to give some advice about what to do.

*T*he trip had taken three hours, but Mrs. Jackson knew she'd find good buys here in the huge factory outlet. Brent and Jenny were excited too. They would be wearing some name-brand items they couldn't afford back home. Soon their carts were filled with shirts, skirts, and jeans. All they lacked were jackets.

Then Brent spotted just the right jacket—in Mom's price range, too. But as he pulled it off the rack, his mother frowned. "We can't buy one of those," she said.

"But Mom, why not? It's perfect—just what I want."

"I know," his mother whispered, "but the sign on the rack says 'Members Only.' I didn't know this was a membership store."

Brent doubled over laughing as he tried to explain. "Mom, 'Members Only' is the brand name! Hey, Jenny, come here! Listen to what Mom said . . . "

◆ TAKE A LOOK / 2 Chronicles 36:10-20

It's sometimes hard to keep track of the trends, fashions, and fads that influence our lives. But most people want to be up to date, to wear "in" clothes, listen to "in" music, drive an "in" car, and be seen at "in" places.

Peer pressure is not a new problem. The Israelites, God's people whose story is told in the Old Testament, wanted to be like other nations. In spite of God's commands and warnings, they imitated the evil behavior of the nations around them. From choosing a king to practicing idolatry, Israel gave in to the pressure. Read the sad story of "Where the 'In' Thing Ends" in 2 Chronicles 36:10-20.

▲ TAKE A STEP

Even today, God's people feel the pressure to be like the world and do what the world does. It's a form of peer pressure Christians can resist by honestly answering these questions:

Do not be yoked together with unbelievers. For what do righteousness and wickedness have in common? Or what fellowship can light have with darkness? What harmony is there between Christ and Belial? What does a believer have in common with an unbeliever? (2 Corinthians 6:14-15).

Or ask it another way: What do the clothes I wear, the music I listen to, the places I go, and the things I do have in common with Christ? Am I like everyone else, or am I what God wants me to be? When it comes to being "in," be sure you're "in" step with Him!

Want to have clout? Know "in" from "out"!

Q

What are the sources of peer pressure?

A

Peer pressure comes from individuals, groups, and the world itself.

PARENT:
Most children fear inferiority. Help your child identify an area of strength and work with him to make that area even stronger.

Hey, friend, give me a nudge in the right direction

*T*he weather's too nice to be cooped up in school," Russ grumbled as he climbed into the car with his friends.

"Well, why don't we just go to the lake?" Mike asked. "Nobody'll even miss us."

"All right!" Steve whooped as he banged the steering wheel with his fist. "We might never get a better chance."

Lou had been silent, but now he said quietly, "I don't think it's the right thing to do. You guys just drop me off at school."

"Can't stay away from the books, huh?" Mike kidded.

Then Russ spoke up. "You know, we could get in real trouble, and it's our senior year. Besides, I've got a report due today."

Steve glared for a moment, then shrugged his shoulders. "Oh, all right. All aboard for Southside High!"

Q

Is all peer pressure bad?

A

Peer pressure can influence me for good or bad.

◆ **TAKE A LOOK / 1 Kings 11:1-13**

The pressure to conform can be tremendous. Sometimes it leads to a wrong decision. Other times, as in the story you just read, it can be an influence for good. It's your response that counts.

Solomon was one of the wisest men who ever lived; but when he yielded to peer pressure, his foolish actions opened the door to sin in his personal life and sin in his nation. Read the account of "The King Who Loved a Thousand Ladies" in 1 Kings 11:1-13.

▲ **TAKE A STEP**

When Solomon married foreign wives who worshiped false gods, he disobeyed God. He chose the wrong crowd and "held fast to them in love" (verse 2). "His heart was not fully devoted to the LORD his God" (verse 4).

You can't get away from peer pressure, but you can choose the peers who influence you.

Do not be misled: "Bad company corrupts good character" (1 Corinthians 15:33).

Your choice is to make friends at school, at work, or in your community who will "pressure" you to do good. Think about the groups you're regularly with—best friends at school, sports teams, community organizations. Which group of peers influences you most? And in which direction? Discuss as a family which influences are helping you, and which are hindering you in your walk with God.

Patty felt sad that her first date with Dan was almost over. His attention during dinner had made her feel like a princess. Later, as they strolled through the mall, she had shivered with excitement when he reached down and took her hand in his. It had been like a dream come true!

But now as they turned onto an unfamiliar highway, Patty felt uneasy. "I guess I didn't explain how to get back very well. You need to take Highway 9 instead of this one," she offered.

Dan smiled as he shifted gears. "I thought we'd go back a different way. There's less traffic."

Then Patty saw a sign: "Covered Bridge—1/2 mile." She remembered hearing some of the girls talk about how romantic it was to walk across the old moss-covered bridge and hear the water swirling underneath. She wanted to spend more time with Dan, but Patty knew this was not the place to do it. "Dan," she said firmly, "I have to be home by 10:30. Let's go back now so we won't be late, okay?"

◆ TAKE A LOOK / Genesis 39:1, 6-20
Though Patty knew some girls didn't mind ending an evening at the covered bridge, she was able to say no firmly but kindly. She had already decided what she would do in that sort of situation.

Joseph, the young man you read about on Tuesday, also had personal convictions. As you read part of his story in Genesis 39:1, 6-20, see if you can discover what guided his behavior even after he was sold into slavery.

▲ TAKE A STEP
Young and old alike, people experience peer pressure. Habits such as drinking, smoking , and using drugs often begin when someone can't say no to a friend. Using bad language, disobeying those in authority, cheating on tests, and watching TV programs that depict immorality often start because "everyone else is doing it."

Like Patty and Joseph, you too can prepare to face certain situations long before the actual temptation comes. Proverbs 4:14 is one verse which might help you. Why not memorize it today!

Do not set foot on the path of the wicked or walk in the way of evil men (Proverbs 4:14).

Have someone write that verse on a sheet of paper and cut it into "word strips" of 3-4 words each. Quick, who can arrange the pieces correctly?

Do you go with the flow or run your own show?

Q

How can I resist peer pressure?

A

Peer pressure is easier to resist when I have already decided to do what's right.

PARENT:
Find out about the groups and organizations your child belongs to. Discover what goes on in those groups and stay in contact with the leaders.

HONESTY

A driver involved in an accident must take a breath test.
A job applicant may have to take a lie-detector test.
An athlete may be required to take a blood test.
A school routinely calls home to verify student absences.
A politician is forced to resign because he's caught stealing.
A department store raises prices to cover the cost of items lost through shoplifting.
A businessman reports extra lunches on his expense account.
A teacher throws out a test because too many students cheated.

◆ THINKING ABOUT HONESTY

In our society it's becoming difficult to find people who really believe that "honesty is the best policy." For many, dishonesty has become a way of life.

"If it feels good, do it," "You're okay if you don't get caught," "If everyone does it, it must be okay," and "Nobody will ever know," are phrases which can be heard in homes, schools, and offices.

Many people seem to think laws are made to be broken and rules must be overturned. For them, the difference between right and wrong is vague, and the only "sin" is getting caught.

Yet God requires that His people live honestly in every area of life.

● KEY VERSE ON HONESTY

Therefore each of you must put off falsehood and speak truthfully to his neighbor (Ephesians 4:25).

▲ TAKE A STEP

Honesty means more than simply not telling lies. Honesty is **truthful words and right actions.**

Begin this week by getting God's viewpoint on honesty. Read Proverbs 6:16-19 and Proverbs 12:22. Why do you think God hates lying but is pleased with those who practice truth?

"Sounds to me like Jack planted a little garden, and every time he described it to his friends, it got a little better."

What's the big deal if I spent the night with Esther instead of Joan?" Sue thought angrily to herself. "Nobody got in trouble like Mom thought might happen."

Sue's mother had learned of her disobedience, and her privileges had been taken away for two weeks. Now every time Sue tried to make plans, her mother gave her the "third degree," asking questions about where Sue was going and with whom.

Over breakfast, the topic of conversation was the concert Sue wanted to attend. Suddenly Sue exploded. "Don't you trust me anymore?"

A long silence followed. "Sue, your dishonesty about spending the night at Esther's did something to my trust in your judgment. You'll have to give it a little time to grow again."

◆ **TAKE A LOOK / Genesis 3:6-13, 22-23**

As Sue discovered, honesty is the basis for trusting relationships with other people. Her own dishonesty damaged her mother's trust.

Man's relationship with God was broken when Adam and Eve sinned. Adam and Eve's response to God after their sin shows how difficult it is—but how necessary—to be honest with God. "Listen in" on their conversation with God after they had disobeyed His command (Genesis 3:6-13). Then read the result of that disobedience in verses 22 and 23.

▲ **TAKE A STEP**

In the Genesis 3 account, nobody was being totally honest with God! Adam blamed Eve; Eve blamed the serpent. No one wanted to admit, "Yes, I disobeyed." But trying to hide sin, or pretending that something isn't sin when God says it is, only shows dishonesty.

Jesus once told the Pharisees (a group of men who pretended to be honest, but really weren't) . . .

"You belong to your father, the devil, and you want to carry out your father's desire. He was a murderer from the beginning, . . . for there is no truth in him. . . . He is a liar and the father of lies" (John 8:44).

Honesty is important because God is truth and Satan is a liar. Dishonesty is sin—something to be confessed and not repeated. Think back to the story of Sue and her mother. What do you think would help rebuild the loss of trust which Sue's disobedience and dishonesty caused?

When you stretch the truth, it breaks the trust

Why is honesty important?

Honesty is important because God is truth and wants me to be truthful too.

Honesty isn't always easy!

Q

Why is honesty sometimes difficult?

A

Honesty is difficult when pride gets in the way.

PARENT:
Identify and define some of the forms dishonesty can take: "white lies," manipulation, stretching the truth, exaggeration, hiding the facts. Actively work to make honesty a part of everyday family conversation.

Bart couldn't believe it! There on his report card was an A in geometry. "It's incredible," he thought as he remembered all those low quiz grades and the C's on tests.

An uncomfortable question began to form in his mind. Was it a mistake? "No," he thought, "I must have done well on the final."

That night, Bart rummaged through his papers and averaged his test scores. No, that A couldn't be right.

The next day Bart hung around Mr. Roberts's room until everyone else had gone. Then he pulled out his report card. "I think it must be a mistake," he said slowly.

Carefully, Mr. Roberts examined his grade book. Then he shook his head. "I did make a mistake, Bart, and I'm sorry. I'll have to change it. But I appreciate your honesty, and I'm going to make a note of it on your record when I change the grade."

◆ **TAKE A LOOK / Acts 4:32; 5:1-11**
Asking Mr. Roberts about the grade was difficult. Bart knew that he would have to let his parents know that he really had made a C instead of an A. But keeping quiet about the grade would have been as dishonest as a spoken lie.

Like Bart, a family in the New Testament also had to make a decision about honesty. And like Bart, their decision was difficult because their pride was involved. Read their sad story of deception and death in Acts 4:32; 5:1-11.

▲ **TAKE A STEP**
Ananias and Sapphira didn't sin in keeping part of the money for themselves. Their sin was trying to deceive God and other people. Deceit—misrepresenting facts so others will believe something untrue—is a form of dishonesty usually caused by pride. Deceit can involve keeping quiet about the truth, telling only part of the truth, or telling an outright lie. God says this about deceit:

No one who practices deceit will dwell in my house; no one who speaks falsely will stand in my presence (Psalm 101:7).

Bragging about achievements that weren't yours, using someone else's hall pass, passing off someone else's grade as your own—it's all deceit in God's eyes. Ananias and Sapphira died because of their deceit, but Brad was rewarded because of his honesty. Which behavior was worth it in the end?

T hree hundred dollars for hubcaps. That's ridiculous!" Doyle thought as he left the parts store. "That's eight more weeks of slavery at the dry cleaners. I'm tired of working after school." Doyle kicked his own dented hubcaps and climbed in his truck.

Three blocks from home, Doyle passed the new four-wheel-drive truck parked in the Stevenson's driveway. As he admired the truck and its hubcaps, an idea struck.

That Friday night, Doyle put his plan into action. Staying in the shadows, he jogged to the Stevenson's house and crouched beside the truck. Just as he pried off the first hubcap, Doyle heard a dog bark. The sound was very loud . . . and very close. Then light flooded the driveway, a door opened, and Doyle was caught!

◆ TAKE A LOOK / 2 Kings 5:15-16, 19-27

Two things were at work when Doyle stole the hubcaps—his own greed and a dislike of hard, honest work. He somehow felt that he deserved to have those hubcaps.

You may remember the story of Naaman, the foreign soldier who came to Israel to be cured of leprosy. God's prophet Elisha instructed Naaman to dip seven times in the Jordan River. Naaman did and his leprosy was cured. He was so excited he wanted to reward Elisha, but Elisha refused any payment or reward. However, Elisha's servant Gehazi, like Doyle, had a problem with material things. Read about "The Greed That Gave Gehazi Grief" in 2 Kings 5:15-16, 19-27.

▲ TAKE A STEP

There are many reasons why people behave dishonestly: They may be trying to avoid punishment; they may not know what's right and wrong; they may be imitating someone else. But one of the main causes of dishonesty is greed—the desire to have more than you've worked for, can pay for, or even really need. God's Word is painfully clear about the path of a greedy or dishonest person:

A greedy man brings trouble to his family, but he who hates bribes will live (Proverbs 15:27).

Gehazi's life is a lesson of just how true that proverb is! If Doyle had taken Proverbs 15:27 to heart, how might his story have had a different ending? If time and weather permit, why not wash the family car together as you discuss the lesson you've learned from Doyle and Gehazi.

Is it just greed or an honest need?

Why are some people dishonest?

A

Greed is the reason for some forms of dishonesty.

Your great internal guidance system

A s the engine died, Mr. Davis angrily pulled his car off the road. Only one week ago he'd had this problem fixed. Now the car had stalled again. "I'll tell that lousy mechanic what I think of him!" And with one simple phone call he did exactly that.

That night, Mr. Davis felt ashamed of himself. Maybe he shouldn't have shouted so loudly or threatened to take his business somewhere else. "But I have a right to be angry! They didn't do a good repair job," he reasoned.

But that little inner voice wouldn't be quiet. As he tried to go to sleep, Mr. Davis thought about the incident again. "Well," he said to himself as he tried once again to shrug it off, "what difference does it make? Who cares?"

Instantly the answer came to his mind, "God cares."

Then and there, Mr. Davis made up his mind to call the mechanic and apologize for what he had said and how he had said it.

Q

How can I develop honesty?

A

Honesty develops as I obey God's Word and keep a clean conscience.

PARENT:
A helpful book for you and your older children to read together is Honesty, Morality, and Conscience *by Jerry White, published by Navpress, 1979.*

◆ **TAKE A LOOK / Acts 24:16**
Like Mr. Davis, you too have a conscience which lets you judge your own actions. Conscience is that inner part of you which forces you to make a choice between obeying God's law or ignoring it. Sometimes the "voice of conscience" comes through loud and clear. At other times it can be drowned out by other voices. But that's one of the reasons God has given you His Word, the Holy Spirit dwelling within, and good Christian friends. Together they can help you use your conscience to stay on the path of honesty.

Look up the following verses, and watch for words which describe the conscience. Put a star beside the descriptions of how your conscience ought to be:

According to . . .	the conscience can be . . .
Acts 24:16	_____
Hebrews 9:14	_____
Hebrews 10:22	_____
1 Timothy 3:9	_____
1 Timothy 4:2	_____

▲ **TAKE A STEP**
Your conscience is a God-given guidance system to steer you in the right direction. It will never lead you to do anything which is against God's Word. How did Mr. Davis's conscience guide him? Share with each other the last time you obeyed the "voice" of your conscience.

HOLY SPIRIT

*B*radley felt important as he entered the sanctuary. The children's worship service had been a special part of his first five years, but now that he was six, Bradley would attend the regular service.

Sitting between his parents, Bradley felt excited that he could find the numbers in the hymnal. He listened intently to the prayers and solemnly put his offering in the plate. But now, as the congregation sang the doxology, Bradley was shocked to hear these words:

Praise God from whom all blessings flow,
Praise Him all creatures here below,
Praise Him above, ye heavenly hosts,
Praise Father, Son, and Holy Ghost. Amen.

With a worried look Bradley leaned over and whispered loudly to his father, "Dad, we don't believe in ghosts, do we?"

◆ THINKING ABOUT THE HOLY SPIRIT

Bradley didn't know that *the Holy Ghost* is an earlier name for the Holy Spirit. It is still found in many old hymns and in some translations of the Bible, but the Holy Spirit Himself is not ghostly. The Holy Spirit is **the helper Jesus sent to be with His followers while He is away.**

When Jesus first told His disciples about the Holy Spirit He made this promise:

● KEY VERSE ON THE HOLY SPIRIT

"I will ask the Father, and he will give you another Counselor to be with you forever—the Spirit of truth" (John 14:16-17).

▲ TAKE A STEP

Jesus knew His disciples would feel like orphans when He went away. His followers then and now would need someone to comfort them, care for and guide them.

Read more of Jesus' promise in John 14:15-20, 25-27. Can you discover where the Holy Spirit lives today and what He does in the lives of God's children?

"I thought you were going to lead me not into temptation."

The Holy Spirit is the Lord Himself

"I hope we don't get lost in here," Michelle said as she and Cathy entered the huge museum. Their tour group planned to meet again at six o'clock, but now the girls had the entire afternoon to explore part of the museum they had missed earlier.

"Don't worry," Cathy said confidently as she approached the information desk. "May we have a map, please?" she asked.

The information agent chuckled. "We can do better than that," he said in heavily accented English as he handed each girl a set of headphones. "Follow the blue line on the floor from room to room. Each exhibit hall has information recorded in ten different languages. You just plug in and press the button for your language. Enjoy your individualized guided tour."

Q

Who is the Holy Spirit?

A

The Holy Spirit is the Lord Himself, sent to guide me into all truth.

◆ **TAKE A LOOK / John 16:5-7**

Wherever Cathy and Michelle went in the museum their electronic guide was there to instruct them. But better than any electronic guide, every Christian has a personal Guide who loves him, understands him, and lives inside him.

Before Jesus returned to heaven, He promised His disciples that He would send Someone just like Himself to guide them and be with them all the time. That person is God—the Holy Spirit. Read Jesus' description of the Holy Spirit in John 16:5-7 and in John 14:16-17.

▲ **TAKE A STEP**

The Holy Spirit, who lives in those who believe in Jesus, is God Himself. Acts 5:3-4 which tells about the dishonesty of Ananias and Sapphira, also shows that the Holy Spirit is God. (Notice who is lied to in each verse!) Another verse that helps us understand about the Holy Spirit is 2 Corinthians 3:17.

Now the Lord is the Spirit, and where the Spirit of the Lord is, there is freedom (2 Corinthians 3:17).

The Holy Spirit is more than a power; He is the third Person of the Godhead, sent to comfort, guide, and teach those who confidently trust in God's Son. In the verses you read in John, He is called a Counselor.

Cathy and Michelle received a "guided tour" of the museum. Their tour was even more enjoyable because their "tour guide" knew so much. How many evidences can you point to that show the Holy Spirit is leading in your family today?

John Sanford, his dad, and his friend Allan were headed to the lake, towing an 18-foot catamaran. Allan, who had never sailed before, could hardly wait. With Mr. Sanford at the tiller bar, the boat surged out of the cove into deep water.

"This is fantastic!" exclaimed Allan, "I feel like a seagull."

Unexpectedly Mr. Sanford tacked into the wind to turn the boat, and Allan almost lost his balance. Mr. Sanford laughed. "Sorry, but if I had tacked with the wind, it would have blown us right over."

"Yeah, Dad," John grinned. "It's a good thing you know how to sail this thing. We'd be sunk if you didn't." Quickly he ducked the wet towel his dad threw at him.

◆ TAKE A LOOK / Romans 8:27

In a poem about the wind, Christina Rossetti asks:

> Who has seen the wind? / Neither you nor I:
> But when the trees bow down their heads
> The wind is passing by.

Whether you're sailing, flying a kite, or just enjoying a breeze, you only see the effect of wind, not the wind itself.

Like the wind, God the Holy Spirit cannot be seen. We know Him because of what He does in the lives of men, women, boys, and girls who have received Jesus Christ as Savior. The action words in the verses below show that even though you cannot see the Holy Spirit, He is alive and well!

According to . . .	the Holy Spirit is active in
Romans 8:27	_____
1 Corinthians 12:11	_____
Romans 8:26	_____
Acts 8:39	_____

▲ TAKE A STEP

The Holy Spirit thinks, gives gifts to believers, prays for us, and performs miracles. But perhaps His most exciting work is bringing people into God's family.

> "I tell you the truth, no one can enter the kingdom of God unless he is born of water and the Spirit" (John 3:5).

What day is your birthday? Do you also have a spiritual birthday when you celebrate your birth into God's family? If so, put that date on the family calendar, and plan now to celebrate that most important work of the Holy Spirit in your life.

Don't look now, but the wind is blowing!

Q

If the Holy Spirit is a person, why can't I see Him?

A

The Holy Spirit is God in spirit form.

The best Teacher you could ask for

I t was an awful day," Hannah moaned as she flopped onto the sofa and kicked off her shoes. "I'm so-o-o glad to be home."

"Yeah, me too," Howard chimed in as their mother sat down to listen to the twins. "We had a substitute teacher who didn't know anything. First, our class was late for library period. Then we missed about half our recess because she didn't know we had to go to the office for equipment. By lunch time she was so confused, kids were trying to mess her up."

"Howie's right, Mom," Hannah said when Howard paused for breath. "And she didn't know anything about our subjects either. She couldn't do our math at all. Everybody's so tired of the confusion. We'll all be glad when Mrs. Edwards gets back."

Q

Why did God send the Holy Spirit?

◆ **TAKE A LOOK / John 16:8-15**
Until now, Howard and Hannah hadn't realized how important their teacher really was. Without her, the class didn't run smoothly and by the end of the day, the students were tired and cross.

Jesus knew His disciples would need a teacher after He returned to heaven. But when Jesus spoke of sending another Counselor (John 14:16), He was not talking about a substitute who didn't know what He knew or couldn't do what He did. Jesus was talking about the Holy Spirit, "another of the same kind," a Person who thought as He did, taught as He did, and would guide His followers as He had done. Jesus explained what the Holy Spirit would do in John 16:8-15.

A

The Holy Spirit was given to reveal Jesus to me.

▲ **TAKE A STEP**
Like any good teacher, the Holy Spirit doesn't talk about Himself. He talks about His subject. He stands behind the scene and explains how real Jesus is in our lives.

"The Counselor, the Holy Spirit, whom the Father will send in my name, will teach you all things and will remind you of everything I have said to you." . . ."He will guide you into all truth" (John 14:26; 16:13).

Howie and Hannah learned very little from their substitute teacher, but Jesus expects His followers to learn everything from their teacher, the Holy Spirit. After you read 2 Peter 1:21, discuss why the Holy Spirit uses the Bible as a "textbook." Aren't you glad that when Jesus went back to His Father in heaven, He sent the best Teacher you could ever ask for!

*E*ight-year-old Gordy was exploring the area behind Grandpa's yard where the trees and underbrush provided homes for birds and squirrels. Suddenly he saw a bush just dripping with blackberries. "Maybe Grandma'll make another pie," he thought, and he quickly picked the berries and put them in his cap.

Minutes later, Gordy burst into Grandma's kitchen. "Grandma, Grandma! Will you make another blackberry pie?" he asked as he handed Grandma the hat full of berries.

But instead of her usual smile, Grandma frowned.

"Gordon," she asked with alarm, "have you eaten any of these?" When Gordy shook his head no, Grandma finally smiled. "These aren't blackberries at all," she explained. "Eating these would have made you sick. Let's get some real blackberries from my freezer and I'll show you the difference. Then we'll make a pie!"

◆ TAKE A LOOK / Galatians 5:19-25

When you look at fruit trees, you expect to find fruit—apples on apple trees, pears on pear trees, and cherries on cherry trees. And when you look at a Christian, you expect to see the fruit of the Holy Spirit.

After promising to send the Holy Spirit, Jesus talked to His disciples about bearing fruit. He said:
"This is to my Father's glory, that you bear much fruit, showing yourselves to be my disciples" (John 15:8).

One way a Christian produces fruit is by letting the Holy Spirit work in his life to make him more like Jesus. Read first about the works of the flesh and then about the fruit of the Spirit in Galatians 5:19-25.

▲ TAKE A STEP

Gordon picked poison berries because he didn't know what blackberries or blackberry bushes are like. Some people won't know what Jesus is like until they see the fruit of the Spirit in a Christian's life.

Reread Galatians 5:22-23. Did you notice that there is only **one fruit** of the Spirit but that it has **nine parts?** Which of those nine do you see in the person sitting next to you? What kind of fruit does he or she see in you? Divide a piece of fruit into nine parts. As your family nibbles, discuss which part of the fruit of the Spirit needs your attention today!

Your life bears fruit when you let God grow it

Q

What does the Holy Spirit do in my life?

A

The Holy Spirit produces His fruit and helps me become more like Jesus.

SUFFERING

A two-year-old boy suffers brain damage from a high fever.
A wife learns that her husband of 20 years is leaving her for a younger woman.

A month before his wedding, an athletic 26 year-old discovers he has cancer.

A father and his two children are killed in a plane crash.

An active 17-year-old girl is paralyzed from the neck down in a diving accident.

A man is imprisoned for life because he dared to believe in Christ.

◆ THINKING ABOUT SUFFERING

No one ever chooses tragedies like these. We'd much rather have the "good life" of minimum pain and maximum pleasure. But suffering is a real part of human experience. In one way or another, everyone suffers.

Suffering is living without the power to change the pain, grief, or hurt you are experiencing. It is **having to put up with something you want to change very much.** It is knowing that something is wrong, but you're powerless to make it right.

You may not be able to choose what, when, and where you will suffer. You may never know the reason why you suffer. But you can choose how you respond to suffering.

● KEY VERSE ON SUFFERING

I consider that our present sufferings are not worth comparing with the glory that will be revealed in us (Romans 8:18).

▲ TAKE A STEP

This week we'll meet four Christians who endured suffering and became better—not bitter—as a result.

Has your family experienced suffering recently? Do you know friends who have?

Suffering is not necessarily good, but its effect in your life can be. Look up 2 Corinthians 4:17-18; what was the Apostle Paul's attitude toward suffering?

Why didn't God move the rock?

S he was a carefree 17-year-old living life to the brim. But on July 30, 1967 she dived into the murky waters of Chesapeake Bay, hit a rock, and broke her spine, becoming a quadriplegic (unable to move her arms or legs).

Joni Eareckson suffered. Her family and friends suffered. She spent the next two years in physical, mental, and emotional anguish. "Why, God?" she demanded. "Am I being punished for my sins? Did You have to do this to get my attention?"

Eight years later, a group of teenagers asked Joni the very same questions. This time she could share the answers she learned from God's Word:

He does not treat us as our sins deserve or repay us according to our iniquities. For as high as the heavens are above the earth, so great is his love for those who fear him (Psalm 103:10-11).

As Joni learned, suffering doesn't mean God loves us any less. Rather, when we experience suffering, He is present in our lives to make us more like Christ. The wise response is to trust God, not to ask, "Why did You let this happen?"

◆ **TAKE A LOOK / Genesis 3:17-19**

You only need to read the first few chapters of the Bible to discover how God can bring triumph out of tragedy.

God created Adam and Eve as free beings in a world which operates by natural and moral laws. Freedom means being able to cause things to happen, to make choices that count. And the consequences of those choices are all around us today.

When Adam used his freedom to disobey God, that choice caused great change . . . and suffering. Read Genesis 3:17-19 to see how Adam's choice brought suffering to him and his world.

▲ **TAKE A STEP**

When we work within God's natural and moral laws for good, we can harness nature and do things that benefit others. But when God's laws are broken—either deliberately or accidentally— people suffer, as Joni did.

But Joni learned that suffering doesn't mean God loves her less. This month, read the biography of someone whose life was changed through suffering. *Joni* and *A Step Further*, both written by Joni Eareckson Tada, are good books to get you started.

Q

Does my suffering mean God no longer loves me?

A

Suffering sometimes results from my choices, but never because God's love for me has changed.

To find life, you first must lose it

Q

What does it mean to suffer for Christ's sake?

A

Suffering for Christ means being willing to act upon what I believe, regardless of the consequences.

PARENT: You and your child can read the story of these five American missionaries in Through Gates of Splendor, *by Elisabeth Elliot.*

*T*he savage Auca Indians, living deep in the jungles of Ecuador, had never been successfully approached by outsiders. Early in January, 1956—after months of praying, planning, and dropping gifts from an airplane —five young missionaries were hopeful the Auca tribesmen would receive them as friends.

They landed their small plane on a sandy river beach in Auca territory, set up camp, and waited. After several days, one man and two women came to the missionaries' camp. They took the man up in their plane and circled low over his village, hoping he would invite them there. But he didn't, and soon the three Aucas left.

Two days later, ten unarmed Auca men walked out of the jungle. This was it—the moment they had been praying for! But suddenly, as the missionaries greeted their visitors, another group of Aucas attacked them from the jungle.

All five missionaries were killed, their bodies left floating in the shallow river.

◆ TAKE A LOOK / 1 Peter 4:1-5, 12-19

Those five young men obeyed the command of Christ to "Go into all the world and preach the good news to all creation" (Mark 16:15). But they also believed what Jesus had earlier told His disciples:

"Whoever finds his life will lose it, and whoever loses his life for my sake will find it" (Matthew 10:39).

Jim Elliot, one of those five martyrs, had considered the risks. He had written, "He is no fool who gives what he cannot keep to gain what he cannot lose." Reading 1 Peter 4:1-5, 12-19 will help you think about what it means to suffer for Christ's sake.

▲ TAKE A STEP

Do you believe anything strongly enough that you are willing to die for that belief?

Throughout history, many men, women, boys, and girls have endured prison, starvation, torture, and even death rather than disobey the commands of Christ. And the world has been changed because of their actions.

Suffering for Christ is not limited to missionaries. You may someday find yourself ridiculed in school, demoted on your job, or mistreated in your neighborhood because of your beliefs. From the verses you've read today, select one to commit to memory—a verse that will help you prepare now to stand firm for your Lord then.

As he stumbled from the burning wreckage of his plane, singer Merrill Womach did not realize how severely he had been injured. He wasn't aware that his face was badly charred nor that his nose and ears were nearly burned away. Though he felt terrible pain, he had no idea that during the next 11 years he would undergo more than 100 operations to rebuild his face.

But even in the car heading for the hospital and during the long, slow journey toward recovery, Merrill Womach still sang. His songs were not bitter cries of pain and self-pity; they were praises to God . . . the One who spared his eyesight and vocal cords . . . the One who would also give him strength to face the future and bring blessing to others through song.

◆ **TAKE A LOOK / Habakkuk 3:16-19**

Merrill and his wife Virginia had learned over the years through their study of God's Word that He can use every circumstance of life for His glory and their growth. When Merrill's tragedy hit, they knew God could and would provide strength to persevere. Their confidence in Him was sure.

Not everyone can sing with a rich, mellow voice like Merrill Womach. But everyone can respond to suffering with an attitude of praise as he did!

Think of some of the Bible characters who praised God while suffering: Paul and Silas who sang in the dungeon, Job who refused to curse God, and David who wrote psalms while fleeing for his life. But one sufferer you may not think of is the prophet Habakkuk. Read his response to suffering in Habakkuk 3:16-19.

▲ **TAKE A STEP**

There's truth in the old saying, "When you're flat on your back, there's no place to look but up." Suffering provides a unique opportunity to sense God's presence. Many who have suffered for weeks, months, or even years tell how real God's presence was to them during those pain-filled hours. Like the psalmist, they told themselves:

Why are you downcast, O my soul? Why so disturbed within me? Put your hope in God, for I will yet praise him, my Savior and my God (Psalm 43:5).

Test your response to suffering by sharing how you faced the last painful circumstance that came your way. How did you respond? Was "Praise the Lord" easy for you to say?

Songs in the dungeon, praise in spite of pain

Q

How should I respond to suffering?

A

Suffering is an opportunity for me to praise the Lord.

Living for the Lord is life well lived

Q

How can suffering help me know God better?

A

Suffering can make me more like Jesus if I respond to it properly.

PARENT:
Johnny Haggai's story is found in My Son Johnny, *by John Edmund Haggai, published by Tyndale House.*

No one expected a baby with such horrible brain damage to live, especially in 1950 when so much of the life support equipment used in today's hospitals was yet to be invented. But by God's grace, the baby did survive.

Knowing that every life has purpose, Mrs. Haggai determined to care for her son Johnny at home. Her tireless, tender care helped develop her son's bright mind that was painfully trapped inside a useless body. And when Johnny accepted Jesus Christ as his Savior, she guided him into his own unique ministry of prayer.

Though he communicated with only two words—yeah and um—Johnny's prayers played a vital role in his father's growing worldwide ministry, the Haggai Institute. After 24 years of suffering pain that continually intensified, Johnny left the prison of his body and went to be with his Lord. He had lived his life fully for God.

◆ **TAKE A LOOK / 2 Corinthians 4:7-12, 16-18**

In writing the story of Johnny's life, his father said, "I dare to tell you that Johnny lived a life of unique significance." Just how significant Johnny's life was may never be fully known in this world. But the lives of Johnny and his mother demonstrate that some of God's most important work is done in and by people who constantly but quietly suffer.

Like Johnny Haggai and his family, the Apostle Paul didn't waste his time in aimless sorrow. His one great goal in life was to know Jesus Christ in the closest way possible.

Paul used every circumstance of his life—whether joyful or sorrowful—as a steppingstone to bring him closer to that goal. Read what Paul has to say about suffering in 2 Corinthians 4:7-12, 16-18.

▲ **TAKE A STEP**

Paul didn't complain about his suffering. Instead, he let God use his times of suffering to make him more like Jesus. He wrote:

Now if we are [God's] children, then we are heirs—heirs of God and co-heirs with Christ, if indeed we share in his sufferings in order that we may also share in his glory (Romans 8:17).

Paul knew that what happens in us is more critical than what happens to us. Take turns sharing lessons you have learned from pain—either in your own life or the life of someone you know—that have caused you to become more like the Savior.

ANGER

"*L* eave that alone!" 11-year-old Julie shouted at her older brother. "That's my money."

But 15-year-old Jason kept taking money out of the box on his sister's dresser. "I don't care," he said. "You took my tape and now it's broken. Dad never does anything to you when you mess with my things, and that makes me so mad. This time you're going to pay."

Jason stormed out the door. Crying with rage, Julie ran to her mother. But Mrs. Walters was angrily scolding the twins for getting muddy.

Ten minutes later, Mr. Walters came home with a scowl on his face. "I'm sick and tired of doing more than my share of work at the office," he muttered. "If there's anything I need tonight, it's peace and quiet."

◆ THINKING ABOUT ANGER

If the truth were known, we are more likely to feel anger—and feel it more strongly—toward family members than toward strangers. Lifelong relationships can be affected by how we deal with anger.

Anger is **the emotion you feel when you think that you or someone you love is being treated unfairly.** Sometimes that emotion explodes into rage or indignation. Or you may bottle it up inside as resentment or bitterness. The Bible has much to say about anger and how to deal with it.

● KEY VERSE ON ANGER

Man's anger does not bring about the righteous life that God desires (James 1:20).

▲ TAKE A STEP

Nearly every day we face things which may make us angry.

Think back to Julie and Jason. Who expressed anger outwardly as rage or indignation? Who expressed it inwardly as resentment or bitterness? Now read Psalm 37:8 to see where anger leads!

"*My temper, my patience, my composure.*"

Should I blow off steam or count to ten?

"Len, I can't believe you're taking money from Granddad!" Troy said angrily to his nephew. "I never took money for doing chores when I was a boy."

"But it's a good deal for both of us, Uncle Troy," Len explained. "Granddad said he'd rather pay me than somebody else. Anyway, I'm saving for a car—I'm not trying to rip Granddad off!"

"Don't get smart with me," Troy shot back.

Just then, Troy's five-year-old son joined in happily. "I'm saving too, Daddy. I'll have $20 when you give me my allowance.

Angrily Troy turned on his son and snapped, "Don't you start, too. One greedy kid in the family is enough!"

A hurt, puzzled look came over the little boy's face. "What did I do wrong?" he wondered as tears welled up in his eyes.

Q

Is anger always sin?

A

Anger expressed with hurtful words or deeds is sin.

◆ TAKE A LOOK / Proverbs 22:24-25; 29:11, 22; Matthew 5:22

Some people think the Bible gives us a green light to be angry. Ephesians 4:26 says, " 'In your anger do not sin': Do not let the sun go down while you are still angry." You may not realize that the Apostle Paul was quoting Psalm 4:4:

In your anger do not sin; when you are on your beds, search your hearts and be silent (Psalm 4:4).

Neither the Apostle Paul nor the Psalmist David is encouraging us to "blow our stacks" before night comes. Rather, these verses encourage us to "calm down, cool off, and think twice" before letting anger express itself in a hurtful way. As you read the following verses, look for words that describe how anger is often expressed. Jot down a word or phrase that tells why angry words and deeds are sinful.

Anger expressed harmfully is sin . . .

Proverbs 22:24-25   Proverbs 29:11, 22
Matthew 5:22   Ephesians 4:31

▲ TAKE A STEP

Anger is sinful when it is expressed in ways that harm you or others. Uncle Troy's son had nothing to do with the situation that made his father angry. What do you think Uncle Troy should say or do to heal his son's hurt feelings? Think of a time you were angry at someone who was innocent. What did you do to make things right?

When Mr. Dobbins called on him in English class, Jimmy mustered his courage and stammered out an answer. Muffled giggles echoed around the room. After class some of the boys started giving Jimmy a hard time.

"Wh-wh-what was that you said in class, Jimmy?" Todd mimicked. "I couldn't understand you. Did you have marbles in your mouth?"

"Maybe it was a foreign language," Wally laughed.

Hearing their cruel taunts made Bob clench his teeth in anger. Bob knew Jimmy had been working hard to overcome a speech problem caused by a birth defect. Now Bob made his way through the sea of students to Jimmy's side. "Come on, Jimmy," he said as he grabbed his classmate's arm, "we're almost late for biology."

Jimmy didn't say a word, but as his eyes met Bob's they clearly said what his mouth could not: "Thanks, friend!"

◆ TAKE A LOOK / Mark 3:1-6

One of the verses you read yesterday was:
Get rid of all bitterness, rage and anger, brawling and slander, along with every form of malice (Ephesians 4:31).

That verse speaks of anger as a sin. But in the story above, Bob's anger was not sinful. Since God cannot sin, His anger is not sinful, either. It comes because of His hatred for sin.

Anger on behalf of someone being treated unfairly is called "righteous anger." Jesus Himself expressed righteous anger when He saw God's Temple being misused. In Mark 3:1-6, you'll read of another time when Jesus showed righteous anger.

▲ TAKE A STEP

Jesus knew that the Pharisees were not using the Sabbath to worship God and serve others. They just wanted to use the man with the crippled hand to trap Jesus into breaking their own Sabbath rules. Jesus knew the Pharisees really didn't care about the suffering man himself, so He showed righteous anger toward them.

Our anger is usually not righteous. We usually become angry when we are hurt, not when someone else suffers unjustly. Think back to the story of Bob and Jimmy. Why do you think Bob's anger was not sinful? Can you share a situation from your life when you were angry without sinning?

There's a time when being mad isn't bad

Q

What is righteous anger?

A

Anger on behalf of someone being treated unfairly is righteous anger.

PARENT:
Discuss Ephesians 6:4 and encourage your child to tell you what he or she thinks of your style of discipline.

Caution: if you let off steam, you may get burned!

Q

What is the best way to deal with my own anger?

A

Anger disappears when I choose to love instead.

Two famous preachers, Joseph Parker and Charles Spurgeon, had large churches in London during the 1800s. Dr. Spurgeon also ran an orphanage. One Sunday the Rev. Parker mentioned the poor condition of children who were taken into the orphanage. Gossips twisted his words and the news came back to Dr. Spurgeon as a criticism of the orphanage itself. As a result, he angrily attacked the Rev. Parker in a sermon.

Now this was news . . . two ministers in a battle of words! But Rev. Parker had been misquoted, misunderstood, and mistreated. Now it was his turn to be angry!

But the next Sunday he stood before his congregation and said, "I know this is the Sunday Dr. Spurgeon usually takes an offering for the orphanage. I also know that he is not there today. So I suggest we take a love offering here for the orphanage."

◆ TAKE A LOOK / Isaiah 53:3, 7-8; 1 Peter 2:23

Rev. Parker had every reason to become angry. But instead of expressing anger in bitter, hateful words, he changed the whole situation with love and forgiveness. The excited crowd filled the collection plates three times with gifts for the orphans, and Dr. Spurgeon later apologized to Rev. Parker.

Yesterday you read about Jesus' righteous anger on behalf of the crippled man. But when Jesus was arrested, beaten, and illegally tried, He remained silent. Unfair treatment did not cause Jesus to express anger. Turn to Isaiah 53:3, 7-8 and notice how those verses describe the suffering Servant, Jesus. Then read 1 Peter 2:23. Can you find a reason why He didn't become angry?

▲ TAKE A STEP

Perhaps you think that "letting off steam" is the best way to handle anger. But studies show that people who express anger forcefully usually become even angrier.

If you believe the truth of God's Word and want to live a life of love, you do not have to express anger in harmful ways. Like Jesus, you can choose to give up your right to be angry because

[Love] is not self-seeking, it is not easily angered, it keeps no record of wrongs (1 Corinthians 13:5).

Read 1 Corinthians 13:5 aloud, but substitute your name for the words "love" and "it." Think of that verse today to help you respond to your own anger with words and acts of love whenever someone mistreats you.

Mr. Robb's fist hit the table hard, rattling the dinner dishes. "Didn't it occur to you to ask me before you wrote that check?" he yelled at his wife. "Now the account will be overdrawn!"

Mrs. Robb winced but said nothing. She could feel her face getting as hot as the dishwater her hands were in. She turned to explain, "It's not what you think. I—"

"It's just plain stupid," he interrupted. "Can't you even add and subtract right?"

"I'm as smart as you are, and I can yell as loud as you can," Mrs. Robb thought angrily. Then, she remembered what the Bible said about anger. She paused.

"I'm sorry," she said quietly. "I did make a mistake and I can explain it. But I don't want to argue with you, and I won't be angry."

◆ TAKE A LOOK / Genesis 4:1-12

How often have you heard someone say, "Count to ten—and if that doesn't work, do it again!" That's good advice for controlling anger, and it really works. The problem is getting people to put that advice into practice!

Ephesians 4:26, which you read earlier this week, is a strong warning that anger must be expressed in a helpful rather than hurtful way. The very next verse explains why:

"In your anger do not sin": Do not let the sun go down while you are still angry, and do not give the devil a foothold (Ephesians 4:26-27).

The first case of anger in the Bible took place between the world's first pair of brothers. Read the story of "The Anger that Ended in Awful Sin" in Genesis 4:1-12. How is God's warning in Genesis 4:6-7 similar to the one in Ephesians 4:26-27?

▲ TAKE A STEP

Anger expressed in a sinful way can lead to something worse. Cain did not learn to control his anger and, in the end, murdered Abel. Much of the violence in families is due to uncontrolled anger.

Three verses show us God's way to handle anger: Overlook the offense (Proverbs 19:11); forgive the one who caused the anger (Ephesians 4:32); and leave vengeance to God (Romans 12:19).

Discuss as a family how Mrs. Robb used those three verses to be a peacemaker instead of an angry participant in the disagreement with Mr. Robb. Did the devil get a foothold?

Count to ten, then count to ten again!

Q

How should I respond to others' anger?

A

Anger cannot grow into something worse when I respond with forgiveness.

PARENT:
When you find yourself in a volatile situation, back off and reflect. Your responses to such situations teach your children more than words could ever say.

YOUTH

The first Sabbath after his thirteenth birthday is a special day for a Jewish boy. By participating in the "bar mitzvah" ceremony on that day, the young man officially takes his place as an adult in the community. He has carefully studied the law of the Old Testament, and from now on he will be held responsible for his own actions. To celebrate the joyful occasion, relatives and friends attend the ceremony in the synagogue and then bring gifts to the home, for on that day the child has become a youth.

◆ THINKING ABOUT YOUTH

One mother exclaimed, "Jesus loved the little children all right, but He didn't have to live with my teenager!" Teenagers could just as easily say, "Jesus may have obeyed His parents, but it's a good thing He didn't have to live with mine!"

Because modern cultures don't really distinguish between childhood and youth, many families face confusion during those years we call the **teens.**

The Bible doesn't use the word *teenager* to describe young people between the ages of 12 and 20, but it does distinguish between childhood, youth, and old age. Youth is **a period of physical, intellectual, and spiritual strength which begins in the teenage years.** God's instructions for youth, then, are also God's instructions for you if you are a teenager.

● KEY VERSE ON YOUTH

The glory of young men is their strength (Proverbs 20:29).

"My Dad got one of those new talking cars. It says fasten your seatbelt, take your keys, and slow down, young man."

▲ TAKE A STEP

At some time, each member of your family will go through the stage of life we call the "teens."

In Psalm 103:2, 5, David compares his youth to an eagle's strength. After reading those verses aloud (and Isaiah 40:28-31 if you have time), take turns sharing reasons why the eagle is an excellent illustration of youthfulness.

"*S*ee you around eleven!*" Connie called cheerfully as she breezed out the door.

"*Where's she going now?*" Mr. Colson grumbled to his wife as he settled down with the evening crossword puzzle.

"*She's going to babysit,*" Mrs. Colson replied. "*She'll be okay.*"

"*No doubt she will,*" her husband sighed. "*I'm just wondering how she does it all. She spends all day in school, every afternoon at basketball practice, and there's an activity nearly every night—Junior Civitan, church group, football games, drama club, running around with friends . . . does she ever sleep?*"

"*Oh, Carl,*" Mrs. Colson chided, "*she's a teenager!*"

◆ TAKE A LOOK
Judges 13:1-6; Numbers 6:2-3, 5, 8

That picture may be exaggerated, but not by much. Young people live life in the fast lane. They take pride in having physical strength, building close friendships, and learning new skills. But physical stamina, growing minds, and a deepening spiritual understanding are strengths God has given young people for a reason.

I write to you, young men, because you are strong, and the word of God lives in you, and you have overcome the evil one (1 John 2:14).

Samson, a young man who lived during the time of the judges, was given extraordinary strength so he could deliver God's people, the Israelites, from their enslavement to the Philistines. Read the beginning of Samson's life story in Judges 13:1-6. Then read Numbers 6:2-3, 5, 8, which describes the Nazirite vow Samson took.

▲ TAKE A STEP

In Numbers 6:8 you read the phrase "consecrated to the LORD" or "holy to the LORD." This means set apart for the purpose of serving God. In the Old Testament, any young person who took the vow of a Nazirite felt that he or she had a special work to do for God.

End your family time by trying to think of at least five ways in which youthful strength can be channeled into God's service. Will you "set yourself apart" to do at least one item on that list this week?

Why sleep if there's anything else to do?

Q

What is special about youth?

A

Youth is a time of special energy and opportunity to serve the Lord.

Hey, every-body! Look at me!

Furious with anger, Frank slammed the door to his room. "Why couldn't Dad let me have the car just once without asking a million questions?" he thought. "He must've never had any fun when he was young!"

"I am old enough to wear mascara," Cherise fumed to her reflection in the mirror as she scrubbed her face. "I may have to wash it off now, but I can always put it on again at school."

"Come on, Dad! Let me stay out past my curfew just this one Saturday! It won't hurt me to miss Sunday school one time. I'll be there in time for the worship service! This party is going to be too good to miss."

"Mom, will you ask Dad to give me my allowance early? Emily and Rachel each bought a blouse and I wanted one too. Now I don't have enough money left to get me through the week. But Dad'll give me some extra money if you ask him, Mom."

Q

What are the opportunities of youth?

A

Youth is a time to harden my heart against selfish desires.

PARENT:
In case you're stumped, the answers above are b, e, d, a, c.

◆ **TAKE A LOOK / Luke 15:11-23**

The opportunities a young person faces today are unique. Information is easily accessible and rapid, efficient transportation brings distant places close. But despite this progress, the temptations young people meet really haven't changed.

Jesus spoke of a young man who faced the temptations of his day but had no strength to stand against them. After you read Luke 15:11-23, match the words in the verses with the words that describe the results in his life.

These Words and Deeds . . . led to these consequences:

____ "give me" (v. 12)   a) Sinful living
____ "got all he had" (v. 13)   b) Self-will
____ "set off for a distant country" (v. 13) c) Starvation
____ "wild living" (v. 13)   d) Separation
____ "he longed to fill his stomach" (v. 16) e) Selfishness

▲ **TAKE A STEP**

In his letter to a young friend named Timothy, the Apostle Paul gave this warning, which still applies today:

Flee the evil desires of youth, and pursue right-eousness, faith, love and peace, along with those who call on the Lord out of a pure heart (2 Timothy 2:22).

With that command in mind, tell what "evil desire" (temptation) you think each young person in the introduction faced, and the advice you would give to help them "pursue righteousness."

I don't think I can stand to read this same story book again!" 13-year-old Dana thought. Then she had an idea. "Elsie," she said brightly, "why don't you read it to me!"

As Elsie recited the much-loved story, her baby-sitter took a bottle of nail polish out of her purse and carefully began coating her fingernails. Elsie's eyes widened in wonder. "Put some on me, Dana, please!" she begged, holding out her tiny hand.

"Okay. But I'll have to take it off before bedtime."

The next morning Elsie's mother heard a sudden crash from her bedroom. Rushing in, she found Elsie watching bright-red nail polish ooze onto the carpet.

"Oh, no," Mrs. Woods moaned. "What were you doing in my nail polish?"

"Dana showed me how last night," Elsie replied innocently, "and I want to be just like her."

◆ TAKE A LOOK / 2 Chronicles 34:1-8, 18, 29-31

Because Dana didn't realize how her behavior affected Elsie's, she unknowingly led Elsie to do something wrong.

After the reign of King Solomon, the nation of Israel was divided into two countries, Israel in the north and Judah in the south. Many of the kings who reigned over these nations were wicked. But one outstanding king was a young man named Josiah who ruled in Judah. He was influenced to do great things for God by the godly example of an earlier king. As you read a portion of his story in 2 Chronicles 34:1-8, 18, 29-31, see if you can find the name of the king whose life influenced Josiah.

▲ TAKE A STEP

Josiah became king at age eight. At 16 he was influenced by the life of King David and began to seek David's God (v. 3). At 20 he destroyed the places where false gods were worshiped (v. 3). At 26 he repaired the temple of the Lord, discovered the lost book of the Law, and led his people back to the Lord. Josiah truly obeyed the command given to a young man in the New Testament:

In everything set them an example by doing what is good (Titus 2:7).

Putting on nail polish seems a small thing, but Dana's example brought unpleasant results for Elsie. What kind of example are you setting where you are observed by someone younger than you?

Be careful what you do; little eyes will watch you

Q

What is the challenge of youth?

A

Youth is a time to be a good example for others.

Haste makes waste; wisdom wins the race

Q

What is the responsibility of youth?

A

Youth is a time to respect those who are older.

PARENT:
If your child doesn't have grandparents living nearby, ask an older person in your church to be an adopted grandparent who will participate in a family activity or take a special interest in your child.

*H*e sure is taking his time—and ours too!" Cal angrily pointed to the car ahead. "I can't keep poking along at 30 m.p.h. . . . we'll all be late to the game!" He gunned the engine and roared past the old man, nearly scraping his fender.

"That old clunker he's driving must be from the 50s," said Mac, frowning. "He's too old to be driving, if you ask me."

"What I can't stand are old people in checkout lines. They always count out their change to the penny as if they had all day," David griped.

"Hey! You guys act like you've never had a grandparent—and never intend to be one," Sam spoke up. "Sure, older people are slower, but I wouldn't take anything for Granddad's stories or Grandma's cooking. And the other day my Granddad gave me some advice that saved me a lot of wasted hours. I'm glad I slowed down and took the time to listen."

◆ TAKE A LOOK / 2 Kings 2:23-25

Cal and his friends—all except Sam—acted disrespectfully toward the old driver. And they criticized older people who interfered with their speed, comfort, and pleasures.

A group of young men in Old Testament times —like Cal and his friends—jeered at Elisha the prophet as he walked along the road. But Elisha had help from a very unusual source. Read the story of "The Baldheaded Prophet and the Brash Young Men" in 2 Kings 2:23-25.

▲ TAKE A STEP

The Bible doesn't say why the young men were jeering at Elisha. But the outcome shows clearly what God thought of their behavior.

God understands youthful enthusiasm, but He also intends that it be balanced by the wisdom and experience of those who are older. He gave this specific command:

Rise in the presence of the aged, show respect for the elderly and revere your God. I am the LORD (Leviticus 19:32).

Until Sam spoke up, Cal and his friends weren't thinking of the ways older people contribute to the lives of those who are younger. Perhaps you too are slow to realize how much your older relatives and friends mean to you. Take turns telling how an older friend or relative has helped you recently.

ENDURANCE

N *ow that the mornings were getting colder, all Charles wanted to do*
was pull the covers over his head when the alarm sounded at 5 A.M.
But he knew the newspapers were stacked and waiting for him at the
pickup point. "I can't quit now—not this close to my goal," he thought.

Five years ago Charles's dad had urged him to begin saving for col-
lege. So he started with a small route in seventh grade, pitching papers
from his bike. But after he learned to drive, Charles was offered a larger
route. Now his bank balance was really growing, and going to college
next fall seemed almost within reach. "I'll hang in there," he said as he
backed down the driveway. "I can take anything one day at a time."

◆ THINKING ABOUT ENDURANCE
When Charles thought about all the harsh winter days ahead,
he wanted to give up his paper route. But when he decided to take
his job one day at a time, he found the will to endure.

Few of us go through life without facing some kind of obstacle—
a paper route in the middle of winter, a teacher who loves to give
homework, a marriage partner who makes life difficult. Endurance
means **sticking with something that is harder than expected in
spite of difficulties or discouragement.** The Bible tells us that God
Himself is the source of endurance.

● KEY VERSE ON ENDURANCE
May the God who gives endurance and encouragement give you a spi-
rit of unity among yourselves as you follow Christ Jesus (Romans 15:5).

▲ TAKE A STEP
Our English word *endur-*
ance comes from the Latin
word which means "to hard-
en." Job was a man who was
forced to endure many
things. Find three phrases in
Job 23:11-12 that show how
he faced his trials. Then turn
to James 1:12 and James 5:11
to find another word that
means the same thing as endurance. What is it?

"Yes. It was hard being cooped up in the ark with
all the animals in the world, but not as hard as be-
ing cooped up in the car with you and your brother."

Setting the pace for our spiritual race

Dad, you should have been there!" Clay laughed as he recounted what had happened at practice. "Coach Rogers always marks out the course everyone is supposed to run before practice. But some of the guys keep goofing off. They hang around the convenience store until the rest of us run by, and then they fall in with us and act like they've run the whole way. They hardly work up a sweat. But today they really got it.

"After school, Coach told us he wanted to clock everybody's time. So he loaded us all on the bus and dropped us off eight miles from the school! Those loafers had to run this time, but none of them were in shape. Everybody else got back before they did. You should've seen their faces when Coach told them we'd run the same course for the next two weeks!"

Q

Why does God command me to endure?

A

Endurance prepares me for the race God has set before me.

◆ **TAKE A LOOK / Hebrews 12:2-3, 7-11**

The team members who hadn't been running lacked endurance. When the test of endurance came, they lagged far behind those who had trained long hours and prepared themselves for the eight-mile run.

God wants to build endurance into your life so you will have the spiritual strength to face life's problems a day at a time. Just as physical endurance is built by exercise, spiritual endurance also comes by discipline—training that develops self-control. In Hebrews 12:2-3, 7-11, how many things can you find that discipline produces in the lives of God's children?

▲ **TAKE A STEP**

Jesus Himself provides the best example of someone who endured hardship without trying to escape from it. Looking at Him gives us confidence as God disciplines us, building endurance into us for future struggles.

No discipline seems pleasant at the time, but painful. Later on, however, it produces a harvest of righteousness and peace for those who have been trained by it (Hebrews 12:11).

How many people in your family are "in training"? Make a list of each activity that requires some kind of training or discipline: after-school sports, music lessons, dieting, night classes, etc. Have each person tell how he or she is "growing" —learning or improving—in his activities. Decide who has the most painful "training program," and reward that person with a five-minute back rub!

S ince he transferred from a school in another state, Walt would be trying out with other boys who had played together for two years.

"But I've got as good a chance as anyone," he told himself as he walked toward the practice field. "I was as good as the others back home."

Even so, a worried feeling tugged at his stomach. He thought about the workouts he had missed, the weight lifting he had hoped to do but never quite got around to. Oh, he had tried to run a few times and work out at home, but the summer months had been so hot and humid. Mostly he had stayed in his air-conditioned house, helping his mom paint and hang wallpaper.

Now as he sat in the bleachers filling out an information form, Walt watched the returning members of last year's team running plays under the broiling sun. "Why didn't I work harder?" he thought to himself. "Every one of those guys is in better shape than I am!"

◆ TAKE A LOOK / 1 Corinthians 9:24-27

As Walt discovered, staying in shape doesn't happen by accident. In pursuit of better health, millions have joined exercise clubs and spend hours working out each week. Fighting flab and strengthening hearts have become national pastimes.

Though the Apostle Paul wasn't an athlete, he knew that physical fitness is a picture of the spiritual fitness God desires in all of us. As you read 1 Corinthians 9:24-27, see if you can spot three things Paul recommends for building—and maintaining—physical and spiritual endurance.

▲ TAKE A STEP

If Walt had read Paul's advice before he went to the tryouts, he might have been in better physical shape. He would have spent the summer in "strict training" (v. 25). He would have made his body his "slave" (v. 27). He would have set goals for his training and not "run aimlessly" (v. 26). In short, Walt would have planned his exercise program so as to:

Run in such a way as to get the prize (1 Corinthians 9:24).

From the smallest infant to the oldest grandparent, every member of the family can build physical endurance by exercising regularly. Start today by taking a brisk family walk together before bedtime. Brainstorm about what other activities you can do as a family to develop physical endurance.

If you don't use it, you'll lose it

Q

How can I develop physical endurance?

A

Endurance is built through regular exercise.

PARENT: Your family might enjoy exercising to inspiring Christian music (15 minutes twice a week is a good schedule to begin). Ask about available exercise record albums at your local Christian bookstore.

You can't cram for God's final exam

Q

How can I develop spiritual endurance?

A

Endurance comes from believing that God is always in control.

*T*hey'll be so disappointed that I didn't get the job," Mr. Hopkins thought as he turned into the driveway. Things were getting tougher for his family since he lost his job three months ago, but it was remarkable how everybody pitched in to help.

He and Betty had carefully figured out what they could cut from the budget. Then the girls started taking lunches to school, lined up extra baby-sitting jobs, and volunteered to take cuts in their allowance.

But even more amazing than all these economy measures was his family's attitude. Not once had Betty or the girls complained because they didn't have the money for some special occasion. And after every job interview, they reminded him that everything would be all right because God was in control.

"Well," he thought as he closed the garage door, "tonight they'll have another opportunity to 'take the test' and keep on praying."

◆ **TAKE A LOOK / 2 Peter 1:3-8**

Mr. Hopkins was referring to the "testing of faith." When things got tough, his family continued to believe that God is in control. They trusted Him to meet their needs, knowing that

The testing of your faith develops perseverance. Perseverance must finish its work so that you may be mature and complete, not lacking anything (James 1:3-4).

Like the Hopkins family, you too need to know that the exercising of your faith develops endurance. As you read 2 Peter 1:3-8, watch for "perseverance" listed among the "building blocks of Christian character." Pay attention to verse 8, which tells why it's important to have these qualities in your life.

▲ **TAKE A STEP**

Living as a Christian often requires perseverance—the ability to bear up under stress or unpleasant circumstances. The Hopkins children encouraged their dad to endure by reminding him of God's faithfulness.

Take turns reading the first eight verses of Psalm 37. Think of someone you know—a friend, relative, or neighbor—who needs a word of encouragement today. Which of those eight verses would you like to share with him or her? Close in prayer together using verses 5 and 6 to express your own commitment as a family to our faithful Father.

Did this thing shrink at the cleaners?" Kirsten groaned as she pulled at the waistband of her skirt. Glancing in the mirror, she saw that the button was a good two inches from the buttonhole!

Hurriedly, she pulled another skirt from the storage bag and tried it on. But it wouldn't button, nor would the pair of slacks she tried next. "What am I going to do?" she muttered. "Mom was counting on these clothes lasting another winter. Oh, I wish I'd skipped those after-work ice cream cones!"

Quickly she went to the bathroom scales. Ten pounds over what she'd weighed last June! Soon Kirsten was sitting at the kitchen table with her mom, planning a sensible diet. "Lean meat and vegetables for a month ought to do it," she laughed. "I hope my will power holds out against French fries and banana splits!"

◆ **TAKE A LOOK / Hebrews 10:35-11:2, 13-16**

Kirsten endured a diet so she could wear her winter clothes. Some people endure exercise for their health. Still others endure hardships to win a prize.

But sometimes you may not have a choice about what you must endure. And sometimes the rewards of your endurance won't be seen—at least not right away. Those persecuted for Christ's sake may not be rewarded in this world. Christians who must endure the pain of a crippling illness may not be cured. Those who are poor may never be rich. Sometimes as God's children we must endure difficulties without any hope of their going away. But read Hebrews 10:35-11:2, 13-16 to find out when and where God's children will be rewarded.

▲ **TAKE A STEP**

You need to persevere [endure] so that when you have done the will of God, you will receive what he has promised (Hebrews 10:36).

One day you will receive what God has promised! End this week's study by making a "survival kit." Have each family member print the word ENDURANCE at the top of an index card. Down the left side, print WHY? and write out Hebrews 10:36. Below that, print HOW? and copy James 1:2-3. Turn the card over and print REWARD at the top. Print WHAT? at the left side and copy Hebrews 13:14. Finally, write WHEN? and add the words of Revelation 22:12. Carry your survival kit in your pocket or purse today. Give a special prize to the first person who can memorize the entire contents of the card!

It's whether you win or lose and how you play

Q

Why is endurance worth the effort?

A

Endurance will be rewarded when God gives me what He has promised.

PARENT: *Encourage your child by reading stories of courage and endurance. Check your library for biographies of missionaries, explorers, and pioneers.*

GOD'S NAMES

*H*ere's a fun multiple-choice quiz your family can take. Match each slogan with the name of the product it advertises.

"Care enough to send the very best."
" _____ has a better idea."
" _____ is it!"
"There's more for your life at _____."
"The quicker-picker-upper."
"Don't leave home without it."
"Reach out and touch someone."

a. Bounty
b. AT&T
c. Ford
d. American Express
e. Sears
f. Hallmark
g. Coke

Answers: f, c, g, e, a, d, b

◆ THINKING ABOUT GOD'S NAMES

Have you ever said, "Well, it's made by _____ , so it ought to be good"? Through advertising, businesses (the sellers) try to influence consumers (the buyers) to ask for their products by name. For businesses and individuals a good name is a valuable asset.

God also gives attention to names. Sometimes in the Bible He names an unborn baby; at other times He gives adults new names to set them apart. But God has also revealed many of His own names. And God's names can teach us who He is and how He works in our lives.

● KEY VERSE ON GOD'S NAMES

Those who know your name will trust in you, for you, LORD, have never forsaken those who seek you (Psalm 9:10).

▲ TAKE A STEP

Knowing God's names will help Christians know Him better.

How we use God's names is important. You'll discover how serious God is about His names by reading Exodus 20:7, Leviticus 22:2, and Deuteronomy 28:58-59. Then look up the word *revere* in a dictionary. Can you think of three things your family does to revere God's name?

"We're having a test on the pilgrims tomorrow, Sir, and I could use the guidance of Providence."

Meeting Valerie's family for the first time at a holiday dinner made Mitch a little nervous. The names of Valerie's father, mother, and two brothers were no problem, but he was getting confused about her grandfather.

Valerie had introduced him as Mr. Abbott, and later Mitch heard Valerie's father call him "Dad," which was easy enough to understand. But it wasn't long before Valerie's mom called him "P.J.," and her two brothers called him "Diddy" and "Pawpaw." And Valerie called him "Grandpop."

"Why does everyone have a different name for your grandfather?" Mitch whispered to Valerie.

"I hadn't realized that!" she laughed. "I guess we each have a name for him because he's special to us in different ways. When you get to know him, you'll see!"

◆ **TAKE A LOOK / Genesis 17:1**

Lots of people have nicknames based on the color of their hair, their resemblance to someone else, an important event in their lives, or something funny they once did.

In Bible times, a person's given name also meant something. For example, Noah means "rest," and Noah rested on God's promises. Moses means "drawing out," and Moses, who was drawn out of the bulrushes as a baby, also drew God's people out of slavery. So the names of Bible personalities describe their lives or characters.

In a similar way, God's names reveal His character. To know His names is to know better who He is and how He works in our lives. In the verses listed below, find the descriptive name of God. Write what you learn about God from these verses:

This verse . . .	tells me that God is . . .
Genesis 17:1	_____
Genesis 18:25	_____
Deuteronomy 6:4	_____
Deuteronomy 10:17	_____

▲ **TAKE A STEP**

God is all powerful. He is the Judge of the earth. He is the true God. And He is above reproach. Truly, His is the name you can trust!

Some trust in chariots and some in horses, but we trust in the name of the Lord our God (Psalm 20:7).

Share which of the four verses listed above you find most encouraging, and why.

Q

Why does God have more than one name?

A

God's names reveal His character and His care for me.

Only one God but more than one name

"Ohhh, I goofed again!" Melissa complained. "I'll never be able to memorize the words to this song. It's like a foreign language!"

Melissa had been asked to sing a popular devotional song at the Sunday evening service. She was working hard to memorize it but kept stumbling over some unfamiliar words. As she took the cup of cocoa her mother offered, she said, "I think I'd do a lot better if I knew what words like Adonai and El Shaddai and El Elyon mean. How I can find out?"

"Well, someone told me that song has something to do with the names of God," her mother replied. "Now that I think about it, I know I haven't seen those exact words in the Bible. Maybe you should ask Dad."

What does God's name "Elohim" teach me?

◆ **TAKE A LOOK / Genesis 17:1; 15:2**

Like Melissa and her mother, you may have heard or read some of God's names but have never seen them in the Bible. That's because they've been translated from the Hebrew language into English.

The three most commonly used names of God in the Old Testament are:

• Elohim, which is translated into English as God.

• Yahweh, translated Jehovah or LORD (a capital "L" followed by small capital letters. We'll talk more about this tomorrow).

• Adonai, translated Lord (capital "L" followed by lower case letters).

Elohim is the name of God first used in the Bible. It describes God's eternal strength and creative power, and pictures Him as the source of all things.

In the beginning God [Elohim] created the heavens and the earth (Genesis 1:1).

A

God's name "Elohim" tells me He is the almighty, eternal Creator.

The prefix "El" is the shortened form of Elohim. When it is combined with Shaddai, it means something like "God the all-sufficient One." (Read Genesis 17:1 to see how it is translated there.) The name El Elyon is found in Genesis 15:2. (Read that verse to see how El Elyon has been translated in your Bible.)

▲ **TAKE A STEP**

In the Bible Elohim and Yahweh are combined with other words to form at least seventeen different names of God. With the two meanings you just learned, what would you tell Melissa the words of the song mean?

PARENT:
Make sure your child knows the significance of his or her name and why you chose it for him.

I n Old Testament times, men known as scribes patiently copied and recopied the Scriptures. Scribes followed strict rules to avoid mistakes. A scribe first read the sentence he intended to copy and said it aloud. Then he wrote it. He did this with every sentence in a book. After he finished copying a book, he carefully checked his copy by counting the letters. If the number of letters in his copy did not match the number of letters in the original, his copy was destroyed.

A scribe honored God's name each time he wrote it by saying, "I am writing the name of God for the holiness of His name." If he made a mistake in copying God's name, he destroyed all he had written and started over. Scribes were very careful indeed! (If you have time, copy today's Bible reading on a piece of paper the way scribes did. Are you usually that careful when you write?)

◆ TAKE A LOOK / Exodus 3:7, 10, 13-17

Of all the different names of God, Yahweh is the one most often used in the Old Testament. This name was considered so holy that it was never spoken. The scribes left out the vowels and would only write the consonants—YHWH—when they copied the Scriptures. When the Scriptures were read aloud, they said the word "Lord," not God's name. In our Bibles YHWH (or Yahweh) is sometimes translated "Jehovah." Often it is LORD, written with capital letters.

The name Yahweh comes from the Hebrew verb "to be." Read Exodus 3:7, 10, 13-17, which describes when Moses met God and asked Him His name.

▲ TAKE A STEP

God used the name Yahweh (or Jehovah) when He revealed Himself to Moses. He said His name is "I AM."

"I AM WHO I AM. . . Say to the Israelites, 'The LORD, the God of your fathers . . . has sent me to you.' This is my name forever, the name by which I am to be remembered from generation to generation" (Exodus 3:14-15).

God's name "I AM" means that He is the One who is. No one created Him. He never changes. And because He cannot change, His promises to us will not change. Because God is "Yahweh," we can trust Him fully.

Write at the top of your own sheet of paper "I AM" (referring to God). Then complete that sentence in as many ways as you can in two minutes.

Be careful with God's name— He's worth it

Q

Why is "LORD" sometimes written with capital letters in my Bible?

A

God's name, Yahweh, written as LORD in the Bible, tells me that He never changes.

God Is So Great That One Name Isn't Enough

Why is it important that I know God's names?

A

God's names help me discover special things He wants to do in my life.

Leann and two of her friends lugged their band uniforms through the kitchen, hurrying to get ready for the game.

"Hello, Mrs. Hutton," Suzy said cheerily. Gail echoed, "Hi, Mrs. H." But Leann's greeting was the one that caught her mom's attention: "Hi, Ellen! Can we eat at six? We need to get to the stadium early."

A few minutes later, Leann returned to the kitchen, seeing that dinner wasn't ready. "Mom! Didn't you hear me ask if we could eat early?" she wailed.

"Oh, yes, I heard you," her mother replied. "But I didn't think you were speaking to me." Leann blushed.

"Leann," Mrs. Hutton continued, "for you my name isn't 'Ellen.' I'm not just one of the girls. I'm 'Mom.' It's a special name because it's a special relationship, and I'd like you to use it whenever you talk to me. Okay?"

"Sure . . . Mom!"

◆ **TAKE A LOOK / Genesis 22:14**

Leann learned that some names are special because they describe a special relationship.

Yesterday you learned about God's name Jehovah (or Yahweh), which means "I AM." That name pictures God as unchanging and eternal. In the Old Testament's original language, Hebrew, the name Jehovah was sometimes combined with other words to make different names. Discovering these combination names in our English Bibles isn't easy, because they have been translated as sentences. Below are four combination names with their references. In each verse the name is translated as "The LORD—." Write what each name means at the right.

God's name . . .	means . . .
Jehovah-Jireh (Genesis 22:14)	_____
Jehovah-Shalom (Judges 6:24)	_____
Jehovah Tsidkenu (Jeremiah 23:6)	_____
Jehovah-Shammah (Ezekiel 48:35)	_____

▲ **TAKE A STEP**

God's names show us different aspects of His character. When we know God's character, we will discover some of the special relationships we can enjoy with Him. Do you need a Provider, a Peace-giver, a God who is always there? Do you need God's righteousness? Pray about a specific family prayer request related to each of the four names above.

CONTENTMENT

O h, Mom, I got everybody the neatest gifts! Lindy said as she stumbled through the door with two shopping bags.

"You're way ahead of me if you've finished all your shopping," her mom laughed. "You know I always have a hard time finding just the right gifts for your great aunts."

Lindy was puzzled. "Why is it so hard to buy presents for them?"

"Well, when I give a gift, I want it to please the person who receives it. But Aunt Rachel always says, 'It's nice, dear, but I really could have used a . . . [whatever].' She's never content with her gift. And Aunt Beatrice is not as well off as Aunt Rachel, so I always try to find something that's a special treat for her. But she always says being with us at Christmas is better than any gift. She's the most contented person I know. Either way, it's hard to find gifts for those two."

◆ THINKING ABOUT CONTENTMENT

Sometimes success is measured by the money a person makes and what he owns. Many people buy new clothes and even new cars—not because the old ones are worn out, but because they're out of style. We get a good education (why?) to get a good job (why?) to buy a nice house and more things. Like Lindy's Aunt Rachel, many have never learned the meaning of the word enough.

God strongly warns us not to love money or to crave things. He wants His children to learn to be content with what they have and to seek His kingdom above all else.

● KEY VERSE ON CONTENTMENT

*Godliness with content-
ment is great gain
(1 Timothy 6:6).*

▲ TAKE A STEP

Contentment is **trusting God to provide what we need when we need it.**

Read Proverbs 15:6, and then tell why you think Lindy's Aunt Beatrice is a good example of a contented person. What would you give to someone who has "everything?"

"I guess we ought to quit complaining about beets and broccoli. Apparently, we could be eating curds and whey and blackbird pie."

The secret that's easy to learn and hard to keep

What's wrong with me, Janice?" Elaine asked her next-door neighbor as she gestured toward her beautiful home. "I have a swimming pool, two cars, and all the clothes and jewelry any woman could want. Don is making more money than we can spend . . . "

Then she began to sob. "But I'm so unhappy. Don travels so much that when he is home, all we do is argue. We were happier when we didn't have half as much!"

Janice put her arm around her friend and let her cry. She and Elaine had often joked about swapping places, and sometimes she envied Elaine. But now she realized that though Elaine and Don were rich, they were not very happy or content. Janice and George—in their small house filled with not much more than love—had the real treasure.

What was Paul's secret of contentment?

◆ **TAKE A LOOK / Philippians 3:8; 4:13, 19**

Like Elaine and Don, many people spend their lives working at jobs they don't like, to make money they don't want, to buy things they don't need, to impress people they don't know.

But Janice and George were content because their needs were being met by a Person, not by possessions. Like the Apostle Paul, they knew the secret of contentment. While in prison, Paul wrote:

"I have learned the secret of being content in any and every situation, whether well fed or hungry, whether living in plenty or in want" (Philippians 4:12).

Prison is never a pleasant place. And though Paul did not always understand everything that happened to him, he was content. You can discover his secret as you read Philippians 3:8; 2 Corinthians 12:7-9; and Philippians 4:13, 19.

A

Contentment comes from letting God control my life.

▲ **TAKE A STEP**

Paul's "secret" was this: (1) He wanted more than anything else to know Jesus Christ and be like Him. (2) He believed that everything that came into his life— including prison and pain, shipwreck and stoning—was there for God's purpose. (3) He was confident that God's strength would see him through even the most difficult circumstances. In short, he gave God control of his life.

Quickly list three things you think the typical family in your community needs in order to be content. Which means more to your family— Paul's "list" above, or the list you just made?

Hey, Dad, this one's only $3,500. Let's just look at it—please?"

Kip had been pleading with his dad not to buy his grandmother's used mid-sized sedan. He wanted a newer, sporty model.

"Kip, even if we have to put a new engine in Grandma's car, that would be cheaper than making payments on what you want. Besides, there's no way you could pay the insurance."

Kip's dad lowered his paper. "I know you'd like to drive a sports car, but Grandma's car is reliable, and its insurance rates are much lower. I've made my decision. Your pride can keep you from driving it, or you can be content just to have wheels. The choice is yours."

◆ TAKE A LOOK / Luke 12:13-23

Kip should have been excited simply about having a car. Instead he felt deprived because that car wasn't new. Kip was comparing what he had with what others had. And the result? Covetousness instead of contentment.

Again and again in the Bible you'll read that God wants His children to be content with what they have. God promises to meet all your needs, but not to give you everything you want. Jesus spoke often of the dangers of greed:

"Watch out! Be on your guard against all kinds of greed; a man's life does not consist in the abundance of his possessions"
(Luke 12:15).

Just after He said those words, Jesus told the parable of "The Man Who Had It Made." Read Luke 12:13-23 to get the whole story; then tell why you think Jesus used such strong language about greed.

▲ TAKE A STEP

Selfish and greedy, the rich man centered his life on his gold instead of his God. He was so concerned about what he owned that he completely forgot God, who owned him. Jesus called this man a fool, for after he died, he had nothing.

Kip may not have been as wealthy as the rich fool, but he had the same wrong attitude. His thoughts were focused on only one thing: getting a sporty car like his friends had. If you were Kip's best friend and you saw what was happening, what would you tell him?

Sacks of silver can't buy the streets of gold

Q

What keeps me from being contented?

A

I am not content when I focus on what others have rather than on God.

PARENT:
Teach your child to live within his means. Help your child make a budget which includes tithing, saving, and the purchase of clothing or school items.

Learning to like the leftovers of life

"I hate squash!" Ginny grumbled as she passed the dish.

"Butter beans—yuk!" said her brother Tim, holding his nose.

"I wish you'd checked with me before planning this meal, Evelyn," Mr. Hatfield said as he sipped his water. "I had ham at lunch today and I really don't want it again."

Mrs. Hatfield shrugged and said pleasantly, "All of you are welcome to do the grocery shopping on our budget any time you like. But until you do, you'll have to eat what I cook or go to bed hungry."

The next evening when Mrs. Hatfield served dinner, there were exclamations of disbelief. "Mother, what are you doing?" Ginny asked. "Oh, no, not again!" Tim groaned.

Mr. Hatfield looked at his wife and said, "You're right, honey. Will you forgive me for complaining?" Then he filled his plate with leftover squash, butter beans, and ham.

How do I know when I'm not content?

◆ **TAKE A LOOK**
Numbers 13:30-31; 14:1-2, 26-34

Grumbling about God's provision is the same as doubting His goodness. God's Word warns of the dangers of discontentment:

Keep your lives free from the love of money and be content with what you have, because God has said, "Never will I leave you; never will I forsake you" (Hebrews 13:5).

When Moses led the Israelites out of their slavery in Egypt, they should have gone straight to Canaan, the land God had promised. Instead, they wandered in the desert for forty years. Find out why by reading Numbers 13:30-31; 14:1-2, 26-34.

A **Contentment is absent when I grumble about what God has done for me.**

▲ **TAKE A STEP**

Here's a short "CQ" (Contentment Quotient) test for you to take: (1) Do you feel sorry for yourself if you don't wear the newest styles, drive a late-model car, or have as much as others? (2) Do you borrow money often so you can have what you want when you want it? (3) Do you feel envious when your friends get something you would like to have?

If you answered yes one or more times, then your "CQ" needs a checkup. Remember, God hasn't changed His mind about grumbling. He wants you to "seek first the kingdom of God, and His righteousness" (Matthew 6:33)!

I wasn't hired to do clerical work," Dot fumed. "If I have to type another letter, I'll go crazy!"
  • "I don't think I can face those students another day," Mr. Jenkins groaned after he shut the alarm off. "Sometimes I wonder if I made the right decision to become a teacher."
  • "If I don't get to play soon, I'll quit the team," Mick grumbled.
  • "The pressures of this job are just too much," Mr. Conway muttered. "I'd quit in a minute if we didn't have two kids in college."
  • "Did I go to college just to wipe runny noses all day?" Mrs. Anderson thought as she watched her three small children argue over their toys. "Maybe I could put the kids in day-care and go back to work . . . "

◆ **TAKE A LOOK**
2 Samuel 15:1-6, 13; 18:6, 9,14-15
God has given each of us different abilities and duties. But every job—from paperboy to president—can glorify God and show others His love.
Absalom was greatly loved by his father, King David. But he had to run for his life when he killed another one of David's sons. For five long years, Absalom remained in exile. Discontented and bitter, he finally returned to Jerusalem to turn the hearts of the people away from his father, the king. Read how he "stole the hearts of the men of Israel" in 2 Samuel 15:1-6, 13. Then read the result of his rebellion in 2 Samuel 18:6, 9,14-15.

▲ **TAKE A STEP**
Absalom's sad story shows how lack of contentment can lead to bitterness and even rebellion. The Bible says:
  No one . . . can exalt a man. But it is God who judges: He brings one down, he exalts another (Psalm 75:6-7).
Even a Christian may be tempted to become rebellious in a routine job. Many part-time jobs filled by young people can be difficult and dreary. If God gives you an opportunity to get a better job, then apply for it—unless by taking it you would disobey God in some other way. Whatever your situation, don't let it cause you to become bitter, rebellious, or jealous. God wants you to be content.
Think back to the five people in the introduction. What would you tell each one about being content?

If God wants you there, you're in the right place!

Q
How can I learn to be content where I am?

A
Contentment comes when I realize that God cares about my situation.

PARENT:
Contentment is an attitude that you can model if you do your job or any unpleasant duties without grumbling.

VALUES

J ames! How many times do I have to tell you to keep your feet off the coffee table?" Mrs. Blake scolded when she walked into the den. *James moved his feet . . . slowly as he gazed out the window at his prized possession—a used car he had bought with his own money.*

A half-hour later, James was engrossed in a TV program, and his feet were . . . you guessed it! Suddenly, something blocked his view. It was his mother, standing between him and the TV set!

"James William Blake," she said, sweeping his legs off the table onto the floor, "this is the last time I'm going to tell you: TAKE YOUR FEET OFF THE DASHBOARD OF MY CAR!"

Startled, James sat up abruptly. Then a smile spread across his face. "Okay, Mom. I get the picture! It won't happen again!" He gave his mother a hug and moved to the recliner.

◆ THINKING ABOUT VALUES

To Mrs. Blake, an attractive home was important. But to James, his car was important. They had different values. What is important to you? Playing sports . . . making the honor roll . . . spending time with friends . . . saving money—lots of things can be "priority one."

Values are **the beliefs and ideas so important to us that they affect our everyday choices and actions.** You may not realize it, but you do have values, and those values can change. You show your values every day by the things you say and do, whether good or bad.

"Every time parental guidance is advised, they exercise it."

● KEY VERSE ON VALUES

"The good man brings good things out of the good stored up in his heart, and the evil man brings evil things out of the evil stored up in his heart" (Luke 6:45).

▲ TAKE A STEP

Turn to John 4:31-35 and read it aloud together. What would you say was the highest value in Jesus' life? Is that value important to your family?

*T*ed Austin hunched over the calculator, checkbook, and the stack of bills. "These house and car payments sure take a chunk out of our bank account," he groaned to his wife. "We've got nothing left over for emergencies. I guess I'd better look for a part-time job."

"But Ted, another job would leave you tired all the time," his wife protested. "Why don't you let me get a part-time job? I've got plenty of time and I want to help out."

"Absolutely not," Mr. Austin said firmly, pushing the calculator away. "My dad never let my mom get a job. He always said a woman's place is in the home—with the children. And I agree!"

Mrs. Austin moved behind him to massage his shoulders. "That's how I feel too," she said softly. "But, Ted, we don't have any children!"

◆ TAKE A LOOK / Philippians 3:4-9

Like Mr. Austin, most of us have inherited many of our parents' values. Things that were important to them have become important to us. Our family, friends, and teachers also have a part in shaping our values. Sometimes it's good to keep the values we "inherit"; sometimes it's not.

As a leader of the Jews, the Apostle Paul was well educated. What others thought and said about him was important to him. But when he became a Christian, Paul's values changed. What he once thought important was replaced with something that had "surpassing greatness." Read Philippians 3:4-9, and you'll see what that something (or rather, Someone) was.

▲ TAKE A STEP

When Paul met Jesus on the road to Damascus, his values changed. Now he could say:
" I consider everything a loss compared to the surpassing greatness of knowing Christ Jesus my Lord, for whose sake I have lost all things. I consider them rubbish, that I may gain Christ" (Philippians 3:8).

Every other person, position, or possession in Paul's life took second place after he discovered the joy of knowing Christ.

In today's story, one of the values Mr. Austin had learned from his parents was that the home is where children are cared for. What are some of your family values? Where did they come from?

Values are as good as their source

Q

Where do my values come from?

A

Values are usually learned from the most important people in my life.

To thine own self be true? Some-times it's hard to do!

Helen looked at the pattern and frowned. "It's a good thing I've got some extra fabric. I'll have to redo this whole piece."

"But Helen," Lois protested, "it's already 5:15 and the midweek youth meeting starts at 6:30. We'd better get ready."

"Count me out, Lois," Helen said, snipping carefully around the pattern. "I've got to start this over and it'll take a while."

"Come on, Helen. You haven't come with me since school started. You promised me you'd go."

"Well, okay. I guess I don't have anything better to do. And I am tired of working on this crazy dress."

"That dress is not crazy—you are!" Lois laughed. "When you get to heaven, you'll probably tell God, 'Well, here I am. I didn't have anything better to do'!"

Q

Why is it helpful to know my own values?

A

My values help me remember what is most important in my life.

PARENT: Rehearse situations your child may encounter involving behavior choices. Determine together the Biblical solutions to such situations.

◆ **TAKE A LOOK / Daniel 1:8-14; 6:3-10**

It's easy for someone to say, "I believe . . ." But the truest test of values is not words, but actions.

Daniel believed he should obey God's laws. But when he was taken from his home in Jerusalem to Babylon as a prisoner, that belief was put to the test. He had to choose what he would do.

Divide your family into two groups. While one group reads Daniel 1:8-14, the other group can read Daniel 6:3-10. Then answer these questions together:

1. What beliefs did Daniel hold?
2. What choices did Daniel face?
3. How did his beliefs affect his choices?

▲ **TAKE A STEP**

When you look behind the scenes in Daniel's life, you'll find that his beliefs showed up in his behavior. God was the most important Person in Daniel's life. By contrast, Helen would have been horrified if her friend Lois had said, "God isn't very important to you!" But that's exactly what Helen's actions were saying.

Sometimes our values—like Helen's—don't always line up with what we say we believe. James puts it this way in his New Testament letter:

"Faith [belief] by itself, if it is not accompanied by action, is dead" (James 2:17).

Can you think of three activities you regularly do as a family because of something you believe with all your heart?

*H*ow was I supposed to know you expected me to pick up Greg?" Nancy said defensively.

Her mother replied firmly, "Nancy, just because we let you drive to school occasionally doesn't mean you can do as you please. Now I'll tell you why you should have known to pick up Greg at his Scout meeting . . . "

Nancy already knew what was coming. She listened sullenly as her mother reminded her that she had been told that morning to come straight home. But after school Nancy had ignored those instructions so she could impress her friends with the car.

"So you knew exactly what to do," her mother said. "If you had obeyed, you would have found the note I left you, and Greg wouldn't have had to wait so long. You really have no excuse."

◆ TAKE A LOOK / Luke 10:38-42

If Nancy hadn't been sidetracked by her own desires, she would have discovered her mother's note and have known what she was expected to do.

God's values are there for all to read in the pages of the Bible and for all to see in the life of His Son, Jesus Christ. But when we get sidetracked by our own desires, we—like Nancy—miss the messages God has given us.

Luke 10:38-42 tells of two sisters who had different sets of values. By reading those verses you'll find that what was important to Martha was not what was important to Mary. How were their values different?

▲ TAKE A STEP

Many people think Christian values are simply a list of do's and don'ts. But Scripture shows that God is just as concerned with attitudes as with actions. His values involve how you relate to Him, to others, and to yourself. When asked what the most important commandment was, Jesus replied:

"Love the Lord your God with all your heart and with all your soul and with all your mind and with all your strength. The second is this: Love your neighbor as yourself" (Mark 12:30-31).

God's values can show you the best way to live. But before you can live by them, you must learn what they are. Like Nancy in today's story or Martha in Luke 10, you cannot learn God's values unless you know where to find them—in God's Word. What would you tell Nancy to do if she truly wanted God's values to guide her life?

God wrote the Book on values

Q

How can I know which values are important to God?

A

Values God wants me to develop are found in the Bible.

PARENT:
Many school systems teach values with no reference to God's Word. Learn what is taught in your child's classrooms and talk about it with your child.

Who's winning the battle for your mind?

In your school classes, have you ever . . .
- *played survival games like "Bomb Shelter" or "Lifeboat"?*
- *been told where to get birth-control devices without your parents knowing?*
- *had classes dealing with witchcraft or meditation?*
- *heard a teacher read you a list of "children's rights"?*
- *discussed personal things with a counselor and then been advised not to tell your parents?*
- *been told that abortion and homosexuality are simply matters of choice or "alternative lifestyles"?*
- *been told there is no such thing as absolute right or wrong?*
- *been encouraged to read books which use bad language or describe immorality in a favorable way?*

◆ TAKE A LOOK / Romans 1:24-32

Everything you read, see on TV, or learn in school is based on someone's values. The situations above are designed to make you doubt Biblical values (which are as changeless as God is).

You can determine the truth of what you are being taught by comparing it with the standard of God's Word. The Bible is the unchanging "yardstick" by which we must measure any idea to decide if we should believe it—or reject it. The Apostle Paul warned about teachings that went against God's Word. He said,

"See to it that no one takes you captive through [the] hollow and deceptive philosophy . . . of this world" (Colossians 2:8).

Read Romans 1:24-32 to see how Paul traces the "decline and fall" of people and nations that turn away from the truth of God.

▲ TAKE A STEP

A battle for your mind is raging—and it's a battle you can't afford to lose! You can guard against false teaching by knowing God's values and by talking often with your parents about what goes on in school.

Suppose you were in a classroom and one of the situations listed above happened. How would you decide the truthfulness of what your teacher was saying? How would you know if you should take part in an activity like that? As a family, discuss one or more of the above situations in detail.

Q

How can I identify wrong values?

A

I can identify wrong values by comparing them to the standard of God's Word.

THANKSGIVING

W hen five-year-old Lila had trouble falling asleep, she would snuggle with her teddy bear and think back over the day.

This week her kindergarten teacher had been reading about thanksgiving celebrations. "I bet the Pilgrims sang songs like we do," she thought. Quietly she began to hum a song she had heard many times. Before long she was singing quite loudly:

> Count your many blessings, name them one by one,
> Count your many blessings, see what God has done.
> Count your blessings, name them one by one—
> And it will surprise you what the Lord has done.

Soon her mother peeked in to see what was happening. "Mom," Lila asked, "would you be surprised if an Indian came to dinner?"

◆ THINKING ABOUT THANKSGIVING

Lila's mother quickly realized that Lila was thinking about the feast at Plymouth Colony in 1621 that is the basis for the holiday Americans celebrate in November. But thanksgiving is more than a holiday. It is both an attitude and an action that God wants all His children to develop and practice.

In Old Testament times, God told His people to celebrate a seven day period of praise every year at the end of the harvest. It was called the Feast of Tabernacles. The New Testament doesn't set aside a particular day or week for thanksgiving. Instead, it encourages us always to practice "thanksliving."

● KEY VERSE ON THANKSGIVING

Give thanks in all circumstances, for this is God's will for you in Christ Jesus (1 Thessalonians 5:18).

▲ TAKE A STEP

Thanksgiving is our grateful response to the goodness of God.

Start this week by reading Psalm 136:1–9. Have one family member read the first half of each verse out loud, and the rest of the family echo the second half together.

"Thank you for the turkey, the dressing, and the squash, which mother so cleverly refers to as pumpkin pie."

Freedoms aren't free until the price has been paid

I pledge allegiance to the flag . . . " the sixth–grade students recited. But out of the corner of his eye, Ben saw Dwight slumped over his desk. He looked bored and sad. "That creep," Ben thought. "Everybody can respect their country's flag."

Later in the cafeteria, Ben noticed how lonely Dwight looked. "Dwight," he said casually, "how come you don't say the Pledge of Allegiance with the rest of the class?"

"Because I think it's a bunch of junk, that's why! You can have your crummy old flag. Just give me back my—" Dwight's lip began to quiver. Ben realized Dwight was about to cry, so he changed the subject. Only later did he learn why the Pledge brought such pain to his friend.

Q

How can I show thanks for the freedoms I have?

A

I can show thanks for my freedoms by knowing and appreciating what they are.

PARENT:
A framed copy of your country's documents of freedom can help your child keep freedom in mind.

◆ **TAKE A LOOK / 1 Samuel 17:20–26, 45-48**

For Ben, the American flag symbolized the freedoms he enjoyed. But for Dwight—whose father had been killed in Lebanon—the flag only reminded him of what he didn't have. Though Dwight didn't realize it, the ability to say freely what he believed is itself a freedom to be thankful for. Since we benefit from these freedoms, we should seek to know and protect them.

Even before he was king, David stepped forward to lead the nation Israel in its fight for freedom against the Philistines. First Samuel 17 tells the well-known story of David's battle with Goliath. But you may not recall why David was angry or why he expected to win against his giant-sized opponent. Verses 20-26 and 45-48 will help you answer both questions.

▲ **TAKE A STEP**

David expected to defeat Goliath, not so much because God was on David's side, but because David was on God's side.

In the same way, Christians today should work to protect the freedoms they enjoy—if those freedoms are in line with God's justice and righteousness. Freedom doesn't mean being able to do whatever you like. True freedom comes when your life reflects God's Word. David wrote,

I will walk about in freedom, for I have sought out your precepts (Psalm 119:45).

The first step in protecting your freedoms is knowing what they are. The word "thanksgiving" has 12 letters, so why not take a few minutes to list 12 freedoms you're thankful for.

B ut Mom! If you talk to Dad, maybe he won't make me go."

"Dad has decided our whole family will take part in our church's planned famine," Mrs. Cranston told 14-year-old Kenny firmly. "Don't worry—you won't starve."

"But Mom," Kenny moaned. "It's not fair! Nine people get roast beef for dinner, half of the rest get sweet potatoes, and everyone else only gets a bowl of rice! What if I get rice and I have to sit next to someone eating roast beef? I'll die! I hate rice."

That Friday Kenny learned a lot about world hunger. "You know," he told his parents later, "the hardest thing was eating that roast beef dinner when everybody around me had nothing but rice. It really made me think. And it made me thankful, too."

◆ TAKE A LOOK / Isaiah 58:1, 3, 6-10

At the church dinner, Kenny realized that millions of people in the world live their whole lives hungrier than he could imagine.

God's Old Testament laws protected the poor. For instance, His people were not to charge interest on loans (Exodus 22:25), nor were they to "reap to the very edges of a field" or go over it a second time, so some food would be left for the poor to gather (Leviticus 23:22).

Years later, one of the sins God condemned was the mistreatment (or oppression) of the poor. Read God's words to His people in Isaiah 58:1, 3, 6-10.

▲ TAKE A STEP

The Jewish nation was told to care for its needy. Jesus fed multitudes. The early church took up collections for famine victims and the poor. Today, centuries later, God has not changed His mind about helping needy people.

Like Kenny, you may not know many facts about world hunger. But you are still responsible to do what you can to help:

If you spend yourselves in behalf of the hungry and satisfy the needs of the oppressed, then your light will rise in the darkness (Isaiah 58:10).

At your next family dinner, set an extra place, but put only a bowl of rice there. How does that make you feel? What would you like to do for that imaginary person? A family offering given to a church or mission program to feed the hungry might help you truly understand thanksgiving!

Saying thanks by giving helps others enjoy living

Q

How can I show thanks for my material blessings?

A

Thanksgiving involves using my material blessings to help others.

PARENT:
Get your family involved in a caring ministry or outreach. Literacy programs, thrift shops, and community meal services can always use help.

Give God praise through all your days

*T*hat first year in the "New World"—America—hadn't been easy. Of the 127 Pilgrims who landed in November 1620, less than fifty survived the harsh winter, the illnesses, the unfriendly Indians, and the lack of food and shelter. At one point only seven people remained healthy, and they unselfishly cared for the rest at the risk of their own lives.

But they did survive! And so in Plymouth, Massachusetts in the fall of 1621, the Pilgrims held a harvest celebration to thank God for their first year in the new land. One man wrote:

> Our harvest being gotten in, our governor sent four men on fowling that we might [in] a special manner rejoice after we had gathered in the fruit of our labors.

Was this the first American Thanksgiving?

Why should I be thankful in trying circumstances?

◆ TAKE A LOOK / Psalm 145:9-21

Surprisingly, Thanksgiving Day didn't become an official American holiday until 1942. The Pilgrims had experienced the hardships of disease and death when they held their feast in 1621. In 1942, when the world was experiencing the horrors of World War II, U. S. President Franklin Roosevelt declared the fourth Thursday in November as a national day of thanksgiving to God.

But wherever you live, God wants you to thank Him—not only when things are going well, but in all circumstances.

Always giving thanks to God the Father for everything, in the name of our Lord Jesus Christ (Ephesians 5:20).

A

Giving thanks in trying circumstances shows that I trust God.

Thanksgiving and praise go together. They're not a magic formula for making circumstances better, but they do demonstrate that you're trusting God with your life— in good times and bad, in plenty and in need. As you read Psalm 145:9-21, a repeated phrase in verses 13 and 17 tells you one important reason why you can praise God . . . even in difficult situations.

▲ TAKE A STEP

God is loving toward all He has made. Like the Pilgrims of 1621, you too can recognize that truth and "rejoice in a special manner" everyday. Let each family member take turns thanking God for these things: 1 difficult situation in your life; 6 specific things God has given you; 2 special people in your life ; and 1 prayer God has answered this year.

M rs. Lane sighed. Her son and his family had
   moved to Canada last year, and the school holi-
days no longer coincided with the American thanksgiving holiday. For the first time, she had been alone.

Suddenly another gloomy thought crossed her
mind: What if the children couldn't come at Christmas
either? Before long, Mrs. Lane felt positively awful.

Then she shook her head. "I sure am being silly,
letting 'what ifs' ruin my day," she laughed. "Life is
'what is,' not 'what if.' I need to turn my eyes upon
Jesus, like the hymn says."

After playing some hymns of praise on her old
piano, Mrs. Lane went to the kitchen. "I'll bake a few
pies and put them in the freezer. Now let's see, mince-
meat is Hal's favorite, and Susie likes pumpkin . . ."

◆ TAKE A LOOK
2 Chronicles 20:2-4, 12-17, 20-26
God commands His children to "give thanks in
all circumstances" (1 Thessalonians 5:18). But like
Mrs. Lane, you probably have found that unhappiness—not thanksgiving—is what you sometimes
feel when things go wrong. You, like Mrs. Lane,
can learn to drive unhappiness away and bring
thanksgiving back when you realize that the secret
of a thankful heart lies in praising God.

The exciting Old Testament story of King
Jehoshaphat shows what can happen when someone praises God in spite of the "what ifs." Jehoshaphat's tiny kingdom was surrounded by powerful
enemies on every side. He knew his people didn't
stand a chance to win the war, but he wasn't ready
to give up. He looked at the enemy's mighty
strength, he looked at his own army's weaknesses,
and then he looked to God for help. Read how
Jehoshaphat faced these threatening circumstances
in 2 Chronicles 20:2-4, 12-17, 20-26.

▲ TAKE A STEP
You can always keep an attitude of thanksgiving if you are willing to say like Jehoshaphat:
"We have no power . . . We do not know
what to do, but our eyes are upon you"
(2 Chronicles 20:12).

Mrs. Lane overcame sad feelings by playing
hymns or praise. Jehoshaphat gained strength to
face the enemy by singing songs of praise. Close
your time together today by singing (or saying)
two songs that include the word praise.

Turn thanks- giving into thanks- living!

Q

*How can I
be thankful
all year
long?*

A

*Thanks-
giving
comes by
praising
the Lord
no matter
what
happens.*

GOALS

"*Hey Drew! I haven't seen you in a long time. What have you been up to?*"

"*Oh, just goofing off, Ron. How about you?*"

"*I'm having some great fun. You remember that old car in my grandfather's garage? My dad and I finally got it running. It was neat to put the engine back together and hear it run like a top. I sure learned a lot about motors. Then I got it painted and put in a stereo system.*"

"*How'd you afford that?*"

"*My folks said they'd pay for half of it if I memorized the whole Book of Philippians—all 104 verses! I thought I'd never make it, but you know, Drew, just a few verses a day did the job!*"

◆ THINKING ABOUT GOALS

Drew aimed at nothing . . . and hit it. Ron set goals and worked toward them. And each boy achieved exactly what he set out to do.

When you hear the word *goal*, maybe you think of a basketball hoop or a hockey net. But you don't have to be an athlete to set and reach goals in your life. All you need is **a clear idea of where you want to go and how you plan to get there.**

Goals are important in all areas of life. Here is a verse that shows that God has spiritual goals for you to reach:

● KEY VERSE ON GOALS

I press on toward the goal to win the prize for which God has called me heavenward in Christ Jesus (Philippians 3:14).

▲ TAKE A STEP

This week our goal is to learn about goals—what they are and how they can help us.

By the way, do you have any goals in your life? Grades to earn, new friends to make, time to spend as a family around God's Word? Now's a great time for you—like Ron—to set goals and hit them!

"*You said I could achieve any goal I cared to set, and I set C.*"

Ten-year-old Matt was trying out his new birthday present—a bow and arrow—when his friend Roger came along.

Roger noticed a series of targets drawn on cardboard boxes. And to his amazement, Roger saw that every target had one of Matt's arrows squarely in the bull's-eye.

"Matt, how did you do that?" Roger asked excitedly.

"It's easy," Matt replied. "Just watch."

Taking careful aim at another cardboard box—this one with no target on it—Matt sent an arrow on its way. It hit the box with a loud "smack!" Matt ran to the box, pulled out a marking pen, and drew the target—with his arrow exactly in the middle!

◆ TAKE A LOOK / Daniel 1:8-19

Matt was learning to become an artist, not an archer, because in order to hit a target you must first have a target to hit!

About 600 B.C. four Jewish boys lived in the land of Israel: Daniel, Hananiah, Mishael, and Azariah. When the Babylonians invaded their country, they were taken far from home to a land where the people knew nothing about their God or their Jewish customs.

There the boys faced a difficult choice: They could either become like their captors and eat the food that Jewish law prohibited—or they could be true to their convictions. Read about their decision in Daniel 1:8-19.

▲ TAKE A STEP

Daniel and his three friends had a goal. Whatever they did and wherever they went, they wanted to please God. Even though the king of Babylon changed their names, he could not change their beliefs. They would not budge from doing what they knew was right!

When you're faced with difficult choices, your goals help you make the right decision. For example, if your goal is to please God and someone asks you to cheat or experiment with drugs or disobey your parents, you will know which path to choose.

"Choose for yourselves this day whom you will serve. . . . As for me and my household, we will serve the LORD" (Joshua 24:15).

What are some of the goals your family can set that will help you serve the Lord in your school, neighborhood, and church?

Aim at nothing and you'll hit it every time

Q

Why is it important to set goals?

A

Goals help to determine what I achieve in life.

You remind me of someone I know!

Four-year-old Mary Beth cradled her favorite doll in her arms. "It's bedtime, Susie. Come here and I'll brush your hair. Doesn't that feel good? Okay, say your prayers and then snuggle down while I read a story."

Mary Beth laid her doll in its crib and tenderly covered it with a blanket. Just then, her mother came into the bedroom.

"Oh, there you are, Mary Beth. I see you've tucked Susie in. Now it's time for me to help you with your pajamas. Let's brush your hair, too. That feels good, doesn't it? Have you brushed your teeth already? Good girl. Now, let's talk to God and then into bed you go. Snuggle down nice and warm while I read you a story."

◆ TAKE A LOOK / 1 Thessalonians 1:4-8

Without knowing it, Mary Beth was becoming like her mother. She was treating her doll with the same love and care that her mother showed her. Even Mary Beth's words sounded like her mother's. She was becoming an imitator of her earthly mother.

Did you know one of God's goals is that you become an imitator of Him? The Apostle Paul says

Follow my example, as I follow the example of Christ (1 Corinthians 11:1).
Be imitators of God . . . as dearly loved children (Ephesians 5:1).

You are to become like your heavenly Father so that you love the things He loves and do the things that please Him.

Was Paul a good imitator of God? Did people learn what God was like by looking at Paul's life? Read 1 Thessalonians 1:4-8 right now and you'll find out. (Notice especially verses 5 and 6.)

▲ TAKE A STEP

Paul made it his goal to become more like his heavenly Father everyday. And because he did, other people also learned what God is like and became imitators of God.

But it didn't happen by accident. Why was Mary Beth able to talk and behave like her mother? Because she spent a great deal of time with her mother. How was Paul able to become an imitator of God? He spent time talking to God in prayer, reading the words of Scripture, and doing things that please Him.

Others can get to know God by getting to know you. Can you think of three ways you can be a good imitator of God today in what you say and do?

Q

What is God's goal for me?

A

God's goal for me is to become more like Him.

PARENT:
Share with your child one goal you have set for your own life. Also, discuss the importance of having friends who share common goals. How does a friendship of this sort give strength in difficult situations?

M om, may I talk to you for a minute?"
"You know you can, Tricia—any time. What's the problem?"

"Well, I need some help with a social studies report. I have to write a four page report on the state government, draw a map of the state, and make a copy of the state flag. I have to use an encyclopedia, a book from the library, and one article from a newspaper. Will you help me?"

"I'll be glad to, Tricia. It sounds like a big project, but if you set some goals, I'm sure you'll find the materials you need to do a really great report. When is it due?"

"Uh . . . "

"Tricia, when is it due?"

"Oh, Mom, it's due tomorrow! I was supposed to work on it all month, but I haven't even started! I don't know where to begin."

◆ **TAKE A LOOK / Nehemiah 4:6-18; 6:15-16**

If Tricia's report sounds like a big assignment, just think about the task Nehemiah faced in about 450 B.C. The walls of Jerusalem had been battered to the ground by the Babylonian army. For more than 100 years, they were rubble. Now it was time to rebuild the walls—all two miles of them! What an enormous job! But Nehemiah knew that:

Those who plan what is good find love
and faithfulness (Proverbs 14:22).

With his goal clearly in view, and counting on God's faithfulness, Nehemiah broke the job into manageable steps. He had each worker build the part of the wall in front of his own house. And when Nehemiah's enemies tried to stop the builders, he came up with a wise plan to keep the project moving along. Read about his plan in Nehemiah 4:6-18; 6:15-16.

▲ **TAKE A STEP**

Nehemiah divided a big job into small steps. But by planning his work and working his plan, the job was done in less than two months—and those walls would stand for 500 years!

Go back to the story of Tricia and her report. Pretend that she still has two weeks before the assignment is due. What steps would you take if you were Tricia in order to be sure the assignment is done well and on time? Why do you suppose she waited so long to begin working on her report?

As parts make a whole, so steps reach a goal

Q

How can I reach my goals?

A

Goals are reached by planning my work and working one step at a time.

Winning isn't everything, but your attitude is!

Beau was obviously upset as he fought back the tears.

"But Dad, it's just not fair. Can you believe it? The ball hit the backboard! It hit the hoop and then bounced away. Why couldn't it have gone in? We really were better. Why didn't it go in?"

"Beau, calm down. I know you're disappointed, but the game's over. Being angry and upset about it won't change the final score."

"I know, Dad, but it was really important to win this one. I've played basketball for seven years. This was my last chance in the league. Now I'll never get a trophy. And we really were better. Why couldn't we have won, Dad?"

◆ **TAKE A LOOK / 2 Samuel 7:1-11**

Everyone likes a good loser—provided it's the other team! In sports, as in all of life, you won't always reach your goal. What then? How should you respond when you've done your best to achieve your goal . . . and still come up short?

King David had a dream—a goal in life. More than anything, David wanted to build a beautiful place where the people of Israel could worship God.

For many years the people had been worshiping God in a tent called the tabernacle. But doesn't the God of heaven and earth deserve something better? David thought so! And being king, he had all the money and manpower needed to build a beautiful temple. But then an unexpected thing happened. Turn to 2 Samuel 7:1-11 and you'll find out what.

▲ **TAKE A STEP**

David wanted to build a house for God, but God told him no. David's goal would not be accomplished during his lifetime.

David could have pouted and fumed when he didn't reach his goal. But that wouldn't have changed anything. Although David didn't completely understand why God said no, he continued to trust God. David discovered this:

Many are the plans in a man's heart, but it is the LORD's purpose that prevails (Proverbs 19:21).

Beau's disappointment at losing the basketball game was understandable, but his response to defeat was just as important as his desire to win. If he had remembered what King David knew, how might his disappointment have been easier to handle?

Q

What if I don't reach my goals?

A

Goals that I miss are new opportunities to trust God and keep trying.

PARENT:
Ask your child to recall a specific disappointment. How does he feel you helped during that time? Tell your child how he has encouraged you when you faced disappointment.

CHRISTMAS MUSIC

*W*hy do bells for Christmas ring?
Why do little children sing?
Once a lovely, shining star,
Seen by shepherds from afar,
Gently moved until its light
Made a manger's cradle bright.
There a darling baby lay,
Pillowed soft upon the hay;
And its mother sang and smiled,
"This is Christ, the holy child!"
Therefore bells for Christmas ring,
Therefore little children sing.
(By Eugene Field. Courtesy of Charles Scribner's Sons)

◆ THINKING ABOUT CHRISTMAS MUSIC

All around the world people celebrate the birth of Jesus. And everywhere one of the most meaningful customs of Christmas is singing.

With opera and oratorio, with carol and cantata, **Christmas music lifts our spirits and turns our hearts in worship** toward the holy child in the manger. With the angels we can rejoice and sing:

● KEY VERSE ON CHRISTMAS MUSIC

Glory to God in the highest, and on earth peace to men on whom his favor rests (Luke 2:14).

▲ LOOKING AHEAD

Long before Bibles were printed, plays were presented in churches and at fairs to teach Bible stories. Easily remembered tunes from these plays soon became popular (sort of a medieval "top forty"!).

Set a timer for three minutes, and as a family name as many Christmas carols as you can before the time is up. Then read Revelation 5:12. Do you know what famous musical work by Handel includes this verse?

"A joyful noise, Philip."

What's so exciting? Come and see for yourself!

Q

Why should I sing Christmas music?

A

Christmas music is a way I can joyfully tell others about my Savior.

See who in your family first remembers the tune to this well-known carol:

> Angels we have heard on high,
>> Sweetly singing o'er the plains;
> And the mountains in reply
>> Echoing their joyous strains.
> **Chorus:** Gloria in excelsis Deo!
>
> Shepherds, why this jubilee?
>> Why your joyous songs prolong?
> What the gladsome tidings be
>> Which inspire your heav'nly song?
> (Chorus)
>
> Come to Bethlehem and see
>> Him whose birth the angels sing;
> Come adore on bended knee
>> Christ, the Lord, our newborn King.
> (Chorus)

◆ **TAKE A LOOK / Luke 2:8-18**

In this carol, the shepherds sing their story to an audience, perhaps of townspeople. "We have heard angels on high!" they announce. In the chorus they repeat what the angels said to them: "Glory to God in the highest!" In the second verse the townspeople ask: "Why this jubilee? What could be so exciting?" The shepherds invite everyone to "come to Bethlehem and see!"

In Luke 2:8-18 you can read what the shepherds actually did after they heard the angels' heavenly message. Which verse in Luke do you think this carol is based on?

▲ **TAKE A STEP**

When they had seen him, they spread the word concerning what had been told them about this child, and all who heard it were amazed at what the shepherds said to them (Luke 2:17-18).

Imagine that you had been one of those shepherds. You saw the glory of the Lord. You heard the angels. You saw the baby. Could anything have kept you from telling others what you saw?

Today we know far more than the shepherds ever did about Jesus. We know that He died for our sins, was buried, and rose again after three days. We know that He went to heaven and that He will come again. The shepherds gladly spread the news of His birth. Can you think of at least one person who needs to know what you know about Jesus?

H ere is the second verse of a beloved Christmas carol written by Charles Wesley, who wrote nearly 6,000 hymns. Can you name the carol?

> Christ, by highest heav'n adored;
> Christ, the everlasting Lord;
> Late in time behold Him come,
> Offspring of the virgin's womb.
> Veiled in flesh, the Godhead see;
> Hail the incarnate Deity
> Pleased as man with men to dwell,
> Jesus our Immanuel!

◆ **TAKE A LOOK / Revelation 5:11-12**
If you're stumped, maybe the chorus will help: "Hark! the herald angels sing, 'Glory to the new-born King!' "

Mr. Wesley used some big words in this famous carol, but every phrase of it is worth thinking about. Listed below are seven passages which will help you understand the song you just read. As you look them up, copy the line of the carol beside the verse it explains:

Truth from God's Word . . .	is in these words:
Revelation 5:11-12	_____
John 17:5	_____
Galatians 4:4	_____
Luke 1:34-35	_____
Colossians 2:9	_____
Hebrews 2:14	_____
Matthew 1:22-23	_____

▲ **TAKE A STEP**
The baby born in Bethlehem was God in the flesh. Jesus did not stop being God, but He became a man too. He put aside His heavenly glory and divine power to live on earth as a man . . . and to die for the sins of mankind.

In Christ all the fullness of the Deity [God] lives in bodily form (Colossians 2:9).

The word *incarnation* describes the unique event when Jesus Christ lovingly humbled Himself. It means "taking on bodily form." Jesus was born as a baby—the Son of God took on humanity. And that's the story of Christmas! So sing together the message of the incarnation with the carol "Hark! The Herald Angels Sing."

God became one of us

Q

What does Christmas music tell me about Jesus?

A

Christmas music tells me that Jesus was God on earth in human flesh.

PARENT:
Plan to include in your busy holiday schedule a musical presentation that exalts the Lord.

There's a song in the air, there's a star in the sky

Many of the carols we know and love came from different lands. "The First Noel" was written in France, "Silent Night" in Germany, and "Joy to the World" in England. But below are the third and fourth stanzas of a familiar American carol. Can you guess which one it is?

How silently, how silently,/The wondrous gift is giv'n!
So God imparts to human hearts
The blessing of His heav'n.
No ear may hear His coming,/But in this world of sin,
Where meek souls will receive Him, still,
The dear Christ enters in.

O holy Child of Bethlehem,/Descend to us, we pray;
Cast out our sin, and enter in,/Be born in us today.
We hear the Christmas angels
The great glad tidings tell;
O come to us, abide with us,/Our Lord Emmanuel.

Q

What does Christmas music tell me about myself?

A

Christmas music tells me that I can have eternal life if I know Jesus as my Savior.

◆ **TAKE A LOOK / 1 Timothy 1:15-17; 2:5-6**

"O Little Town of Bethlehem" was written by an American preacher after he visited the tiny village where Jesus was born. When you sing the well-known first verse, you can almost feel the crisp, clear air and see the sparkling stars as if you were there on that holy night. But the third and fourth verses (above) help you realize that you can understand the true meaning of Christmas only if Jesus has come into your life.

First Timothy 1:15-17; 2:5-6 explains why Christ came into the world and what we must do in response.

▲ **TAKE A STEP**

Think about that night in Bethlehem. Use your imagination: Was the night warm or cold, cloudy or fair? Was the manger in a cave or a shed? What did the animals think about their "guests"? What did baby Jesus look like?

It would be nice to know those things, but the Bible focuses clearly on what we need to know—that Jesus was God's Son.

For there is one God and one mediator between God and men, the man Christ Jesus, who gave himself as a ransom for all men (1 Timothy 2:5-6).

With each person contributing his or her own ideas and talents, write a poem, draw a picture, make up a song, or design a Christmas card about that long ago night in Bethlehem when a manger became a bridge between heaven and earth.

*T*he words and music of this stirring Christmas carol were written by Americans. Do you recognize this final stanza?

> For lo! the days are hast'ning on,
>   By prophets seen of old,
> When with the ever-circling years,
>   Shall come the time foretold,
> When the new heaven and earth shall own
>   The Prince of Peace their King,
> And the whole world send back the song
>   Which now the angels sing.

He came to earth once, and He's coming again

◆ TAKE A LOOK / Philippians 2:5-11

For many folks, the Christmas season is a time of joy—with families gathering, people worshiping, and children playing.

The main cause of joy at this time of year, though, is the familiar story of Christ's birth, heard again and again in Scripture, music, and pageants. But have you ever thought how the Christmas story ends?

In the Bible, the facts of Christ's birth are recorded by Matthew and Luke. But the meaning of that great event is explained by the Apostle Paul.

Paul does not begin his Christmas record with the census or the shepherds, as Luke does. In fact, Paul doesn't even mention Bethlehem, Mary, Joseph, or the angels! And he doesn't end with the visit of the wise men or the flight of Jesus' family to Egypt. Read Paul's unusual version of the Christmas story in Philippians 2:5-11.

▲ TAKE A STEP

Paul's Christmas story starts at the actual beginning—in eternity past, before Jesus took on human form. In these few verses you see that the birth of Jesus in Bethlehem was just one part of God's plan—not the whole story. Paul looks forward to the end of the story, the time when Christ will return from heaven as King of Kings, and

> Every tongue [will] confess that Jesus Christ is Lord, to the glory of God the Father (Philippians 2:11).

The stanza at the top of this page is the third verse of "It Came Upon a Midnight Clear." Close your family time today by singing that carol. Then ask yourself this question: Am I ready for the Christmas story to end?

Q

What does Christmas music tell me about the future?

A

Christmas music reminds me that Jesus is coming again.

PARENT: *Take advantage of any opportunity your church offers for your child to participate in a choir or receive musical instruction.*

FEAR OF THE LORD

I can't believe we're going to see him!" Lori whispered. "Yeah! It's kinda scary, isn't it?" Ross whispered back.

As they glanced at the two Secret Service agents riding with them in the elevator, the teenagers squeezed the hands of the children with them.

Two days ago they had learned that the President was visiting their city. They decided to see if somehow they could bring the 10 children they cared for each day after school to meet him.

Last night a phone call informed them that the President would see them! All night questions had swirled through their minds: What should I wear? What if I stutter? What will he say to me?

Now the wondering was over. The elevator doors opened. The excited children walked nervously into the splendid Presidential Suite. Then the President walked in, smiling. Excitement gave way to awe as he bent down to shake the hand of each child.

◆ **THINKING ABOUT FEAR OF THE LORD**

How would you feel if you could speak personally to the leader of your country? You might be just a little bit afraid—not with terror, but with awe. And you'd certainly be on your best behavior!

That idea can help you understand what the Bible means by the phrase "fear of the Lord." Fearing the Lord doesn't mean cringing in terror because He might punish you. It does mean **that you honor and respect God because of who He is and what He has done.**

"If you think the Lord moves in mysterious ways, you should see long division."

● **KEY VERSE ON FEAR OF THE LORD**

Let all the earth fear the LORD; let all the people of the world revere him" (Psalm 33:8).

▲ **LOOKING AHEAD**

One way to understand what it means to fear the Lord is by reading Psalm 33:6-11. What reasons did the psalmist find to fear—or revere—the Lord? Are they your reasons, too?

*E*very time he looked at the aquarium, 10-year-old Grayson thought how hard it had been to move to the new condominium. But he knew that Maggie, his collie, wouldn't have been very happy here, and he understood why he had needed to give her away when the family moved.

Grayson often thought about the difference between Maggie and the mollies swimming in the fish tank.

Both depended on him completely for food and care, but only Maggie had understood that Grayson would never deliberately hurt her. She loved him even when he had to give her medicine or spray for fleas. But though Grayson fed the fish every day, they always swam away when he came near. Unlike Maggie, they never figured out that he had only their own good in mind.

Yep, he sure missed Maggie.

◆ **TAKE A LOOK / Deuteronomy 10:12-13**

God made us with the ability to understand who God is and what He does for us. He wants us to trust Him as confidently as Maggie trusted Grayson, not to run away in terror or go our own way like mollies in an aquarium.

God commanded the people of Israel to fear Him:

> "*Fear the LORD your God and serve him. Hold fast to him . . . He is your praise; he is your God, who performed for you those great and awesome wonders*" (Deuteronomy 10:20-21).

One of those great and awesome wonders which causes us to fear God is the universe, which He created and keeps going from day to day.

We also owe God our praise because He is totally holy. Yet because of His love for sinful people, He sent His only Son Jesus to pay the death penalty for our sins.

Read Deuteronomy 10:12-13; Psalm 34:11-14; and Proverbs 8:13 to learn what God desires for those who fear Him.

▲ **TAKE A STEP**

Of all the creatures on earth, only humans can think about their Creator. But many still refuse to fear God. Some even say that He doesn't exist!

Proverbs 8:13 gives us a clue as to why people refuse to fear the Lord, and John 3:19 tells us plainly. After reading those two verses, what would you say is the main reason some people don't fear the Lord?

Fearing God leads to trust, not terror

Why should I fear the Lord?

A

Fear of the Lord is the reverence God deserves because of who He is.

God has spoken ... but are you listening?

Q

How do I express fear of the Lord?

A

Fear of the Lord is expressed when I obey Him willingly.

PARENT:
Are you careful about obedience? Something as small as instructing your child to tell a caller that you're not home when you are, conveys a careless attitude toward sin.

Come on, Corey, let's take the short cut. We'll get soaked if we don't." Brandon pointed to the clouds overhead and turned his bike toward the highway.

Corey shook his head. "Look, the only reason my dad lets me ride to the hobby shop is because I promised I'd stay off the highway. If I do, he won't ... "

Just then they heard a sharp clap of thunder, and the rain flooded down. As fast as he could, Brandon pedaled out onto the shoulder of the highway ... and Corey followed. Suddenly Brandon heard the squeal of tires. He glanced back to see a car spinning and Corey flying over the handlebars of his bike.

When Brandon and the driver reached Corey, he was staring at his twisted bike and his badly scraped legs. "Dad's gonna kill me!" he cried wildly. "When he finds out, he'll kill me!"

◆ **TAKE A LOOK / Deuteronomy 6:13-19, 24-25**

When Corey's father heard of the accident, his first reaction was thankfulness, not anger. But because Corey had knowingly disobeyed, Corey's first feeling had been fear of his father's reaction.

Fearing God does not mean being afraid because of possible punishment. It does mean honoring God because of who He is and what He can do. We express it by willingly obeying His commands. What does Deuteronomy 6:13-19, 24-25 say about obeying God?

▲ **TAKE A STEP**

When we fear the Lord, we acknowledge that He is totally holy. He hates sin. And what is sin? If God has told us in His Word to do something and we don't, that's sin. If He has told us not to do something and we do it, that too is sin.

Just like earthly fathers, our heavenly Father wants us to obey Him out of love, not terror. Jesus said:

"If you love me, you will obey what I command" (John 14:15).

Sometimes you may be pressured to do something you know is wrong, as Corey was. Would you:

1. Do it anyway if you think you won't get caught?
2. Not do it because you're afraid you might get caught?
3. Not do it because you know it's sin?

Which attitude would please your earthly parents and your heavenly Father?

How come he gets all the breaks?" Andy muttered as Grant's name was called to receive the award. Ray grinned. "Do I detect some 'sour grapes,' old pal?" he said, slapping Andy on the back.

"Oh, come on, Ray. You know me better than that!" Andy replied. "It's just that a lot of us make about the same grades as Grant does, and you and a couple of other guys are a lot better on the football field. But Grant seems to get every school award that comes along. What is it about him?"

"Well, you forget who votes on those awards. We don't —the teachers do. And Grant is involved in just about everything. He's worked at getting on the teachers' good side since first grade. He's got their blessing, that's all."

◆ **TAKE A LOOK / Psalms 25:12; 31:19; 33:18-19**

You probably know people who always seem to win the awards or get chosen to help the teacher. You and your friends may even say that those who receive such special treatment are "teacher's pets." But much of the time they have earned that special favor.

God doesn't play favorites. Everyone is equal in His sight. But He does look with favor on those who fear Him and keep His commandments. On the lines at the right, list the special favor each verse promises those who fear the Lord:

To those who fear Him . . .   the Lord promises:
Psalm 25:12   _____
Psalm 31:19   _____
Psalm 33:18-19   _____
Psalm 103:11   _____
Psalm 111:5   _____

▲ **TAKE A STEP**

God promises guidance, goodness, protection, love, and provision to those who fear Him. Psalm 128 sums it up this way:

Blessed are all who fear the LORD, who walk in his ways (Psalm 128:1).

The word *blessed* simply means "happy." Can your family think of five ways people today try to find happiness and fulfillment—without God?

From what you've learned this week about fearing the Lord, do you think anybody can be truly happy unless he or she fears God?

Find yourself in God's favor

What does God promise those who fear Him?

A

Fear of the Lord is the path to receiving His blessings.

Fear will flourish when it's God you cherish

*A*ll during the campaign, the Harrison family worked hard in support of the candidate they thought would be the best mayor for their city. Mr. and Mrs. Harrison contributed money and attended rallies; their teenage daughters did telephone surveys; even eight-year-old Evan stuffed and stamped envelopes.

Now the election was over . . . and their candidate had lost. But since the whole family had been involved in the campaign, Mr. Harrison decided they should watch the winner's speech on TV.

As the new mayor began to speak, Evan started booing. But his father's stern words stopped him: "Evan, he is now the mayor. We may disagree with his views, but we must always show respect for the office he holds."

Q

How can I develop a proper attitude of fear?

A

Fear of the Lord grows as I learn more about Him.

PARENT:
One way you can help your child learn to fear the Lord is to explain how he can participate in your church's worship service and be attentive during the sermon.

◆ TAKE A LOOK / Daniel 4:28-37

Though they disagreed with the new mayor's politics, the Harrisons honored him simply because he was now the mayor. The office to which he was elected set him apart from all the other candidates.

God is set apart from all created beings, for He is the only one who can create and save. His ways are always true and just. So we honor Him simply because He is God. Fear of the Lord is respect and awe for who He is and what He does. But the fear of God and pride of humans simply won't mix.

During the days of Daniel, King Nebuchadnezzar learned to fear the Lord the hard way. When the Lord saved Daniel's three friends from the fiery furnace (Daniel 3), the king acknowledged God's power. But later the king became lifted up with pride, for he didn't fear the Lord. After he had a strange dream, he asked Daniel to tell him what it meant. Read the story of "Nebuchadnezzar's Nightmare" in Daniel 4:28-37.

▲ TAKE A STEP

Fear of God does not come from treating Him like a buddy. Rather, it grows when we learn more about Him and His commands. Read Nebuchadnezzar's words again:

"Now I, Nebuchadnezzar, praise and exalt and glorify the King of heaven, because everything he does is right and all his ways are just. And those who walk in pride he is able to humble" (Daniel 4:37).

What do you think Nebuchadnezzar would say now if you could ask him, "What does it mean to fear the Lord?"

GIVING

I t sometimes seems hard to believe / That on the birthday of my Lord, / I think of gifts I should receive, / And get them all, a generous hoard. / This year, I'll change all that around; / Three gifts for Jesus are my plan: / A mind that's pure, a body sound, / And hands to serve my fellow man.

"Whose Birthday?" copyright 1971 by David C. Cook Publishing Co. Elgin, IL 60120. Used by permission.

◆ THINKING ABOUT GIVING

When we think about giving during the holiday season, we usually picture brightly wrapped boxes filled with things we hope to get.

But giving and receiving Christmas gifts is only a tiny part of what true giving is all about. Actually the idea of giving began with God, who "gave His only Son" to be the Savior of mankind.

As God's children, we give to meet others' needs. True giving is **joyfully providing what others need without worrying about what it costs me.**

● KEY VERSE ON GIVING

Just as you excel in everything . . . see that you also excel in this grace of giving (2 Corinthians 8:7).

▲ LOOKING AHEAD

Do you know how to excel (or do your best) in giving? This week we'll learn that the best kind of giving comes out of a heart filled with love for God. We can love God because He first loved us.

Remind yourself of His great love-gift to you by reading John 3:16 aloud together. Then read another description of that most wonderful gift in Galatians 1:4.

For a Christmas project that's fun and meaningful, wrap a large box inside and out with beautiful paper. Leave the lid off, stand the box on edge, and arrange your nativity scene inside. Attach a silver bow to represent the star. Let it remind you of God's gift to you!

"I'll bet Cinderella was surprised when she got that fairy godmother's bill."

With no strings attached you can't yank it back

Lucy dropped her schoolbooks on the table. "May I go to Stephanie's slumber party Friday night?" she asked her mother.

"Well, I guess it'll be okay," her mother replied hesitantly. "But it seems as though there was something else Friday night . . . ."

Later that evening Lucy overheard her mother and father talking in the den. "I'm having trouble finding a baby sitter for Friday night," her mother said. "I meant to ask Lucy but I forgot. I've already told her she could go to the slumber party. I hope I can work something out. We haven't been to the symphony for so long."

Lucy heard the disappointment in her mother's voice. She knew her parents hadn't been out on a "date" in quite a while. She walked in the den and hugged them both. "Hey, you two! I'll baby-sit! And since you didn't ask, consider it a gift from me to you. Spend the money you would have paid a baby sitter on dessert after the concert."

Q

Why should I give?

A

Giving joyfully and freely shows I appreciate what God has given to me.

◆ TAKE A LOOK / 2 Corinthians 8:1-7

Lucy could have made her gift conditional: "If you can't get a baby sitter, I'll do it." She could have given it grudgingly: "Oh, all right, I'll baby-sit. But it's going to cost you!" Or she could have said nothing at all and gone to the slumber party. But Lucy's offer was a gift of love freely given.

As Paul traveled around preaching the gospel, churches he had visited would often send money to help him. You can learn a lot about giving in a God-pleasing way by reading about the churches of Macedonia in 2 Corinthians 8:1-7.

▲ TAKE A STEP

Though they were very poor, the Macedonian believers asked for an opportunity to help others. They gave freely and generously because they had enjoyed God's generous love for them. And in return, they had "given themselves to the Lord."

Many gifts today are given with strings attached. That way, people can "reel them back in" if they want. But God's way of giving—with no strings attached—is described in the instructions Jesus gave his disciples:

"Freely you have received, freely give" (Matthew 10:8).

Think of someone who needs something that you or your family can give. Will you ask God right now to help you give it joyfully, lovingly, and with no strings attached?

Joshua loved the offering time in Sunday school. He liked to drop his pennies one by one into the little plastic "church" that sat on the table beside the door. As the three-year-olds filed by the table, Mrs. Marshall would tell them that they were giving their offering to Jesus. Later, Mr. Kearns would quietly open the door a crack, reach his hand in for the bank, and empty the money, adding it to the offering from the other classes.

But this time when Mr. Kearns picked up the bank, the bottom fell out! Clinking and clattering coins rolled all over the floor. As Mr. Kearns opened the door quickly to scoop up the loose change, Joshua shot from his chair like a jack-in-the-box. "Look, Teacher," he exclaimed, pointing to the red-faced Mr. Kearns. "Is that Jesus coming to get our money?"

◆ TAKE A LOOK / Deuteronomy 12:5-7

Little Joshua may not have understood exactly what "giving to the Lord" meant, but he was learning a holy habit. Giving to God is not a choice. It is something He expects us to do.

In Old Testament times God's people gave 10 percent of their crops to support the leaders God had chosen to take care of the temple and conduct the worship. They also gave to support the poor.

Read one of God's Old Testament instructions for giving in Deuteronomy 12:5-7. Then, from these New Testament verses, tell which groups of people should receive our help: 1 Timothy 5:8, 17-18; Acts 4:32; Galatians 6:6; and Matthew 25:35-40.

▲ TAKE A STEP

Instead of priests and Levites, the church today has pastors, teachers, missionaries, and other leaders. God says we are to support these leaders with our gifts. We must also give to help family members, fellow believers, and others in need.

Jesus cannot have our hearts without having our money. The way you give shows who rules your life—you or God.

"Store up for yourselves treasures in heaven. . . For where your treasure is, there your heart will be also" (Matthew 6:20-21).

What sort of plan do you have for laying up treasures in heaven? After you discuss the ways your family gives to the Lord, you might want to make a family commitment: "To show that our treasure and heart are in the right place, we will give $_____ or _____% of our income to God."

Give God your best—He deserves nothing less

Q
To whom shall I give?

A
Giving to the Lord is one way I show that He rules my life.

PARENT:
You set the example of giving for your child. Your cheerfulness in giving others your time, attention, and money will speak louder than any words you could say.

Give yourself to God, then give yourself to others

Q

What should I give?

A

Giving is best expressed when I follow Jesus' example and give of myself.

Many years ago in Europe, a young minister was eager to begin preaching the message of God's love. Finally the day came when an older minister took him out on a preaching mission.

As they walked along the dirty cobblestone streets of the town, the old pastor stopped to chat with a widow in the marketplace. Then he paused to dry the tears of a young girl who had scraped her knee. With a kind word, he gave a coin to a beggar. By quoting Scripture he comforted a mother whose baby had recently died. Later he helped a peasant lift a heavy load onto a horse-drawn cart.

The younger man grew more and more frustrated. He wondered when he would have the chance to preach. Finally, as the sun was setting, the older pastor began walking back to the church. "But I thought we were going to preach," the young minister cried.

The old man smiled and said, "I have given myself to God. Now I give myself to others—a helping hand, a coin, a smile, a word from God. You see, I've been preaching all day long!"

◆ **TAKE A LOOK / Luke 4:16-19**
[Jesus] did not come to be served, but to serve, and to give his life as a ransom for many (Mark 10:45).
By giving himself to serve others, the old pastor was following Jesus' example. Read Luke 4:16-19 to discover how Jesus gave Himself to serve others.

▲ **TAKE A STEP**
Jesus gave Himself to serve people who were spiritually poor and blind, and burdened by sin. You can enjoy a special form of giving by serving others who are in the same condition—suffering physically, spiritually, financially, or emotionally.

Perhaps your family could treat a less fortunate family in your church to a night of just plain fun. Enjoy supper at a fast-food restaurant with them, then go bowling or skating together—your treat. An elderly or blind person might appreciate an outing to a holiday music concert. A social service agency can give you the name of a prisoner's family that could use a helping hand.

And don't forget those people who are burdened by loneliness because they are far from their own family. Sharing holiday celebrations with them is a great way to share God's good news. Pick one of these ideas and get started!

Patrick counted the money he had saved. Only three more dollars and he would have enough to buy the train set he wanted!

But at supper Patrick's happiness disappeared. His dad explained that a family in their church had lost their house and all their possessions—even their car—in a fire. "At least our church will be taking up an offering Sunday to help them," he said.

That night Patrick lay thinking about that family—and about his money. He thought about how hard he'd worked and how much he wanted the train. But he also believed God wanted him to give his money to help that family in need. It wasn't a lot, but it would help. "I'll do it," he decided. "I'll put my money in the offering to help them." With that, he turned over and fell asleep.

◆ TAKE A LOOK / Mark 12:41-44

Nobody forced Patrick to give all his money to help the fire victims. He could have given just part of it or none at all. But Patrick gave sacrificially. He gave up what he wanted because he believed God wanted him to help someone else.

On one occasion Jesus was watching people put their offerings into the temple treasury. He told the disciples that a poor widow who had put in two "pennies" had given more than the rich people who had contributed large amounts. Read Mark 12:41-44. Which offering do you think pleased God more: the widow's pennies or the rich men's sacks of money? Why?

▲ TAKE A STEP

How are we to give? The Old Testament law required a tithe (which means one-tenth). Today many people use that as a general rule for giving. But you should keep in mind that God really owns everything you have.

Giving a tenth of what you have is a good place to begin. Some people have extra money after they give their regular offering and pay their bills, so they are able to give more. In any case, God honors sacrificial giving—meeting others' needs by giving up something you need or want—as in the case of the widow:

"She, out of her poverty, put in everything—
all she had to live on" (Mark 12:44).

Would you give your money to someone who needed it, as Patrick did? Can you think of a way you can give sacrificially?

Whether large or small, God owns it all

How should I give?

A

Giving sacrificially is one way I show my willingness to obey the Lord.

PARENT:
Encourage your child to give God a portion of any money he or she receives—including earnings, allowances, and gifts. Again, your example is crucial.

CHRISTMAS

*A*s a family, decide whether these statements are true or false according to the Bible. You may need to refer to Matthew 1-2 and Luke 2.

1. Christmas has always been celebrated on December 25.
2. The innkeeper told Mary and Joseph there was no room.
3. The angels told the shepherds to look for a baby in a barn.
4. A manger is a feeding trough for animals.
5. Three wise men visited Jesus the night He was born.
6. The wise men stopped in Jerusalem to tell King Herod about the new king.
7. The shepherds hurried to Bethlehem because they were afraid of the angels.
8. Mary and Joseph were in Bethlehem to visit relatives.
9. The name Jesus means "Jehovah [God] is Savior."*

◆ THINKING ABOUT CHRISTMAS

Christmas—which comes from the phrase "Christ's mass"—is **a celebration of Jesus' birth.** Through the centuries, different ways of celebrating that event have resulted in a variety of traditions around the world. But the facts of Christmas have never changed. Taking time to get those facts straight will help you remember the true meaning of Christmas.

● KEY VERSE ON CHRISTMAS

"Today in the town of David a Savior has been born to you; he is Christ the Lord" (Luke 2:11).

"There goes my wiseman part in the Christmas pageant."

▲ LOOKING AHEAD

Plan a family project that will help you keep the true meaning of Christmas in mind this year. (You could act out the story of Jesus' birth, draw a series of pictures illustrating it, or compose a song about Christmas.)

*Answers: 1F, 2F, 3F, 4T, 5F, 6F, 7F, 8F, 9T.

"**T**his is a neat spaceship game," Leon said as he played with the gift he had unwrapped a few hours ago. Then a puzzled look crossed his face. "Dad, are there people living on other planets?"

"I don't know, Leon," his dad answered thoughtfully.

Leon walked over to the picture window and looked up at the sky. "What about UFOs—what if they're messengers from outer space?"

"Well, we really don't know, son. There's certainly no hard evidence that they exist. So far, it's all speculation."

"You know," Leon continued, "I wonder why Jesus didn't come to earth in a UFO, or fly in with an army of angels. Why was He just born like an ordinary baby?"

◆ **TAKE A LOOK / Matthew 1:18-25**

Leon isn't the first person to ask that question!

Because of their disobedience, Adam and Eve became sinners, passing on their sinful nature to every human being born since then. And God's punishment for sin is death. So how could anyone ever be saved?

The situation seemed impossible: In order to deal with the problem of sin, there must be one man without sin who could set humanity free—one man who could pay for the sins of others. But after Adam, no human being was free from sin.

God alone knew the solution. He Himself would become a man. He would experience everything that human beings experience—even a human birth. Though born a man, He would not inherit the sin of Adam because He would have a sinless body, formed by the Holy Spirit, and would be born of a virgin.

But before it actually happened, God knew even the smallest details of this miraculous birth. Read God's explanation of this unique birth to Joseph, Mary's husband, in Matthew 1:18-25.

▲ **TAKE A STEP**

That God would come to earth as a human being is a mystery we will never completely understand this side of heaven. But we—like Mary—can take comfort in the words of the angel:

"For nothing is impossible with God" (Luke 1:37).

Every time you open a gift today, pray a silent prayer of thanks for God's gracious gift to you—that He became the baby of Christmas.

Born as a baby to die as a sacrifice

Q

Why did Jesus have to be born?

A

Christmas celebrates the time when God became a man so He could die for my sins.

Jesus put all the puzzle pieces in place!

I love having Martine for a pen pal" Joyce laughed as she opened the letter from France. "I feel like I already know her just by reading her letters."

"You do have a lot in common," her mother said.

"Yeah we do. Martine is my height and has the same color hair. We both love ice skating and ballet. Did I tell you she paints too? Let's see what she wrote . . . oh! She says they'll be visiting the U.S.! They're going to the Grand Canyon next June. Hey—that's when we're going! I'll have to write and tell her the exact dates . . . ."

The months quickly passed. At last the day arrived. Joyce scanned the crowd overlooking the North Rim of the Grand Canyon. She spotted a tall girl with dark hair intently peering at the crowd. "Martine!" she yelled.

"How did you find me?" Martine asked excitedly as she hugged Joyce. "I've been looking all over for you!"

Q

Why are the details of Jesus' birth so important?

◆ **TAKE A LOOK / Isaiah 7:14**

Joyce was able to identify Martine because she already knew a lot about her from their letters.

In a similar way the Jewish people who accepted Jesus as the Promised One, recognized that the details of His life matched the promises God had made to them.

Look up the following prophecies in the Old Testament; then match each with the detail it foretold about Christ's birth.

A

The details of Jesus' birth show that God kept His promises about the coming of the Messiah.

The Old Testament . . .	foretold these details:
1. Isaiah 7:14	a. His birthplace
2. Micah 5:2	b. His name
3. Genesis 3:15	c. Member of Abraham's family
4. Genesis 22:15-18	d. Member of David's family
5. 2 Samuel 7:12-16	e. God Himself
6. Isaiah 9:6	f. Offspring of the woman

▲ **TAKE A STEP**

In recording Jesus' birth, Matthew explained: *All this took place to fulfill what the Lord had said through the prophet (Matthew 1:22).*

Jesus' birth, life, death, and resurrection fulfilled every detail of Old Testament prophecy about His first coming—proof that He is who He claimed to be. Can you think of another event that has been prophesied but has not yet happened? (Find a clue in 1 Thessalonians 4:16-17.) How should we react to that promise?

PARENT: Answers to the matching quiz are: 1b, 2a, 3f, 4c, 5d, 6e.

S kidding on the slick pavement, the station wagon failed to stop in time and slid into the sports car. **Crunch!** Fortunately, no one was hurt.

Days later in traffic court, witnesses argued about the details. One reported: "I was walking near the intersection as the driver of the station wagon turned left. He had the right of way. The traffic light was red further up the road, and I'm sure that sports car should have stopped at it."

Another witness explained: "I was at the corner gas station. The sports car had been parked and was pulling out when the station wagon turned into it. The sports car was in the clear."

If you were the judge, which report would you believe?

◆ **TAKE A LOOK / Matthew 1; Luke 2**

The two witnesses saw the same accident from different viewpoints. Each account included details the other did not see. But both were right!

The accounts of Jesus' birth are given in the New Testament books of Matthew and Luke. Both accounts are true and accurate, but each one includes details not found in the other.

Turn to Matthew and Luke. Let's try to discover how and why the two accounts are different.

Who sees an angel appear in Matthew 1:20? Who hears from an angel in Luke 1:26-27? Who saw the angel in a dream and then led the little family to Egypt (Matthew 2:13)? Who spent a long time thinking about the things the shepherds had said (Luke 2:19)?

▲ **TAKE A STEP**

Answering those questions shows you that Matthew's account seems to be written from Joseph's point of view, while Luke tells the story as Mary experienced it. But both versions are . . .

An account of the things that have been fulfilled among us, just as they were handed down to us by those who from the first were eyewitnesses (Luke 1:1-2).

Because Matthew was a Jew and Luke was a Gentile, their viewpoints are different. With that in mind, why do you think Matthew began with the family tree of Jesus? Here's a hint: Do you remember what God promised Abraham and David, and how important that was to the Jewish people? (See Genesis 12:3, Isaiah 9:7, and Matthew 1:1.)

Two accounts are better than one!

Q

Why are there different accounts of Jesus' birth?

A

Different accounts of Jesus' birth stem from the authors' different viewpoints.

You're invited; won't you come to the party?

Balloons dangled from crepe paper streamers, brightly wrapped presents were piled on the table, and 16 candles sparkled on the cake. "Surprise! Happy Birthday!" The shouts of excited friends greeted Sheila as she stepped into the den. Soon the stereo filled the room with happy music.

As the group stood around the table eating ice cream and cake, Norm noticed that the girl next to him seemed bored, even unhappy. "C'mon, celebrate!" he encouraged. "It can't be that bad!"

The girl shrugged. "I don't even know Sheila," she said. "I was with one of her friends and just came along for the ride. Ya know, a party's not much fun if you don't know the guest of honor."

◆ **TAKE A LOOK / Luke 2:17-20**

She's right—parties are more fun when you know the guest of honor. And that's true with the Christmas celebration, too.

So how can you best celebrate Christmas? First of all, you need to know Jesus as your Savior. Though we are celebrating His birth, Jesus didn't come just to be born. He came to die for our sin. Because of Jesus' death and resurrection, God can say to anyone who trusts Jesus for salvation, "Your sins are forgiven. You're a member of My family."

Once you belong to God's family, how can you best celebrate Christmas? Find out by reading Luke 2:17-20!

▲ **TAKE A STEP**

To celebrate Christmas, the shepherds spread the news of Jesus' birth. Imagine them going through the little town excitedly telling everyone that they had found the Christ Child.

To celebrate Christmas, the shepherds who heard the good news passed it on. God Himself was born a man! They may not have understood, but they did marvel. So should we!

Finally, to celebrate Christmas,
The shepherds returned, glorifying and praising God for all the things they had heard and seen, which were just as they had been told (Luke 2:20).

If you haven't experienced something, you can't tell others about it. And if you don't know the party's guest of honor, you really can't celebrate. Have each person go to a different room in your home to pray about this question: "How should I celebrate Christmas?" Then regroup and sing "Joy to the World."

Q

How can I best celebrate Christmas?

A

Christmas is best celebrated when I know Jesus as my Savior.

PARENT:
Extend the holiday joy by planning now to celebrate the Epiphany (the coming of the wise men) on January 6 by inviting friends to dinner.